Mixed-up Kids?

Race, identity and social order

Tina G. Patel

RHP

Russell House Publishing

First published in 2009 by:
Russell House Publishing Ltd.
4 St. George's House
Uplyme Road
Lyme Regis
Dorset DT7 3LS
Tel: 01297-443948
Fax: 01297-442722
e-mail: help@russellhouse.co.uk
www.russellhouse.co.uk

British Library Cataloguing-in-publication Data:
A catalogue record for this book is available from the British Library.

ISBN: 978-1-905541-38-6

Typeset by TW Typesetting, Plymouth, Devon

Printed by the MPG Books Group

Russell House Publishing

Russell House Publishing aims to publish innovative and valuable materials to help managers,
practitioners, trainers, educators and students.
Our full catalogue covers: social policy, working with young people, helping children and families,
care of older people, social care, combating social exclusion, revitalising communities and
working with offenders.

Full details can be found at www.russellhouse.co.uk and we are pleased to send out information
to you by post. Our contact details are on this page.

We are always keen to receive feedback on publications and new ideas for future projects.

Contents

Acknowledgements

I would like to express my heartfelt thanks and gratitude to the following for your continuous academic support: Professor P. Marsh and Dr N.J. Britton. Your patience, expert guidance and belief proved invaluable.

I would also like to thank Russell House Publishing in particular Geoffrey Mann, and also Toyin Okitikpi for comments and support in the production of this book.

Thanks also to the Postgraduate Student Body of 2000–2004, at the Department of Sociological Studies, University of Sheffield, and my colleagues at the School of Social Science, Liverpool John Moores University, whose encouragement, advice and humour never failed to keep me moving forward.

Love and thanks also go to my partner (D.P.H.) and my family, especially my sister (L.P.). Your support and grounded advice helped me at the most difficult of times, and will always be remembered.

Thank you also to Professor J. Sim for comments on earlier drafts, and to my grammarian, Miss E. Ross. Last, but not least, my deepest thanks and respect goes to all the adoptees who participated in the research study on which this book is based. I hope I've done justice to your experiences, views and beliefs.

Dr Tina G. Patel

Dedication

. . . In loving memory of Bapa (C.F.P.)

Preface

This book is concerned with the racial identity development process amongst the mixed-race population, in particular transracial adoptees, children of mixed (interracial) parentage, and the children of immigrants. Producing an exact figure on this proportion of the population that can be classed as 'mixed' is by no means an easy task. What is certain is that the numbers of those who are located across traditionally fixed racial, ethnic, religious and cultural lines are not only large in their numbers and increasing at a steady pace, but also that the very content of their mixed-ness is also growing in variety. This is producing a population group whose identities question essentialised notions, and instead present complex, flexible and diverse categories. In terms of the transracial adoption debate, an updated re-think is warranted. It is a re-think which also can be applied to the children of mixed (interracial) parentage, and the offspring of immigrants. These are two other groups in society whose identities are all too often essentialised and problematically discussed. The time for such a consideration is long overdue. The issues of race, identity and social order are continuously the focus of public discussion, media attention or government debate. This is partially because it makes a social comment on the state of society, not only in terms of race, but also in terms of family formations, societal relationships and the politics of identity rights issues.

This book provides a strong and progressive statement that readers can engage with in the areas of race, identity and social order. It allows this to be done through reference to the case studies of transracial adoption, and to a lesser extent, the children of mixed (interracial) parentage, as well as the offspring of immigrants. It contextualises the key points and arguments of the debate, offering empirical evidence, and makes statements readers are invited to reflect upon and critically engage with. In doing so, the book is of interest to academics, researchers and students in the social sciences, especially in the disciplines of sociology, social work and family/community studies. The book is also useful for child, family and community support workers both directly as a handbook on which to base policy/practice, and indirectly, as a tool for considering key issues in the area. This is because it provides a critically reflective analysis of the existing body of literature as well as presenting the actual narratives of six adults who had been transracially adopted as children. In addition, because the interviewees were aged between 21 and 43 years at the time of interviewing, they were able to comment reflectively and wholly on a fairly mature life span that varied across time, space and social context. What is also unique here is that they speak for themselves, in their own ways and on their own terms, about their views and experiences, some of which were negative as well as positive.

It is also of interest to other more directly affected members of the population, those who are themselves adoptees or the children of mixed (interracial) parentage, or the offspring of immigrants. This is because it links into what is expected to be a shared set of experiences. It provides commonality of experiences, as well as sociological comment on these experiences. More importantly, it also provides validity to what is later termed a 'mixed heritage' status that these groups, amongst others, share and so argues that their rights to recognition and self-naming be catered for.

The book is also of interest for those with a broad interest in the area, as well as those interested more generally in the dynamics of relationships in society and the impact of these factors on our sense of self and the functioning of broader social relationships. This is so whether one is considering these on political, sociological, or even historical and psychological levels. This is because the presented narratives also comment on other areas and social situations. These include: being black minority ethnic or mixed race in a predominantly white society; being the offspring of immigrants; having been an intercountry adoptee and experienced global placement practice; having been orphaned or abandoned at birth and spending time in institutionalised care; being raised in a step-family or by a single parent; experiences with other children, such as negotiated play contexts during childhood; being at a private school, and having experienced bullying; and building personal relationships in relation to gender and sexuality.

The arguments and ideas covered in the book analyse these issues as they have implications for a group of individuals who, although growing in size, nevertheless remain marginalised in terms of their voices and their right to self-determination. Firstly, an informed base is used. These are empirical data, in the form of life history interviews with six adults who had been transracially adopted as children, and whose experiences were real and varied across a given period of time, i.e. at the time of interviewing, the eldest adoptee had been born in 1959. Secondly, a sociological perspective to identity formation is utilised. This is the view that identity is something that is socially constructed, as opposed to being essentially based. It is developed in an ongoing social process of negotiation. In doing so, the book seeks to provide a valid and updated contribution, along with a legitimate call for its analysis and recommendations, to be seriously considered by students of relevant disciplinary studies, by practitioners in the field, as well as by those more generally interested in advancing the identity rights of marginalised populations in society.

In doing so, a number of questions are raised in the book: Why do essentialist ideas about a single black identity tend to dominate? What are the consequences of this for social service policy and practice? What are the consequences for those who actively choose not to identify themselves as having one singular racial identity? What can be done to improve the situation? In considering these questions, the book aims to challenge orthodox accounts and analyses by providing an updated re-think on the racial identity debate. It calls for the recognition of these and like groups of people, offering prescriptions for interventions on how to best serve their needs and facilitate access to racial identity rights.

About the Author

Tina G. Patel is a lecturer in Criminology at the University of Salford. Her main research and teaching interests are: 'race', identity and the racialisation process; crime, deviance and violence, in particular racist violence; and police accountability.

Introduction

Despite the growing numbers of children being raised in mixed-race families and social settings, such as transracial adoptions, children of mixed (interracial) parentage, and the offspring of immigrants, child and family placement services have been dominated by a tendency to follow restrictive policy and practice guidelines which are themselves based on outdated and heavily problematic ideas about essentialised racial identities. This has been underpinned by the supposed need for children to fully commit to a singular racialised identity, usually the black minority ethnic one, in order to develop a healthy and positive sense of self. These views are also commonplace in other child, family and community support services, be they health, welfare, housing, education, employment or criminal justice. They are also reflective of the dominant ideas about race, identity and the family that exist more generally within society, including in the everyday thinking and attitudes amongst its lay members, in the presentations of the media, and in political speak.

Although a common view, it is argued here that this 'binary world view and essentialised ideology' (Okitikpi, 2005: 1) are restrictive, inaccurate, crude and offensive for those who develop for themselves a multi-racial identity. At its best, it misidentifies a growing section of the population who do not see themselves in singular racialised ways. At its worst, it completely ignores their most fundamental identity rights. This book therefore aims to explore this issue in greater depth. However, it does so from a sociological perspective, which in utilising a social constructionist approach to racial identity development, challenges the traditional and essentialist based thinking behind dominant ideas. The book uses transracial adoption as a case in point. It draws upon the reflective narratives of six adults, aged between 21 and 43 years at the time of interviewing, who having been transracially adopted as children, talked in depth about the external pressures to conform to a singular racial identity and the ways in which they negotiated these pressures in order to emerge with a positive and healthy multi-racial identity which they felt most accurately reflected their own mixed heritage.

The significance of race

In all aspects of citizenship, it would be naïve to ignore the fact that in Western societies, such as Britain where there is a white majority, that there is a serious problem of racial disadvantage and discrimination against members of its black minority ethnic population. This is so both in terms of institutional policy and practices and certainly in terms of commonsensical lay attitudes. Commentaries of personal experience and documented high profile cases such as that of Stephen Lawrence (MacPherson, 1999) illustrate this reality. It would be impossible to claim otherwise, given that as a society born out of Imperial rule and its consequences, such as slavery, economic exploitation, discourses of racial superiority, to name a few, such a country can be anything else.

Of greater concern is the way in which Britain remains a home for many individuals experiencing institutionalised and lay racism on a daily basis. The overwhelming majority of these are members of the black minority ethnic community, or to put it more crudely as is often the case, all those who are non-white. It is important to recognise here that although skin pigmentation remains a strong basis on which distinctions are made, the politics of race and non-whiteness is a much more complex issue. Here, for example, it can also refer to individuals whose skin colour appears white, but whose culture or ethnic origin is not that of a white, western and therefore supposedly superior advanced society, like the Polish, the Lithuanians, and still to some degree, the Irish. These individuals, who continuously battle with the personal love–hate relationship that being a minority ethnic individual living in countries such as Britain brings with it, also continue to struggle with the fight to obtain full citizenship and equality rights.

On another level, however, it is important to recognise that the debate goes much further than a binary black/white conceptualism allows. Here, recognition should be given to the way in which Britain is a multi-cultural, multi-ethnic, multi-racial, diverse society. For example, in April 2001, the black minority ethnic and mixed-race population in Britain was 4.6 million, which is 7.9 per cent of the total population, and a 53 per cent growth from 1991 (ONS, 2001). Furthermore, 2 per cent of marriages in April 2001 were interethnic marriages (ONS, 2001). Hence, the claim that there are two distinct binary opposites, that of blackness and that of whiteness, should be seriously questioned and challenged.

However, the promising growth and diversity of racialised identities can not escape the reality of there being an over-representation of children from black minority ethnic and mixed-race backgrounds who are subject to institutionalised care or intervention from the various child, family and community support agencies and organisations. The reasons for the possible over-representation of these groups are discussed later in the book, but for the moment it is suffice to say that racism is a powerful contributory factor. Because of the significant role played by these agencies and organisations, it is especially important to examine their approach to issues of race, racism and identity, particularly in the context of the argument presented in this book, this being the ways in which their policies and practices may actually serve to restrict the development of *newer* forms of racialised identities.

A note on terminology

The ways in which we talk about 'race', racism and identity is in itself a complex, political and contested process. Terms of reference are constantly changing, being negotiated and updated on a variety of local and global levels. For example, consider the replacement of the once commonsensical term of 'coloured', used to refer to all those of non-white origin, by that of the term 'black', and more recently the use of other labels to represent the different sub-categories within the black label, such as South Asian, mixed-race, African Caribbean, and so on. Permanent settlement on racial labels is not possible. Neither should it be expected in a society in which attitudes are constantly being re-defined and re-negotiated. In addition, the use of racial labels are in themselves often based on crude, inaccurate and offensive stereotypes, particularly when these are used to dominate, discriminate and as a basis for justifying abuse. Indeed, as the reader will go on to see in a fuller sociological discussion of 'race' in Chapter 1, 'race' is only a social construct of the perceived relationship of 'race'. However, because humans continue to act as if 'race' is real, and thus organise behaviour and social relationships accordingly, meaning that individuals become 'racialised', a critical examination of this issue is warranted. This explains the publication of this book.

The terms **race** and **racial** are used to refer to the set of stereotypical ideas and beliefs, which are exhibited in the attitudes and behaviour of individuals. Race is both socially constructed and a contested concept. However, it continues to be used as something that is a real and substantial marker of difference. It therefore has social significance. To highlight these issues, the terms are often used in inverted commas, thus 'race' and 'racial'. Although this book agrees with this, the terms have not henceforth been used in inverted commas. This is because, given the focus of the book, which brings with it the regular use of these terms, the readability of presented typology would be lessened with the continuous use of the terms in inverted commas.

The term **black** is often used in the English language as something crudely associated with negative connotations. Following the US Civil Rights Movement of the 1960s, and later activism in Britain, it became a political term, used with a capital letter: **Black** (in addition to use of 'people of colour' in the US) to indicate the unified inclusion of all those people who suffered inequality, discrimination and racist violence because of their *non-white* skin-colour, i.e. largely those of African, Caribbean and South Asian origin. It also indicated political solidarity against such racial discrimination (British Sociological Association (BSA), 2007: 1–2). However, this book argues that the term can no longer be viewed as a singular political label which brings with it the same set of meanings. As such, the term is used in lower case type: **black**. In addition, the term is rarely used on its own. When the term is used though, it is done either to refer to the perceived notion exhibited by others of a singular essentialised or politically unified identity, or in quoting its use by others. Where this is the case, a note is also given to remind the reader of the implications bound up in its particular use.

In addition, the terms **black minority ethnic** (where residence is in a *white* majority society) and **minority ethnic** are used as preferential terms of reference. Alongside these, more detailed ethnic terms of reference are also used. This highlights labels that have been re-negotiated and moved away from an essentialised notion of a *black* identity. For example, **South Asian** is used to refer to those with recent origins in any of the Asian countries, and more specifically, **British Asian** (Modood, 1994: 1), is used to refer to those individuals with recent origins in South Asia, who were born, raised and now are living in Britain. **African Caribbean**, **African**, or **Caribbean** is used to refer to those with recent origins in the Caribbean and/or Africa. More specifically, **British African Caribbean** is used to refer to those with recent origins in those countries, who were born, raised and are now living in Britain. Where the identity is in a *white* majority society, the term **black** in its presented form (lower case) is also inserted. Where the identity is also a politicised one in addition to being in a *white* majority society, the term **Black** in its presented form (capital letter) is also used.

The terms **white** and **white European** have often been presented in *race* talk as neutral, that is, when they are used, they are done so to refer to all those who reside in 'a dominant but usually unquestioned cultural space that is neutral and normative', a space that is 'an unnamed, hegemonic position of privilege and power (which) becomes the point of reference for measuring others' (BSA, 2007: 6). They are also bound up by similar implications that are associated with essentialised notions of *blackness*. This book uses the terms reluctantly to refer to all those who are of non-black minority ethnic status.

The term **mixed-race** is used to refer to individuals whose biological parents are of at least two different *racial* origins. It has been argued that the term is problematic and disputed because it assumes that a pure race exists (BSA, 2007: 4). However, despite this, it is still viewed as having social meaning and significance, and is also an advancement on previous terms of reference such as *half-caste*. It is for this reason that the term is used.

The term **multi-racial** is used to refer to those individuals who regardless of their parent's *race*, view themselves as having no singular racial identity, but rather possess a socially constructed combination of *racialised* ones.

Racialisation is used to refer to the socially constructed processes by which a population group is categorised as a *race*, and the meanings that are attached to this category and the effects of this assigned label.

An explanation on the lack of use of the term *ethnicity* is required. This refers to 'cultural markers such as language, religion and shared customs' (Pilkington, 2003: 11). It has been pointed out that in looking at identity, the term *race* 'can deflect attention from cultural and religious aspects' of identity (Runnymede Trust, 2000: 6). As such, its use should be limited in place of *ethnicity*. However, it is argued that although *race* and *ethnicity* share their similarities and as such often overlap, their use also has important distinctions. Here, the markers of difference drawn on the basis of *race*, i.e. 'physical markers such as skin pigmentation, hair texture, facial features' (Pilkington, 2003: 11), continue to present its own set of distinct issues, which remain the focus of this book.

In talking directly about child placement and adoption, the term **transracial** is used to refer to the placement of a child into a family who are of a different race to that of the child.

This is often, although not always, the adoption of *black minority ethnic* and *mixed-race* children by *white* families (Turner and Taylor, 1996: 262). The term **inracial** is used to refer to those placements where the child and the adoptive family are of the same *race*. The term **intercountry** is used to refer to those placements where the child is from another country. This is often, although not always, the adoption of a *minority ethnic* child from a 'poor' country by *white* parents in a 'rich' country (Frost and Stein, 1989: 106).

The book may present variations on the given terms of reference, as well as the occasional use of additional key concepts. Where this is the case, a note explaining their use will be given accordingly. When describing or quoting the work of others, including the adoptees who were interviewed for the study on which this book is based, their own terms of reference have been used.

Race, the family and mixed-up kids?

The family is seen as one of the key agents for assisting development of a racial identity. Indeed, in terms of racial identity development, many view it as *the* most important agent. Here, a growing body of studies have been undertaken highlighting in particular the strengths and resilience of Black African Caribbean and African American family units (Genero, 1998; Hill, 1971; Logan, 1996; McAdoo, 1998; and Smith, 1996 in the US, and Hylton, 1997; Modood et al., 1997; Small, 1998; and Prevatt Goldstein and Spencer, 2000 in the UK). Although not quite as huge in volume, a similar body of literature has started to emerge on the familial strengths of other ethnic groups (see for example Hylton, 1997 and Jones, Jeyasingham and Rajasooriya, 2002). What these studies highlight is that despite a past history that has been filled with racial oppression in the form of forced migration, slavery and genocide, these oppressed communities have through struggle, resilience and mobilisation of strengths, survived and in many cases thrived. A significant element contributing to this survival strategy has been the black family.

Hill (1971) notes that there are five key strengths of the black family which have been culturally transmitted from one generation to the next:
1. a strong kinship bond
2. a strong work orientation
3. a strong achievement orientation
4. flexible family roles
5. a strong religious orientation.

Others after Hill (Hylton, 1997; Jones, Jeyasingham and Rajasooriya; 2002; Sudarkasa, 1997), have also supported this view. It is therefore argued that the black family have a unified outlook that is based on years of having experienced and survived racism. This outlook allows such families to assess risk, project protection, build up an effective wall of resilience, and harbour success for its members. This strength is partially due to the unique ability of black minority ethnic families to retain strong familial links with members in both Britain and abroad, and the ability to act as a positive black role model for children (Cheetham, 1986; Rashid, 2000).

However, black minority ethnic families continue to be dogged by negative and very often offensively inaccurate racist stereotypes. In addition, the characteristics of some black minority ethnic family units also suffer from contrasting perspectives in the press. For example, in August 1993, two images were presented about the black African Caribbean family. Firstly, there was *Newsweek* magazine's piece on the 'endangered black family', suffering from 'absent fathers' and hustler fathers, producing 'hopeless children and frustrated teenage mothers'. In the same year, *Ebony* magazine released a piece 'celebrating black families, by focusing on their determination, strength and diversity' (Johnson, 1997: 94). These contradictions exist in sociological studies also. For example, although their analysis was based on the same Census data-set, Moynihan (1965, in Johnson, 1997: 95) 'reported a deteriorating black family and recommended social policies that would encourage changes in the black family's structure and values', whereas Hill (1972, in Johnson, 1997: 95) 'observed the resilience of black families and recommended social policies that could build on the strengths of black family values and structure'.

These problematic contradictions also exist in Britain, where, as Rashid (2000) rightly notes, black families have had a contradictory response to their presence. Cheetham (1986) points out that stereotypes about black minority ethnic families persist in views that 'West Indian families are weak because of some ill-understood relationship with the ways of life enforced upon them as slaves; West Indian children are said to suffer from low self-esteem because, it is argued, they have no firm cultural roots. Asian parents are likely to experience insoluble conflict with their children. Muslim families will systematically suppress their female members' (Cheetham, 1986: 7). Cheetham observes that while there are some black minority ethnic families who have these characteristics, it is dangerous to assign these stereotypes to *all* black minority ethnic families, and indeed as Alexander (in Rashid, 2000: 15) argues further, use them to characterise the entire black community and all black people.

In particular, partially as a response to the criticism of black family formations, especially given the recent hostility generated largely by the media about 'baby-fathers',[1] and following comments such as that made by Britain's Commission for Racial Equality chairman Trevor Phillips in March 2004, implying that some absent fathers were partially to blame for the under-achievement of black boys at school, many have highlighted the significant role played in the formation of resilience and collective identities by female members of the black minority ethnic family that are re-produced in their everyday activities. Indeed, Anthias and Yuval-Davis

---

[1] 'Baby-father' is Caribbean slang for a man who does not live with his children – who often have different mothers. It is an affectionate Jamaican word which has somehow gained a negative meaning in Britain.

rightly suggest that 'women play a vital and unique role in the re/production of ethnic collectivities' (1992: 115). For example, Ali (2005), highlights the importance of cooking food and telling myths and stories and utilising memories for the development of these identities. James (1993), emphasises the whole mothering process, and what she calls 'othermothering'. This is 'the acceptance of responsibility for the welfare of non-blood related children in their community' (James, 1993: 44). She goes on to argue that:

> While western conceptualisations of mothering have often been limited to the activities of females with their biological offsprings, mothering within the Afro-American community and throughout the Black diaspora can be viewed as a form of cultural work ... othermothers can be defined as those who assist blood mothers in the responsibilities of child care for short-to-long-term periods, in informal or formal arrangements. They can be, but are not confined to, such blood relatives as grandmothers, sisters, aunts, cousins or supportive fictive kin.

(James, 1993: 44–5)

Similar work has been produced in the UK by Cheetham, 1986; Rashid, 2000 and Reynolds, 2001.

Diversity and the black family

Although the value of the family unit is not being disputed, especially in terms of its ability in providing an environment in which racial, ethnic and cultural identities can be formed – families are after all the key sites where stories are told, traditions and customs passed on, etc., it is argued that there is no one universal black family. Indeed, as McAdoo argues 'when one is asked to make a definitive statement about 'the Black family', it is now more difficult to respond. The diversity of Black families, their value systems, and their lifestyles, makes it impossible for any one person to be "the expert" on Black families. This is as it should be' (McAdoo, 1997: xx). Each black minority ethnic family varies according to, amongst other things, ethnicity, religion, politics and the history of the country from which it most recently originated. Within each of these variations exists sub-categories.

Each new offspring generation brings with it a new way of being. In recognising the diversity of black minority ethnic families then, it is also vital that we recognise the diversity of black minority ethnic racialised identities and to move away from the idea of a universal black identity. To do this is not to ignore the historical and ongoing struggle of black minority ethnic people living in racially discriminatory societies. Rather, it is to allow a fairly small, but significantly growing body of individuals the right to identify themselves in their own way. Using the social constructionist approach provides a means by which their experiences can be most appropriately understood.

This would mean developing a more accurate representation of the growing numbers of children experiencing such mixed upbringings, such as those from transracial adoption, children being born from mixed-race relationships, and the children and grandchildren (and even great-grandchildren) of immigrants, who came to the UK in the 1960s and 1970s, not to mention all those who came to the UK before and after this period. All these children share the key commonality of being considered by the wider society, policy makers and often by themselves to be 'mixed', either in terms of crude biological references or in terms of cultural differences. For them, an essentialist emphasis on Blackness as a political racial definition is problematic. Although to some degree these individuals may still experience racial discrimination, because as Small argues, the majority white society discriminates against anyone who has 'the slightest taint of Black' (Small, 1986: 92), one can nevertheless not escape the reality that these mixed individuals have a varied set of identity issues that an essentialised and wholly political Black label no longer caters for.

Indeed, what does it mean to be 'mixed', especially when talking about how such mixed individuals identify themselves? Traditionally, such individuals were often perceived to be susceptible to a variety of problems if they failed to adhere to a notion of Blackness, such as identity conflicts and an inability to deal with experiences of racism (Tizard, 1977). The idea being that they would never fully belong in a society where notions of binary blackness and whiteness are so embedded. Although at face value the points made appear sensible and logical, one cannot help but be concerned at the lack of empirical weight given to such arguments, and the emergence of what we see is a generation of mixed (racial, ethnic or cultural) individuals who choose to identify themselves, their lives, experiences and their identity in more complicated, flexible and diverse ways, which despite not adhering to essentialised notions of binary blackness and whiteness, are nevertheless emerging as positive and healthy identities.

Indeed, my own biographical experience is itself reflective of these issues. My father's parents, with whom we lived, came to Britain after spending time in both India and Kenya, bringing my father, aged 13 at the time, and his two siblings, in 1967. My father met my mother in 1971, a fellow Indian who had been born in Kenya and raised in India, and with her own family moved to Britain in the late 1960s. Together they went on to have three children, of which I was the middle child. Being raised in Wolverhampton, in the West Midlands, I was surrounded on a daily basis by a plethora of vibrant mixed and multi-racial communities. I was lucky enough to have a large extended family and a racially mixed social network, which provided me with a comfortable arena in which I could develop a racial identity that I felt comfortable with. However, on leaving home at the age of 18 years to study at university, I found myself in a new city where issues of race and racism differed. That is not to say that these issues did not exist whilst I was in Wolverhampton. Indeed, let us not forget that Wolverhampton was the then town of Enoch Powell, and the site of much racial tension from the 1970s onwards. Rather, as a Social Science student of black minority ethnic origin in a largely white majority university, itself located in a city with a dubious reputation in matters relating to race and racism, I began to mull in some great depth those issues associated with race and belonging. I now found myself increasingly encountering individuals and groups who assumed that I had been 'white washed',[2] using my lack of support for essentialist Black politics, not to mention my choice of partner who was a white Protestant male from Northern Ireland, as supposed clear evidence of this. It was here that my struggle to project my own racial identity, that of a British-born, brown-skinned woman of Indian heritage, began to be muffled. This attempt to silence me and have instead inaccurate politicised Black labels thrown upon me, led me to ask how others in similar situations responded to such essentialist and politicised racial labels.

The role of race in adoption

So how do black minority ethnic and mixed-race children who are most forcibly faced with these issues cope? One growing section of the population for whom these issues are prominent are black minority ethnic and mixed-race children in the care system. For a variety of reasons, many children cannot be raised by their birth families and this means that many of these children often find themselves in care. For example, there are approximately 60,000 to 85,000 children in care in Britain at any one time. Although the overall numbers of children entering the care system is decreasing, their actual length of stay once in the system is increasing (DfES, 2006a). Many want to be placed with a permanent alternative family (via adoption or long-term fostering), and so the importance of seeking permanent placements and avoiding temporary care is widely recognised as being an urgent necessity, largely because of the perceived problematic effects of temporary care. For example, it is argued that after a life in care 'young people in their teens are particularly vulnerable' and in particular report feeling lonely, having little support, confusion about their past, and suffering from poor access to housing and employment skills (Marsh, 1999: 69). It is clearly vital, therefore, that permanent care should be secured for these children as soon as possible.

Within this number there is a clear over-representation of black minority ethnic and mixed-race children in care (Ahmad, 1989; Barn, 1993; Frost and Stein, 1989). However, due to the lack of a national data collation of the racial and ethnic background of children in care, it is impossible to give any exact figures.[3] However, one count states that 'children of mixed-parentage (8 per cent) and black children (8 per cent) remain over-represented in the care system' (Barn, 2006: 4). Compared to their numbers in the general population and in comparison to their white counterparts, it is clear to see that there is a disproportionate number of black minority ethnic children in care. A variety of reasons and explanations have been offered as to the reasons for this. This includes the view that the British family services system is racist, and as such discriminates against black minority ethnic children in families. Therefore, it is seen as more ready to remove children from homes and then to discriminate

---

[2] This is an offensive term used to refer to a black minority ethnic individual who is viewed as having taken on stereotypical white characteristics over black ones.
[3] In 2000, the Department of Health recognised this problem and made initiatives to start recording and collecting data on black and ethnic minority service users (DoH, 2000c).

against prospective black minority ethnic parents wishing to adopt, largely because it views black minority ethnic families as feckless and problematic (Almas, 1992; Chand, 2000; Chimezie, 1975; Sunmonu, 2000).

Transracial adoption

It is therefore not surprising that many black minority ethnic children are transracially adopted. The adoption of these children by parents of a different race is like any race related issue, a contentious and controversial area of debate. Within Britain, it has been estimated that the transracial adoption of black minority ethnic and mixed-race children by white adopters make up more than half of all adoptions (SSI, 1997). And it is for this reason that this type of transracial adoption has particularly attracted a lot of attention by those who either view it as a viable option, or by others who contest it. It is important to note here that there is very little support for the practice of transracial adoption as an option in its own right. In other words, as an option to cater for that growing fraction of contemporary society who come from a mixed biological, or indeed cultural, background. Rather, those who do support this practice tend to do so on the basis that it is a 'next best thing' option, in the sense that an inracial placement would ideally be preferred, but failing the opportunity for that situation to be met, then a transracial one does offer some benefits and can, if carefully managed, work. This means that the first choice preference is still for an inracial placement – a black minority ethnic one, even if the child is of mixed parentage or of a different religious background.

However, in instances where an inracial placement can't be found, then those supporting the transracial adoption of black minority ethnic children by white parents have referred to evidence and theoretical arguments to suggest that it does not seriously harm or lead to identity problems for the black adoptee (Bagley, 1993; Brooks and Barth, 1999; Feigelman and Silverman, 1984; Simon and Alstein, 2000; Zastrow, 1977). Such support has also been reflected in adoption policy guidelines. For example, *Adoption: Achieving the Right Balance* (DoH, 1998), *The Prime Minister's Review of Adoption* (DoH, 2000a), the *Children Act 1989*, and the *Adoption and Children Act 2002* all make statements in line with guidance that: 'due consideration to the child's religious persuasion, racial origin and cultural and linguistic background' must be addressed (Children Act 1989, section 22(5)(c)). However, they also note the balancing of needs:

> These are . . . only some among a number of other significant factors and should not of themselves be regarded as the decisive ones. Where no family can be identified which matches significantly closely the child's ethnic origin and cultural heritage, the adoption agency's efforts to find an alternative suitable family should be proactive and diligent . . . the Government has made it clear that it is unacceptable for a child to be denied loving parents solely on the grounds that the child and adopters do not share the same racial or cultural background.

(DoH, 1998, sections 13–14)

Nevertheless, it is the arguments of the anti-transracial adoption camp which continue to dominate actual adoption practice. Although providing some evidence in support of their claims, the opposing camp's call to stop transracial adoption have largely been conjecture and underwritten by the argument that black children suffer serious identity problems as a result of having been raised in a white home, usually away from any Black culture or social network. The lack of sufficiently detailed or in-depth research into transracial adoption and identity development means that 'the agenda of debate was set by other priorities than discovering what was actually happening in the hearts and minds of those intimately involved' (Cohen, 1994: 60). The little research that does exist on the topic is contradictory and inconclusive. Its empirical evidence is problematic and open to interpretation. Its theoretical arguments are based more on a political perspective and conjecture rather than a firm sociological understanding of the issues involved. The consequence of this means that there is much confusion and disparity across Britain in terms of how social work agencies balance the child's welfare needs and the perceived need to be placed with a family of similar racial background.

It would be fair to say that there is something about transracial adoption, especially the transracial adoption of black minority ethnic and mixed-race children by white parents, which continually generates heated debate. Although it is something that has been practiced for many years, it would be fair to argue that the practice really came to be the focus of attention with what appeared to be a noticeable increase in its use in the 1960s. From this period onwards, there has been at the very least a fairly steady level of interest in the public arena. Although attention in the debate and subject matter have shifted over the years, the key elements of the debate, involving arguments about subsequent racial identity problems of the black minority ethnic adoptee, have never really disappeared. More recently though, there has been a resurgence of attention in transracial adoption, highlighted in the very least with a growing number of celebrities choosing to opt for transracial and intercountry adoptions. For example, consider the adoption by Mia Farrow of children from India, Vietnam and Korea, and more recently Madonna and Guy Ritchie's adoption of a child from Malawi, and Angelina Jolie and Brad Pitt's adoption of children from Cambodia and Ethiopia. Such an increase in celebrities choosing to adopt in these ways has also been reflected in lay society, with, for example, claims that requests for intercountry adoption have doubled since the Jolie-Pitt Ethiopian adoption (Adoption Advocates International, 2007). As mentioned before, we should also consider recent UK adoption policy which has noted that although due consideration must be given to the racial, cultural, religious and linguistic needs of the child, they should not be regarded as the decisive factors in placement practice (DoH, 1998, sections 12–14). Given this surge of recent interest in the rights and wrongs of transracial adoption, and the developments made in the race thinking since the last set of debates about transracial adoption took place, the time is now right to consider the issue again.

Why *another* book on race, identity and the family?

The claims about mixed racial identities made by this book are not new. Indeed, even the suggestion that not all black minority ethnic people view such mixed identities or transracial placements as problematic is also not a new one. For example, consider the work produced by Howard, Royse and Skerl in the late 1970s, whose study found that 'the majority of blacks do not support the militant position against transracial adoption and, in fact, favour such adoption when the alternative is institutionalisation' (Howard et al., 1977: 184). This book's value lies in the way in which it provides valid claims, and an illustration, about how mixed individuals develop a culture of their very own, one that is neither wholly black nor white but contains elements of both. This study is based on empirical research, and is thus able to offer a sound application of findings to a growing population of individuals who have moved beyond definitions based on appearance and colour, and identify themselves in such flexible, diverse and mixed ways. In doing so, a key contribution is therefore made to the discussion on race, identity and the family. A contribution, it should be noted, that seeks to balance a debate that continues to be dogged by limited discussion on the development of mixed identities in contemporary society.

In order to consider this on a deeper level, the book moves away from restrictive essentialist ideas about race and identity. Instead, it is argued that we need to consider the ways in which healthy, positive, mixed identities can be developed, and more importantly, with reference to the actual narratives of mixed individuals, to illustrate how they can develop and exist. This is not to say that they do not experience difficulties, but rather to demonstrate how such difficulties are negotiated and overcome, without having to surrender to an essentialised and ill-fitting notion of a universal and singular black identity. This book seeks to address these issues. Firstly, it provides an updated consideration on the social construction of a multi-racial identity. Secondly, it argues for multi-racial identity being viewed as valid in its own right, and an obtainable positive outcome for a growing number of individuals residing in society today. Thirdly, the relevance of this updated re-think is offered to both family placement and community link practitioners in the field, offering suggestions on how to best serve the needs and facilitate access to racial identity rights.

In order to provide an illustrative exploration of these issues and a sound foundation for the given argument, the case of transracial adoption is utilised, with the arguments then being applied to the cases of children of mixed (interracial) parentage[4] and the children of settled immigrants. However, it is important to note that in its challenge to the prevailing orthodox accounts, this being the essentialist and politically based arguments about a fixed Black identity that are used in the transracial adoption debate as well as wider discussions on racial identity development, this book does not seek to undermine the work of black minority ethnic

---

[4]This term is borrowed from Okitikpi (2005: 2).

social workers who have worked so hard and come so far to gain positions which allow them to ensure equality via a delivery of appropriate welfare provision for black minority ethnic people. Indeed, I have recognised elsewhere the importance of the role that such welfare workers make,[5] and the significance of 'a "black professionalism" beginning to replace a "white professionalism"' (Frost and Stein, 1989: 106). Rather, this book argues that an updated re-think of the essentialist ideology regarding identity is required if it is to represent the lives and experiences of a growing population of individuals who do not wholly identify themselves as either black or white. It also offers issues for welfare professionals to consider in their work with children. As Okitikpi (2005: 6) rightly recognises in his own work, a view which is applied to the arguments raised in this book:

> Some practitioners may well be aware of some of the issues but that many may need to review these in light of the debates and research findings . . . [the] 'meanings' for practitioners . . . are complex ones which must be filtered through the knowledge, skills and practice wisdom of individual practitioners . . . there is a plea to policy makers to open up a space where a thoughtful and innovative practice can be developed.

Organisation of the book

Based on a research study carried out between 2000 and 2003, this book seeks to redress the inconsistent nature of the debate by critically examining from a sociological position, the ways in which racial identity development theory has been applied to the transracial adoption debate, and how the same line of theorisation has then been used to comment on the lives of other mixed individuals, i.e. children of mixed (interracial) parentage, and the settled immigrant children for far too long. In its place, an updated consideration on the social construction of a multi-racial identity, that is valid and positive in its own right, is offered. It does so by looking at the problematic nature of the presented empirical evidence. Additionally, it discusses the findings of data produced from a sample of adults who were transracially adopted as children. At the time of interviewing, the interviewees were aged between 21 and 43 years, meaning that a wide range of narratives were given based on experiences which varied across time and context. In doing so, the book supports the idea of a changing identity, such as that described by Jenkins: 'identity is not just there, it must always be established . . . (and) can only be understood as a process of "being" or "becoming" . . . it is never a final or settled matter' (Jenkins, 1996: 4). The book then goes on to discuss the relevance of this perspective for those involved in both the family placement and community link sectors, offering suggestions on how to best serve the needs and facilitate access to racial identity rights.

Chapter 1 provides a contextualisation to the key debates by tracing the underpinnings of existing racial identity development arguments. It explores the possession of a racial identity

---

[5]See the author's other work, for example, Wright, Standen, John, German and Patel (2005).

in modern society, considering the existence, shape and ownership of multiple racial identities as opposed to a singular core racial identity. It is here that a critique of the Black radical perspective's arguments about blackness as an essentialised identity is offered. In doing so, a consideration of the social construction of racial identity, and in particular the Symbolic Interactionist theory is presented, utilising the ideas of theorists George H. Mead, Erving Goffman, and Herbert Blumer. The chapter closes by outlining identified social variables commonly found to shape and influence racial identity development.

Chapter 2 examines more precisely child, family and community support work. It begins by discussing the ways in which those working in these fields cater for the needs of members of the black minority ethnic and mixed-race populations. The chapter then goes on to examine more closely the case of child and family placement services, and its practice in matters relating to race and adoption. It provides an understanding of adoption practice, as well as a comparative consideration of practice in various countries around the world, such as the US approach to the pursuit of inracial placements and Korea's intercountry adoption programme, and then provides a more detailed consideration of practice in Britain. A statistical atlas of transracial adoption patterns is also given to locate the relevance of the debate. Throughout the chapter, critically reflective evaluations of existing legislation, including UK-wide legislation such as *Adoption (Intercountry Aspects) Act 1999*, and *Adoption of Children Acts, 1926, 1950, 1958, 1976* and *2002*, together with social work policy and practice followed in Social Service Organisations across the UK and advocated by specialist organisations, is drawn upon. In doing so, the chapter illustrates how the current approach is problematic and open to interpretation. In addition, the neglect of appropriate service delivery and the implications of this for those who do not define themselves in racially singular ways is also discussed.

Chapter 3 presents the narratives of a group of individuals of black minority ethnic or mixed-race origin who were transracially adopted as children. Their racial biographies are even more complex when considering that some of them are also intercountry adoptees, of mixed (interracial) parentage, and/or the offspring of immigrants. Their experiences are discussed, in particular the ways in which they negotiated the transracial experience, their birth heritage and other elements of their racial biographies in order to emerge with a racial identity that they felt comfortable with and considered best represented who they were. For example, areas considered include the place of race in the adoptive family home and its influence on the building of relationships with significant others in the adoptees transracial environment; the extent to which one's birth heritage will always act as an important link to the development of identity; whether they had searched for information and/or experience of their birth heritage, and whether such contact constituted their attempt to find answers or to establish connections; and did adoptees feel a need to gratify and fulfil a core essential racial identity? The chapter also reports upon and explores adoptees' ambivalent and ambiguous experiences of racial integration and racial isolation.

Chapter 4 asks what constitutes a transracial identity? In doing so, it explores the notion of having a positive or problematic multi-racialised identity, when deviating from expected racial stereotypes or supposed essential elements of a particular racial identity. The chapter also therefore explores the possibility of controlling racial signifiers when attempting to re-negotiate a more fitting racial identity, or racial identities. In illustrating the process of social construction, interaction and constant re-negotiation of a fluid racial identity, a key argument is made via the utilisation of a racial identity continuum.

In having made a call for a more updated and sophisticated level of thinking in matters relating to race and identity, and illustrated the way in which to achieve this, Chapter 5 applies the arguments to the case of children of mixed (interracial) parentage, and settled immigrant children. It does so because of the readily transferable status of the arguments made and its direct applicability to the given cases. In doing so, it argues that these groups also negotiate themselves a flexible multi-racial identity that is not just a black *or* a white one, but a combination of both. This multi-racial identity is a healthy and positive one that best represents who they are. Furthermore, the usefulness of this perspective is also applied to members of the wider black minority ethnic and mixed-race population, and their rights to the delivery of a more fitting body of child, family and community support services as a whole.

By drawing on some key conclusions, the final chapter applies the findings and arguments made in previous chapters to the policy development and placement practice in matters relating to child, family and community support, in particular for race and adoption. In doing so, it offers a series of realistic and readily useable recommendations for adoption best practice, as well as for other agencies and organisations working with black minority ethnic and mixed-race children. Finally, it indicates not only how permanent care can be secured, but also how a space to develop racially diverse and positive identities can be provided.

Race, racism and identity in a black and white society

Despite a recognition of the problematic notion of this 'entity' which is referred to as 'race', individuals in society continue to form ideas, develop attitudes and behave in accordance with socially constructed ideas about race. On a regular basis there is evidence of the social and political issues that demonstrate the power of race ideology. These can commonly be found in the political strategy of national politics, 'commonsensical' lay thinking and taken-for-granted notions, and an unquestioned belief in the media presentation of news. The messages about race that are projected by these institutions and collective organisations indicate the variety of ways in which ideas about race, that are themselves inaccurate, crude, offensive and based on a power imbalance where often being of black minority ethnic origin equals disadvantage and discrimination, continue to dominate.

The projection of these ideas continues to represent and sustain the idea that there is a clearly divided binary black and white society. The problem with this is the variety of implications it holds for those individuals who consider themselves as having moved away from a singular essentialised notion of racial identity, and instead have developed multi-racial identities. Considering this fact means that modern Britain is no longer the racially polarised society that many consider it to be. Rather it is host to a variety of spatial struggles where the politics of race, as well as ethnicity, continue to draw flexible boundaries between each other, which are themselves based on renegotiated notions of 'us' and 'them'.

In order to reconsider the emergence and prevalence of these outdated essentialist ideas, and this book's argument about the need to consider the social construction of multi-racial identities, a consideration of race, racism and identity issues in a binary black and white society such as Britain is presented.

Scientific racism

The concepts of race and racism did not always exist. It would be fair to argue that it only really began with the global expansion of European societies which occurred from the late fifteenth century onwards. This transforming period saw a rise in a new way of viewing natural and social phenomena, which was a level of thinking that was more and more orientated towards a scientific approach (Mason, 2000: 5). Global expansion brought with it contact with other human societies, and 'what appears to have struck explorers most forcefully, particularly those from England, were the differences in physical appearances ... the most striking of which was that of skin colour' (Mason, 2000: 5). It is important to remember that at this time skin colour characterisation was very significant because the colours of black and white were emotionally loaded concepts in the English language, in that they were 'polar opposites in which 'white' represented good, purity and virginity, and 'black' was the colour of death, evil and debasement' (Jordan, 1974, in Mason, 2000: 6).

By the mid-nineteenth century, the discipline of 'race science' had become fully established. These hierarchical scientific and enlightened ideas about race and biology were tied to mistaken ideas about human biology, and this included the idea that man was descended from apes (which we now know is untrue, although both man and apes probably developed from similar earlier forms of life), and in particular how black African Caribbean people were thought to be closer to the ape than the other races. Indeed, the biological differences between human races are relatively minor,[1] and all races are far more similar to each other than any modern ape. For example, it has been argued that no two human beings living today 'are likely to be further apart than fiftieth cousins' (Ely and Denny, 1987: 1). Indeed, Tizard and Phoenix argue that 'when genes have been mapped across the world it has been found that trends in skin colour are not accompanied by trends in other genes . . . 85 per cent of genetic diversity comes from the differences between individuals of the same colour in the same country, for example, two randomly chosen white English people' (Tizard and Phoenix, 2002: 2).

Racial hierarchy

Clearly this strand of 'scientific' thinking 'characterised human diversity as a division between fixed and separate races, rooted in biological difference and a product of divergent heritages' which then became linked to 'a notion of hierarchy in which all differences, both of history and future potential, were seen as a product of biological variation' (Mason, 2000: 6). Here black people were seen as savage barbarians (Ratcliffe, 2004: 16). Although empirically under-weighted for a variety of reasons, this enlightenment thinking continued to dominate societal relations. Despite the lack of any direct discussion on race, enlightenment thinkers, including Charles Darwin (1872), Frances Galton (1869) and Charles Linneaus (1735), to name a few, clearly held racist views (Malik, 2001).

Although enlightenment thinkers at first believed that all humans were potentially equal, and in principal all persons could reach a state of civilisation, in practice, however, the reality is that society fails to reflect this philosophy, which led enlightenment thinkers to argue that 'certain types of people were by nature incapable of progressing beyond barbarism, and they were therefore naturally inferior' (Malik, 2001: 3). The following comment illustrates this view:

---

[1] We now know that in terms of skeletal features, whites when compared with blacks and Asians are farthest in respect of jaw protrusion, but closer to apes in respect of their pronounced brow ridges, and the pronounced concavity of the spine in the blacks lower back region makes them the least ape-like of human groups in body form; in non-skeletal features, the thin lips and greater hairiness of the whites place them closer to the apes than are blacks (Ely and Denney, 1987: 1).

'there is in the world a hierarchy of races . . . those nations which eat more, claim more, and get higher wages, will direct and rule the others, and the lower work of the world will tend to be done by the lower breeds of men. This much we of the ruling colour will no doubt accept as obvious' (Murray, 1900, in Fryer, 1984: 173).

Indeed, this strand of thinking is still with us today, for example, if we consider the recent growth of interest in human genetics. Such an understanding has even filtered through to the everyday commonsensical usage of the term, which continues to create boundaries between groups of peoples and distinguishes these groups on rather a crude biological basis of colour, whereby white equals good and pure, and black is associated with evil (Mason, 2000; Tizard and Phoenix, 2002), as in, say, the commonly used phrase 'the black sheep of the family'. These negative connotations surrounding the term black continue to be associated with 'having undesirable qualities which prompt others to adopt strategies of exclusion and avoidance' (Britton, 1999: 134). More seriously, these ideas have been used to justify many atrocities, including Adolf Hitler's notion of the Final Solution and the master Aryan race, the US slavery period and 'Jim Crow' practices, and the apartheid system in South Africa. Similarly, such ideas are used to generate both fear and panic. One need only look at the recent 'race riots' of northern England and in the Los Angeles region of the US, and the observations concerning different populations following the aftermath of Hurricane Katrina in the US.

As a result of these 'race science' arguments and of the assumptions about race in everyday commonsensical society, race developed in the Western language as a means of creating boundaries and hierarchies. These then became 'a means for states to achieve their goals of domination, exploitation and extermination' (Guillaumin, 1999: 355). They also allowed for such ideas about essentialised identities, and the need to satisfy these, to form.

A sociological understanding of race

These 'race science' arguments were sharply questioned when the discipline of sociology began to recognise how race was a concept to which people were 'assigned' and which was then used to 'create' groups of people who either suffered racial oppression or a privileged position in society (Ignatiev, 1995: 1). Here it was recognised that colour and race is heavily dependant on contextual meanings, for example, 'in Spanish speaking parts of America no sharp line is drawn between black and white' (Banton, 1997: 54). Sociologists therefore became interested in this process of *racialisation* – that is, the social processes by which a population group is categorised as a race, the meanings attached to this and the effects of the assigned label. In studying race and the process of racialisation, sociologists are concerned with examining the causes and consequences of the socially constructed division of population groups according to what has been referred to as their race – whether this is something that has been self-assigned or allocated by others.

Contesting the 'race' concept

Although all sociologists agree that race is something that is socially constructed as opposed to being naturally given, there is some dispute as to the status of the concept of race. Many see race as a crude biologically based label. It is argued that this is because the term 'reflects and perpetuates the belief that the human species consists of separate races' and therefore 'can deflect attention from cultural and religious aspects' of identity (Runnymede Trust, 2000: 6). Hence many sociologists have rejected the term. To demonstrate this they have either highlighted its 'contested character' by using it in inverted commas, or stopped using it altogether (Mason, 2000: 8).

However, other sociologists point out how race 'remains a legitimate concept for sociological analysis because social actors treat it as real and organise their lives and exclusionary practices by references to it' (Mason, 2000: 7). Many sociologists, therefore, take the view that although there is no such thing as races *per se*, 'large numbers of people behave as if there are' and it is this that sociology must examine (Mason, 2000: 8). In particular, sociology needs to examine the 'social relationship of race' (Pilkington, 2003: 17), and the ways in which via the generation of the ideas and beliefs around 'the social and cultural relevance of biologically rooted characteristics' this 'relationship presumes the existence of racism' (Mason, 1995, in Pilkington, 2003: 17).

The polarisation of black and white

Sociological understanding of the construction of race and blackness has focused on the polarisation of blackness and whiteness. It has found that over time the polarisation of race in this way has been justified through a variety of means. This includes references to religion, politics and the so-called 'race science'. For example, Dyer discusses the polarisation of blackness and whiteness and how 'non-white' people 'became seen as degenerative, falling away from the true nature of the (human) race' (Dyer, 1997: 22). Dyer stated that these views were justified by references to religion. For example, Johan Boemus in 1521 proposed that all humans 'descended from the sons of Noah, these being Ham, Shem and Japeth, and argued that the descendents of Ham degenerated into 'blackness', whereas those civilised descended from Shem and Japeth, and so remained white' (Fredrickson, 1981, in Dyer, 1997: 22).

For sociologists, however, black and white are socially constructed via a power relationship in society where being white equals privilege and superiority, and being black equals disadvantage and discrimination. They therefore can be seen as socio-political concepts in that their meanings and usage are based on ideas that are developed and maintained in social human interaction through dialectical and behavioural processes. There has been sociological work, supported by actual psychological and scientific tests, which show that humans are not divided into biological races, and which also disprove dated ideas around the so-called problematic nature of black minority ethnic people, such as having poor IQ levels, a proneness to violent behaviour, untrustworthiness and sexual promiscuity. However, dated ideas continue to dominate, and show themselves in a variety of discriminatory practices and attitudes. In suggesting reasons for this behaviour many writers have pointed to intentional and unintentional racism and discriminatory practices, by both black and white groups, which mean that a power imbalance between whiteness and blackness, and indeed within each, continues to exist and perpetuate itself.

There are serious problems in the effects of the social construction of blackness and whiteness in this way. Firstly, because of the way in which black and white are held as distinct and separate, which means that all those who either do not want to, or do not feel as if they wholly belong to one or the other group, are then marginalised or deemed to have identity problems. This is often the case for those people who are mixed-race, and who find themselves frequently marginalised or deemed as having psychological, emotional and social problems as a result of their supposed conflict by being raised between two distinctly different racial groups. Secondly, the polarisation means that there is unequal treatment of one group at the hands of another. For example, Owusu-Bempah and Howitt argue that black people continue to be seen as 'flawed psychologically, morally and socially' (Owusu-Bempah and Howitt, 2000: 95), not only as individual black people, but in terms of their cultures and family life, and indeed every aspect of their lives. This leads to the third problem of white being accepted as the norm against which everything is then measured. As Dyer argues, 'in other words, whites are not of a race, they're just the human race' (Dyer, 1997: 3). Here, the idea that black people have culture, and white people have civilisation is perpetuated and it is this perpetuation that needs to be challenged and changed (Khan in Ely and Denney, 1987: 12).

Clearly, Dyer argues that we need to look at the construction of whiteness. However, I suggest that we also need to do so alongside or in parallel with an updated (re)consideration of the social construction of blackness. Therefore, not only do we need to look at the construction of whiteness and 'dislodge it from its centrality and authority' (Dyer, 1997: 10), but we also need to question the politicised essentialist ideas around blackness that have dominated, and limited, debates. Hence, as well as a rejection of the idea that race and blackness are natural categories, the existing usage of the term black and the ideas around notions of blackness within society, politics, sociology and so on, are also contested and re-examined.

Imposed universality of blackness

Sociological discussions around the concept of blackness have seen some sociologists, such as Small, using the term black to refer to a supposed 'common experience of Afro-Caribbean and South Asian people who are the subject of racism and their collective will to struggle against it' (Small, 1991: 62). Although Small and others like him recognise that there are other groups who experience discrimination, like the Irish, race is considered by Small as it 'relates to the more visible groups' because the experiences of those visibly black are more difficult than those not visibly black (Small, 1991: 62).

The problem here is that Small, and others sharing this view, fail to consider how the black label or concept of blackness is rejected by those very people he assumes to be black. As Cohen points out, this is because having been initially reduced to being 'a biological category', blackness is 'then reconstructed as a 'political colour' so that it can be magically expanded to include a large number of honorary blacks . . . on the grounds that they have a long and honourable history of resisting racism' (Cohen, 1994: 59).

Modood has highlighted how the blackness concept actually harms British Asians because of how such homogeneity is imposed. It is important to note that Modood (1994: 859) does not actually so much criticise the concept of blackness, but rather he criticises that of the 'assumed homogeneity'. For Modood, the problem is that British Asians suffer from a form of 'doublespeak' which labels them black depending on the convenience or politics of the speaker/writer and not on the Asian in question. They therefore suffer from 'false essentialism' because black for Asians refers to features from African Caribbean history and their experiences are assumed to fit in with or be the same as these. Modood also argues that the black homogeny also means marginalisation for British Asians because for them black is no more than a political colour that is imposed upon them, with other areas being neglected, since for the majority of British Asians, religion is central to self-definition (Modood, 1994).

Similarly, MacAnghaill refers to the work of Back (in MacAnghaill, 1999: 62), to highlight how the current usage of the term black is not suited to the UK black, South Asian or other minority ethnic origin populations because the ideas around black identity has its roots and significance in the African American Civil Rights and Black Power movements in 1960s America. As a result, the homogeneous application to members of the diverse British black minority ethnic peoples, and in particular the South Asian population, is inaccurate, and this inaccuracy is also offensive. The inaccurate reference is also a hindrance to any real progression. This is because a particular population's historical roots are not being accurately recognised, recorded or respected.

Identity essentialism

This leads us to consider the essentialising of racial identity, a politicised approach that has often been used in the theorisation of black minority ethnic people, including those of mixed-race. Ballis-Lal provides an outline of the essentialist arguments, stating that the essentialist view is that there is one clear and authentic set of 'black characteristics' which are unique to all black people and which do not alter across time. According to this 'identity essentialism' model, not only does 'one facet of a person, such as race . . .'trump' all other conceptions of selfhood' but 'it also determines experiences and life chances' (Ballis-Lal,

1999: 56–7). The model also 'emphasises the benefits of knowing who you are as a consequence of either biological descent or socially constructed attributes such as race, and of participation in collectivities organised around an essentialist identity' (Ballis-Lal, 1999: 57). This means that the individual's 'primary identity' is the Black one, which is pre-fixed and determines their experiences. It also means that the individual needs to be raised in an environment that can nourish this Black identity, namely to be raised in a black family within a black community. This is because it is argued that there is 'uniqueness to being black, that one has to be black in order to understand it and transmit its meaning' (Simonton, 2000: 1).

Indeed, this essentialist view is something that is supported by many practitioners, researchers and authors within the field. For example, Maximé argues that the 'inner core racial identity has an ethnographic substance . . . and that racial identity is developed by nurturing it in a positive way. Therefore racial identity needs to be stimulated and reinforced' (Maximé, 1994: 2). Small has commented extensively on the issue, largely through his work with the Association of Black Social Workers and Allied Professionals (ABSWAP, 2007), a British based organisation which 'contributed to a radical shift in the ideological base of social work practice' (Prevatt Goldstein, 2000: 9), and which led a huge drive in inracial placements. Here, as a foundation for his work, Small has placed great emphasis on the psychological damage that is likely to occur when the black core identity of these children is not recognised (Prevatt Goldstein, 2000).

Realising a Black core

In line with this essentialist thinking, many theories have 'attempted to explain the various ways in which blacks can identify (or not identify) with other blacks' (Helms, 1990: 5). Here, the possession or development of a positive and healthy black identity has been measured by:

* Racial group preferences.
* Racial self-identification.
* Knowledge, awareness and experience of one's own racial group.

For example, Clark and Clark (1939, 1940, 1947, 1950), used dolls to test black children's racial preference and racial self-identification. In their 1947 study the Clarks presented 253 three to seven-year-old black children with dolls that were identical in every way except skin and hair colour. Two dolls were brown and had black hair, which the Clarks referred to as 'coloured', and the other two were white and had yellow hair (white) (Clark and Clark, 1947: 169).

In attempting to measure racial preferences, the Clarks asked each child to give them 'the nice doll', upon which 150 chose the white doll. Each child was then asked to give the researchers 'the doll that looks bad', whereupon 149 chose the black doll. To measure racial self-identification, the Clarks asked the children to give the researchers 'the doll that looks like you'. In response, 166 children chose the black doll and 85 chose the white doll. From this demonstration, the Clarks suggested that the black children had low self-esteem because they had negative views of black people and inaccurate views of themselves. The primary reason for this was because they internalised white people's negative views of their black race. The identity confusion was therefore seen as a result of them having denied their own colour.

This type of test, using either dolls or photographs, was replicated by others. Johnson, Shireman and Watson (1987) used the Clark doll test with a sample of adoptees between four and eight years old. The sample contained 42 transracial adoptees and 45 Black adoptees who were adopted by black families. They found that at age four, the transracially adopted black children had a greater awareness of their race in that they had correctly identified the doll as having a race similar to their own, and had a greater preference towards dolls of their own race at an earlier age than the inracially adopted black children. However, at age eight, both groups of adopted children were found to have expressed similar levels of awareness and preference.

Some argue that this study, and others finding similar results, showed a drop in the number of black children who were not identifying themselves as black because of the positive contributions made by the black civil rights movement. Others say it is due to the use of more accurate and realistic dolls or photographs. However, Tizard and Phoenix (1989) point out that a significant number of studies measuring racial identity and self-concept levels have still found that 'a substantial proportion of young black children continue to say that they prefer, or would prefer to be like, the white doll or photograph' (Tizard and Phoenix, 1989: 429).

Looking at black racial identity development, Cross's 'Nigrescence model' (1971) outlined a view of the developmental process by which a person 'becomes black'. In this sense, the Black identity 'is defined in terms of one's manner of thinking about and evaluating oneself and one's reference groups rather than in terms of skin colour per se' (Helms, 1990: 17). The model aimed to separate those aspects of black identity development which resulted from racial oppression, from those which occurred 'as a normal part of the human self-actualisation process or the need to be the best self that one can be' (Maslow, in Helms, 1990: 17). Hence, according to the model, an over-identification with white culture was not only seen as unhealthy, but also a consequence of an identity crisis. Helms (1990) and Maximé (1986) each provide good outlines of Cross's five stage model.

The first stage was the 'pre-encounter' stage. In this, the black individual has a 'euro-centric' or white orientated view. They identify with white culture, whilst rejecting or denying their membership in black culture, and even denying the existence of racism. Some may even develop anti-black attitudes. The second stage of the model is the 'encounter' stage, where the black individual has an actual experience of racism that is so strong that it forces them to reinterpret their world. They reject their previous identification with white culture and instead seek identification with black culture. Next is the 'immersion-emersion' stage. Here the black individual attempts to identify completely with black culture and debases white culture. In the fourth 'internalisation' stage, the black individual successfully internalises black culture. In the final fifth stage of the model, the 'internalisation-commitment' stage, the black individual continues to internalise black culture, but in addition fights general cultural oppression by, for example, becoming involved in black groups or in black community issues (Helms, 1990: 12; Maximé, 1986: 108).

Mixed-race individual's adherence to blackness

However, when looking at these black racial identity theories and models, one should consider the place it allocates for those who are mixed-race. In this area, traditionally a society where there is a white majority, and with it white privilege and power, the 'one-drop rule' has been used to mark out those who are of mixed-race. These individuals' blackness has often been noted and racially classified[2] for hierarchical purposes, which though placing them closer to whites, nevertheless marked them as black, often for economical and inheritance purposes (Owusu-Bempah, 2005: 28). A by-product of their blackness being forced upon them led to their mixed-race status being ignored.

Based solely on theory and presented with an absence of empirical evidence, the idea of mixed-race people having such independent viewpoints was raised by Robert Park in 1928 and later developed by Everett Stonequist in the 1930s. Park wrote that certain individuals are 'predestined to live in two cultures and two worlds' (Park, in Tizard and Phoenix, 2002: 43). In discussing this type of person, whom Park called 'the marginal man', the case of mixed-race individuals was referred to, although today the concept also extends to transracial adoptees. Park argued that although 'the marginal man' was condemned to a life of living between 'two diverse cultural groups' and hence could develop 'an unstable character' (Park, 1928: 881), the position also brought with it the benefit of 'the marginal man' having the unique experience of being able to 'fuse' the two cultures and 'widen their horizon' (Park, ibid). Stonequist (1937) developed Park's ideas. However, he instead pointed out that the 'the marginal man' faced serious psychological problems as a result of being torn between the two opposite cultures: 'the individual who lives in, or has ties of kinship with, two or more interacting societies between which there exists sufficient incompatibility to render his own adjustment to them difficult or impossible he does not quite 'belong' or feel at home in either group' (Stonequist, 1942: 297).

Also, according to these theories and models, it is argued that there should be no difference made between children who are black and children who are mixed-race. Small provides some ideas as to possible reasons for this. Firstly, he says that: 'when most people use the term 'mixed-race' they do not mean a child of Indian and African parents, nor a Chinese and a person of African descent, they generally mean the child of a white person

---

[2]Traditional racial classifications that have been used made reference to 'sambo'; someone who was of '87.5 per cent "black blood"'; 'mango'; someone was '75 per cent black'; 'meamelouc'; someone who was '6.25 per cent black'; and, 'sang-mele'; someone who was '1.56 per cent black'. Indeed, these crude classifications still exist today. Consider for example commonly used terms such as 'mixed-breed', 'half-breed' and 'half-caste' (Owusu-Bempah, 2005: 28).

and any other person who is not white ... (and) in this society, any child who has the slightest taint of black is seen by the majority as black ... for those children there are no "in-betweens" '. Secondly, the term mixed-race itself is deceptive because it leads 'transracial adopters to believe that such children are racially distinct from other blacks. Consequently, they may neglect the child's need to develop a balanced racial identity and thereby a well-integrated personality'. Thirdly, 'many black people find the term "mixed-race" derogatory and racist because they feel it is a conscious and hypocritical way of denying the reality of a child's blackness' (Small, 1986: 91). This is problematic at the very least because a somewhat militant pro-Black position is imposing this label on mixed-race individuals, regardless of their own wishes (Alibhai-Brown, 2001: 5).

Others also disagree with the labelling of mixed-race people as wholly black. This is because it is nevertheless viewed as a way of 'socio-politically scraping out their white heritage' (Owusu-Bempah, 2005: 28). For example, in reporting part of a wider study, Tizard and Phoenix looked at the racialised identities of 58 young people of mixed black and white parentage, whom they refer to as people of 'mixed-parentage' from in and around London. Of the young people, 60 per cent lived with both parents, 12 per cent with a single black parent, or a black parent and a black step-parent, and 28 per cent with a single white parent, or a white parent and a white step-parent. The authors found that 'people of mixed-parentage do not always wish to be viewed as "black" – even though they are likely to share experiences of racism with black people'. This is partially because to define themselves as black would involve them denying their white parent (Tizard and Phoenix, 2002: 219).

Similar results were also found by the sample of mixed-race people in Alibhai-Brown's (2001) study. It is therefore argued that 'mixed-parentage' people 'have independent viewpoints' due to the 'mixed' race status of their birth, and often they used a special term to reflect this 'mixed-parentage', such as 'half-caste' and 'mixed-race' (Tizard and Phoenix, 2002: 219–21). Indeed, as Wilson found in her study of mixed-race youngsters: 'mixed-race children do not necessarily conform to the stereotype of the social misfit, caught between the social worlds of black and white. Not all mixed-race children are torn between the ethnic loyalties of their parents and not all spend their lives trying to make themselves acceptable to one ethnic group' (Wilson, 1987: 176).

However, in addressing Small's use of the term Black in an essentialised way, Prevatt Goldstein (2000), who also rests her own arguments on 'a political and inclusive understanding of the word "black" ' (Prevatt Goldstein, 1999: 286) is keen to note that Small's and indeed it follows, her own 'inclusive use of the word "black" to refer to those of South Asian, African and African Caribbean and black and white parentage, reflects the striving for black political unity of the 1980s and is open to misinterpretation by those who adhere to the more recent fragmentation of "black" into its ethnic components' (Prevatt Goldstein, 2000: 14). Although this may be both Prevatt Goldstein and Small's base in their selected usage of the term black, one should nevertheless consider what it serves to take away from those who are not perceived, by themselves or by others, as wholly black, either biologically, socially, politically or otherwise. Moreover, as Dean (1993, in Owusu-Bempah and Howitt, 2000: 111), points out, 'there is now a need for progression away from a simplistic conceptualisation of ethnicity based on a crude black/white dualism towards a more comprehensive understanding of the complex factors that contribute to the establishment of a personal and group identity' (Dean, 1993: 33).

Owusu-Bempah and Howitt provided a valid critique of the supposed problems faced by the marginal man and those residing in such similar positions, this being the idea that 'culturally and socially, the marginal person was said to live in limbo. Psychologically, marginal individuals were perceived to experience torment, to experience psychiatric and emotional problems, low self-esteem and identity confusion' (Owusu-Bempah and Howitt, 2000: 96). They go on to argue that such views, especially those of the Black self-hatred thesis, are 'essentially conjectural and suffer from tunnel vision' (ibid: 97), and even more so, dangerous in that such views are 'accepted virtually without question' (ibid: 100). They further argue that nevertheless the 'myth' about Black self-hatred and low self-esteem continues to exist.

The social construction of identity

Identity is viewed as something that is largely, although not wholly, socially constructed. Racial identity is therefore shaped by social relations, whilst also acknowledging that to some degree, an individual's biology plays some conditioning role. Ballis-Lal rightly argues:

> . . . identity is orientated to affiliations based upon consent . . . as well as social bonds based upon descent . . . individuals and groups see themselves with respect to others in many different ways. Self-conception is a creative process, both changeable and self-interested although subject to constraints, such as the understandings and behaviour of others in particular situations and conventions and norms.
>
> (Ballis-Lal, 1999: 60)

The social constructionist perspective and in particular the Symbolic Interactionist theory, views race and blackness as labels that are socially constructed in an ongoing process between:

- The individual.
- The individual's social contact with other individuals.
- How the individual thinks others perceive them.
- The individual's social environment.

The reported study therefore rejected the idea that race and blackness are natural categories. Instead it supports the ideas of Britton, who in her study of collective racialised identities argued that:

Having a non-white skin colour does not indicate a related uniform experience specifically because, first, skin colour accounts partially for processes of racialisation and, second, defining oneself and being defined as black is always, to a certain extent, negotiable . . . the common-sense prioritising of skin colour as the key to explaining the racialised social world tends to disguise the complexity of processes of racialisation.

(Britton, 1999: 152)

In this instance, racial identity development is examined from a social constructionist perspective. It argues that the boundaries of racial groups are subjective and fluid, and that racial identity development is socially constructed in transactions which occur at and across permeable boundaries of group classification (Jenkins, 1996). Therefore, racial identities are actively and creatively produced by human beings in their everyday social interaction and can be best understood as an 'ongoing synthesis of (internal) self-definitions and the (external) self-definitions of oneself offered by others' (Jenkins, 1996: 20). Such a social constructionist perspective therefore moves away from the essentialist ideas of racial identity being something that is wholly naturally given.

Symbolic Interactionism: Mead, Blumer and Goffman

In particular, the use of this perspective in this study involves a construct of identity based on the works of Symbolic Interactionists George Herbert Mead (1995), Herbert Blumer (1969) and Erving Goffman (1982). The Symbolic Interactionist theorisation of the 'self' being developed in ongoing social communication and symbolic interaction is used to guide the theorising of racial identity development. This means there is an emphasis on the importance of the negotiation of racial categorisations found in the language, meanings and symbols of human symbolic communication, and how such racial categorisations are constantly being negotiated and (re)negotiated. To understand this process, a consideration of the Symbolic Interactionist theorisation of identity development is now given, which is then followed by its application to the theorisation of racial identity.

Mead (1995) argued that the construction of 'self' is a social process. It is something that 'is structured from the outside to the inside, (and) reflects the structure of role models, games, rules, generalised others, and the institutions in the individual's social world' (Baldwin, 1986: 112). As such, 'the self . . . is essentially a social structure, and it arises in social experience' (Mead, 1995: 367). This is because of 'the human capacity to be reflexive and take the role of others' (Macionis and Plummer, 2002: 156). For Mead then, 'the individual possesses a self only in relation to the selves of the other members of his social group; and the structure of his self expresses or reflects the general behaviour pattern of his social group' (Mead, 1995: 373). As the human social self is seen as inseparable from wider society, this means that the community has some degree of power over the individual's formation of social self and the way in which they identify themselves, because 'the individual takes . . . the organised social attitudes of the given social group or community' (ibid: 370), and absorbs them into their own self.

In addition to this, individuals are seen as having 'multiple selves', because 'we carry on a whole series of different relationships to different people . . . (and) we divide ourselves up in all sorts of different selves with reference to our acquaintances' (ibid: 368). However, in suggesting this, Mead disputes the idea of there existing any sort of identity conflict. For example, he argues that 'we can discuss politics with one and religion with the other (because) there are all sorts of different selves answering to all sorts of different social reactions' (ibid: 369). This means that we are not only just one person, but rather that we can be different people at different times.

Although at times this may produce contradictory selves, this is nevertheless viewed as perfectly normal and healthy. For example, Kathleen Hall collected and used the examples of several stories given by second generation British-Sikh teenagers growing up in Leeds to illustrate how cultural identity formation is an ongoing process. Hall found that the British-Sikh teenagers' construction and negotiation of alternative ways of being a British-Sikh teenager in modern England was based on 'a compromise' which had been the result of them having negotiated multiple forms of identity that were available to them in their homes and communities. This had meant that the British-Sikh teenagers 'act and react, fashioning their identities creatively, within the ambiguous space in between their British and Sikh selves' (Hall, 1995: 258).

Harris and Sim, in their study of mixed-race adolescents' construction of race, support this view by arguing that the 'boundaries of racial groups vary both over time and across social contexts . . . people need not have a single racial identity that they carry with them from birth to death (but) rather people may be born one race, live as a second race, and have yet a third racial identity at death' (Harris and Sim, 2000: 4–5). According to this, race is assigned depending upon:

- Whether the individual identifies themself, or has their racial identity defined by someone else.
- Their ancestry, whether this is real or, as is usually the case, imagined.
- The context in which they find themselves, for example, the other(s) race, ideology, familiarity with the individual, racial composition of the context, etc.
- Their own personal history.

(Harris and Sim, 2000: 4–5)

As previously mentioned, this social constructionist theorisation clearly emerges from the works of Symbolic Interactionists Mead (1995), Blumer (1969), and Goffman (1982). In the development of social life and individual identity, Mead emphasised the importance of how individuals negotiate 'language' and 'symbols' that are presented in everyday social relations. These ideas were developed by Blumer who stated that the theory of Symbolic Interactionism consisted of three key concepts. These were 'meaning', 'language', and 'thought'. Meanings referred to the way in which humans naturally assign meaning to people and things, and then act accordingly. This is a central principle of the understanding of human behaviour according to the Symbolic Interactionist theory. The next concept is that of 'language' which is the source of meaning. This is because language gives humans a means by which to negotiate meaning through 'symbols'. The third concept is that of 'thought', which refers to the individual's ability to take the role of the other during social interaction. As thought is a mental dialogue that requires role taking, or imagining different points of view, this then allows the individual to develop their own understanding of the other and of their own self. This is where Mead's ideas about the 'I' and the 'Me' emerge. The 'I' is the active portion of the self, capable of performing behaviours and the 'Me' is the socially reflective portion of the self, providing social control for the actions of the 'I'. The combination of the 'I' and 'Me' equals the self. It is important to recognise that according to the Symbolic Interactionist theory, the self is seen as a process as opposed to a structure because the 'I' acts out action and the 'Me' defines the self as reflective of others as a result of the action (Mead, 1995).

Goffman further developed Blumer's ideas around Symbolic Interactionism by highlighting the importance of symbols and rituals in everyday life. He looked at what he called 'the interaction order'. This is 'what we do in the presence of others' (Goffman, 1982: 2). In his analysis, Goffman used the metaphor of the theatre to argue that individuals 'perform' roles, and the individual's 'performance' can be seen as a 'presentation of their self', that is, the individual's attempt to create a specific impression in the minds of others (Goffman, 1982). In addition, according to Goffman, individuals not only 'perform', they also watch from the audience, meaning that they are also able to observe performances.

In terms of this research study, Goffman's illustration of the deeply textured way in which societies are ordered through an array of human social interactions, helps to highlight the Symbolic Interactionist theorisation of individual behaviour being dependent upon and influenced by other individuals in a network of social interaction where symbolic communication lies at the heart of explaining individual identity and social life. Goffman also considered the role of 'stigma' in the way in which one is perceived, and hence the way an individual is able to negotiate their social identity. Here, possession of a certain stigma attribute, such as race, means that 'an individual who might have been received easily in ordinary social intercourse possesses a trait that can obtrude itself upon attention and turn those of us whom he meets away from him, breaking the claim that his other attributes have on us. He possesses a stigma, an undesired differentness from what we had anticipated' (Goffman, 1963: 14).

Key variables in influencing racial identity

The Symbolic Interactionist theorisation is used to show that racial identity is developed in an ongoing process of social interaction, where the individual negotiates a racial identity that reflects their immediate social environment. This racial identity will be one that the individual feels most appropriately fits in with, and reflects, the shared norms and values of that environment, as well as being the one that they feel most comfortable with. The flexible nature of the racial identification process also means that the individual is able to construct themselves multiple racial identities, each able to modify and adapt to a variety of sub-settings within society. For example, at certain times they will be required to lean more towards a particular racial identity, and at other times towards another. The requirement to do so will be largely based upon the other social actors and the significance/meanings attached to a particular racial identity within that sub-setting.

Clearly then, the application of the Symbolic Interactionist theorisation of identity to understanding racial identity development allows an appreciation of not only the social constructed status and negotiated creation of racial identity, but also to understand its complex, diverse and fluid nature.

A number of variables can therefore be identified in the formation of racial identity development. These will be discussed at greater length in the following chapters, but in brief they are:

- physical features
- gender
- age
- immediate family
- friends
- immediate and wider social networks
- religion
- history
- geographical location

These highlight the socially constructed ways in which both biological and cultural elements are defined and negotiated. Theorising about their role and significance in the racial identity development process allows us to consider the ways in which they are in a constant state of being negotiated and renegotiated, as and when required to do so.

CHAPTER 2

Serving the needs of black minority ethnic and mixed-race children

In its broadest sense, family placement and other community link services in the UK refers to the body of various agencies and organisations whose goal it is to promote the emotional, mental, physical and economic welfare of those individuals in society experiencing social suffering, disadvantage and exclusion. This is attempted by the use of preventative measures and relief packages. Within this body exists family support groups and child placement services whose focus is on ensuring the care and support of those children, young people and families identified as vulnerable or at risk. When referring to one of the most vulnerable sections of the population, that is, children who are of a black minority ethnic or mixed-race background, it is vital that family placement services and community links work hard to provide a service that is underpinned by an ethos of representation, equality and fairness, as well as one that is needs appropriate.

Although guided by national government policy and legislation, each of the regional sectors of these groups and services often conceptualise their role and policy practice differently. This practice is largely determined by locally based variables such as the historical context of child care, cultural norms and available resources, as well as the politicised views of practitioners. These considerations enter another level of complex thinking when issues around race are taken into account. Given the focus of this book, what is of concern here are the ways in which policy makers and practitioners undertake duties in matters relating to the needs of black minority ethnic and mixed-race children, particularly in terms of decisions made about child care and family placement. In light of this, an historical mapping of adoption practices and patterns is given, and in doing so, this chapter also considers the use of adoption in contemporary society. In particular, legislative ruling, policy formulation and practice implications are considered with reference to issues of race.

Disadvantage and discrimination in support services

Black minority ethnic service users report being faced with inappropriate services, which, underlined by racial prejudice, fail to meet their needs (Chahal, 2004). This situation has been heavily influenced by race theories and stereotypical beliefs about a binary racial order and an essentialised ideology about race and identity. It would appear that support services in the areas of health, welfare, housing, education, employment and criminal justice for black minority ethnic and mixed-race members of the population have historically been based on fixed, racist and stereotypical ideas of particular cultures and their supposed needs. This has occurred at both practitioner and organisational levels. In all these cases, these black minority ethnic people have been problematised, both individually and as a community as a whole. They are seen as weak, oppressive and incapable of change. Today, these ideas continue to dominate.

Consider, for example, the attention paid by the British press to the case of teenager Shafilea Ahmed, whose decomposed body was found in the river Kent in Kendal, Cumbria, in February 2004. Allegations soon followed that her parents had abused her and attempted to force her into an arranged marriage (*The Independent*, 9 January 2008). What then followed in the press was a claim that this sort of attitude was found largely amongst families of Asian origin, and who, if we believed these media reports, were all forcing their young daughters to marry men, many of whom were much older, often in order for them to enter the UK. Such reports were designed not so much to highlight the plight of a vulnerable group, which in a small minority of cases do exist, but more so to strike at the very core thinking of all white British people, the threat of a continued *Asian invasion* that would soon outnumber the white majority.

Consider the negative press given to black African Caribbean single mothers. Song and Edwards (1997: 233), highlight that although 'black lone mothers constitute a relatively small proportion of all lone mothers in Britain', this being 'just under 5 per cent of lone mothers, as compared with over 90 per cent of white lone mother households' (1991 Census, in Song and Edwards, 1997: 233), they continue to be demonised and presented as 'folk devils' (Cohen, 1972). This is done via the presentation of links between them and the receipt of welfare benefits. In reality, it is worth noting that black lone mothers are in fact 'much more likely to be economically active and in full-time employment than white lone mothers' (Bartholomew, Hibbert and Sidaway, 1992, in Song and Edwards, 1997: 238).

Many of these ideas also have a particular gendered aspect, in order to intensify the perceived threat of danger. As a result, young black minority ethnic men experience a particular type of stereotyping, one that is even more laden with negative connotations and presentations of the dangerous other. Consider here the cases of 'baby-fathers', school excludees, the radicalisation of young Muslims and coverage of the race riots[1] of both the 1980s and more recently in the Northern cities of England in 2001. In each of these cases, particular racial, ethnic and religious categories of young black minority ethnic men were presented in their own ways as a threat to wider society, due to their supposed weak,

---

[1] Benyon and Solomos (1987) make the point that we must view such race riots, or what they call 'disorders', in terms of broader social injustices that are related to political, social, cultural and economic issues. For this reason, many prefer to use terms such as 'uprisings', 'unrest' or 'demonstrations' in place of 'riots'.

immoral,[2] fickle, lazy, backward attitudes and criminal tendencies.[3] They are in their very being considered to pose a threat to the idea of a civilised society, and all that is British. With this view, it is no wonder that support services not only feel that discriminatory behaviour is legitimate, but also that it is necessary.

Specialist intervention

On a more sinister level, this stereotypical attitude is matched with the introduction of specialist schemes to combat the so-called problems considered unique to black minority ethnic communities, such as the UK Forced Marriage (Civil Protection) Act 2007. Although this was beneficial on a human rights level because it provided protection for those forced into situations of marriage, the frenzy surrounding its passing not only failed to distinguish adequately between forced marriages and arranged marriages, but also suggested that both types were unique to the Asian culture only. Another example of the power of racial stereotyping and scaremongering is the recently released guidance on the need to tackle the promotion of extremism in the name of Islam within higher education institutions (DfES, 2006b).

Any response of the black minority ethnic community to question or struggle against such racially discriminatory forms of management is itself considered as a further indication of their deviance, and then used to justify greater control measures. For example, a key contributory factor leading to the 1981 Brixton riots was the Metropolitan Police Force's 'Operation Swamp 81' which saw officers' heavy and discriminatory use of the so-called 'sus-law', which allowed the stopping and searching of individuals on the basis of a mere suspicion of wrong-doing. When the riots occurred, additional heavy handed and discriminatory measures were adopted. More recently, reasons of self-segregation and anti-British hostility have been given by the mass media, politicians and policing officials for the motivations of the 2001 Northern rioters (McGhee, 2005). The demonstrators' frustration at having been marginalised and racially discriminated against in every aspect of their lives was not taken to be a serious consideration in explaining the occurrence of the demonstrations.

Implications of discrimination

Research shows that even in spite of any good intentions of individual practitioners and outreach workers, such as those who have attempted to pursue anti-racist practice, it would seem that structural discrimination and a reluctance by institutions to seriously implement anti-racist and equal opportunities has resulted in a situation where an inadequate service is still often the outcome (Barn, 1993; Humphreys, Atkart and Baidwin, 1999; O'Neale, 2000).

---

[2]Following the 1981 Toxteth riots, the then Merseyside Chief Constable Kenneth Oxford described black Liverpudlians as 'the product of liaisons between white prostitutes and black sailors' (Channel 4 History, 2007).

[3]The power of the media and politicians to have successfully presented such a strong image of black criminality was later highlighted when, following the 1981 Toxteth riots, evidence was presented which indicated that a significant number of participating 'rioters' were actually white (Jacobs, 1986).

This is because these services have largely failed to address two core issues. Firstly, to self-scrutinise their own problematic ideas which underline their intervention and service provision, and secondly, to pay seriously appropriate consideration to the diversity of black minority ethnic groups.

The consequence of this situation has been that the needs of black minority ethnic service users have not been adequately delivered. In its place, it has been left up to a number of grassroots organisations to fill the gaps. These groups have harnessed the principles of self-help and empowerment, via social capital. This consists of networks of co-operation and reciprocity, civic engagement and a strong sense of a community identity (Bourdieu, 1986; Putnam, 1995). These groups have done very well to support the excluded and contributed a great deal to assist successful transitions (Wright et al., 2005), and often they have done so on a voluntary basis with limited resources.

Although the value of these groups is not being dismissed or denied, what is being questioned are the ways in which, at times, some of these groups too have often attempted to achieve success through essentialisation of racial identity. So, although this effort has produced an area where members of the black minority ethnic community can achieve inclusion and empowerment, it has often done so at the expense of overlooking the rights of those, who, on the basis of race, are experiencing discrimination and inadequate service delivery, but nevertheless do not want to identify themselves in racially singular or inaccurate ways. Rather, these other multi-racial groups need to reside in a space where a more representative collective identity could be formed and specific empowerment requirements be achieved. It needs to be a space that fairly represents the specifics of their own multi-racial background, as opposed to an area whose membership rests on a forced adherence to an essentialised notion of a racial identity. For example, Owusu-Bempah (2005: 37), observes that the mixed-race child is placed under severe pressure when 'childcare professionals join or collude with others to pressure them to accept or confirm the social identity we impose over their self-concept; that when this happens, feelings of confusion, isolation and loss of orientation frequently result'. He states that this adds to their 'continuing marginalisation' (ibid: 38). A supportive space should instead be provided which seeks to understand and fairly represent that given multi-racial identity, and in doing so not be motivated by a conspiracy to steal individuality (Alibhai-Brown, 2001: 118). Such an accurately representative space and progressive level of thinking would also help to achieve a fairer and more effective body of service delivery in a wide range of child, family and community support services. Also, it would help to avoid the problem of children 'becoming hypersensitive to situations in which others or groups attempt to define them in ways which are inconsistent with their own self-definition' (Owusu-Bempah, 2005: 37). This is discussed in later chapters.

Child and family placement services

Estimates suggest that there currently exists significant numbers of children in temporary institutional care who are awaiting adoption. For example, it is estimated that there were approximately 65,000 children in care in England and Wales at the end of March 2005, of which only 40 per cent will return to their biological parents and of which only 4,000 were adopted (After Adoption, 2007). These children have been removed from their biological families either through co-operation or force, and seek the opportunity for a stable, secure and permanent family life, largely through adoption. For these children, adoption is seen as bringing many benefits, namely the opportunity to have one's welfare, emotional and psychological needs met by permanent movement into a family home.

It is important to note here that Western society's ideal of the 'normal' family has 'tended to be equated with the nuclear family, that is, with conjugal, small, independent households' (Lambert and Streather, 1980: 18). In such households, the normative and healthy functioning of the conventional family is seen as leading to the fulfilment of important societal functions (Parsons, 1949, in Lambert and Streather, 1980: 18). The traditional classic model of such a conventional family is that of the nuclear family. It consists of the following elements:

- *The father who is the head of the household and economic provider.*
- *The mother who is the homemaker and provides domestic care and socialises the children.*
- *The helpless and dependent children, whose emotional, financial and welfare needs are met by their parents.*

(Raport et al., 1977, in Lambert and Streather, 1980: 19)

The family is therefore seen as a key institution in a society in which these needs are provided for. This is because the family unit not only raises offspring, catering for their survival requirements, but more so because it socialises them, instilling values and the skills necessary for them to develop into healthy people who can contribute to a prosperous society (Lambert and Streather, 1980: 19–20). This theorisation and support for the conventional family in its nuclear unit form, in itself raises a number of issues tied into debates about the functions of the family. For example, questions can be raised about the assumption that the family is a wholesome nourishing agent, which in doing so fails to consider the problems of abuse, violence, and neglect within the family. It also fails to consider the value of various family formations in contemporary society. However, on this latter point, it can be argued that adoption policy has progressed in line with the development of changing family formations in contemporary society, meaning that the two-point-four family type is no longer considered to be an essential requirement. Thus single people, co-habiting couples, and single-sex couples are among the many variants of the typical family unit who are encouraged to apply to adopt. As a whole, it is fair to say that the family unit is viewed as vital to providing a child with the permanent support, care and attention they need, especially in comparison to prolonged institutional care.

These ideas about permanence and familial stability are viewed as elements of a successful adoption. In this sense, adoptive families are like 'natural' families, although with an additional set of duties, as Lambert and Streather (1980) note:

> Adoptive families are like other families in that they are legally constituted with rights and responsibilities common to 'natural' families. They seek to meet all the major functions of the conventional family with respect to the needs of the adults and children. And after children arrive they experience broadly similar developmental processes to other families. But there are some differences, and in particular adoptive parents must contend with a problem of identity resolution parallel to that facing their child, who must experience and resolve complex identity problems.

(Lambert and Streather, 1980: 36)

Despite these additional tasks, the adoptive family is seen to offer 'reliable love', as well as 'material support', and for these reasons adoption is seen to 'work' (Whitfield, 1999: 113).

Understanding adoption

Although it is difficult to give any precise time in history that the practice of child adoption began, it is suggested by Goody (1969, in Barton and Douglas, 1995: 72), that the practice was historically a common one, bound by legal ruling, in ancient civilisations such as Rome, India and Mesopotamia. Goody states that 'its purpose was to provide an heir for a childless man', as opposed to being primarily directly concerned with the welfare needs of the child (ibid: 72). However, a radical shift in this practice of 'heir provision' occurred, and which saw its relative disappearance. Goody notes that the reason for this shift was the heavy influence of the Christian Church at the time, which discouraged the practice of adoption in an attempt to persuade heirless individuals to leave their wealth to the Church instead (ibid: 72). Although the practice of adoption did not formally make a significant reappearance again in the European and American world until the nineteenth century, it is clear that the practice continued, albeit at reduced numbers, in unofficial forms in Western societies. Adoption also continued in various informal forms in other societies. For example, there is a long tradition of informal adoption and 'othermothering' in African and Caribbean societies (Cheetham, 1986; Hill, 1977; James, 1993; Rashid, 2000; Reynolds, 2001).

Many adoptions across societies were usually kept secret from extended family members, the immediate community and even the adopted child themselves. This can be explained by an attempt to assist the child's settling in and to make them feel that they are a 'real' member of that family. It can also be explained by the stigma surrounding the whole process of adoption and a number of reasons can be suggested for this. For example, the view that these children were illegitimate or troublesome if they had been taken into care, or that individuals seeking to adopt may have been forced to do so for very personal reasons, such as their own inability to biologically produce children of their own, and consequently viewed as a personal or unnatural failing of the individuals concerned. Although not considered to be such a stigma in contemporary society the practice of keeping the adoption secret for a variety of reasons, if possible, is still quite common. There are two types of adoption today, domestic and international. The first refers to the adoption of a child born within the country, and who is from institutional care, foster care or from their birth parents. The latter refers to the adoption of a child from another country, also referred to as intercountry adoption. These two types of adoptions occur in two different forms. Firstly, there is the public form, which is carried out by local government controlled social service departments, and secondly, a private adoption, which is carried out by family placement agencies, based either on a not-for-profit or for-profit basis (Morrison, 2004: 174–5).

In terms of UK legislation regulating practice, *adoption* is defined as the 'process by which the legal relationship between a child and their birth parents is severed and an analogous relationship between the child and the adoptive parents is established' (DoH, 1990, para. 2). According to the 1989 Children Act, the general criteria to be satisfied states that the person to be adopted must:

(a) Be under 18 years old (section 71(1)).
(b) Be at least 19 weeks old and had a home with the applicant at all times during the preceding 13 weeks, if either applicant is the child's parent, step-parent or relative, or the child was placed with the applicant by an adoption agency or by order of the High Court (section 13(1)). If the applicant does not meet those criteria, then the child must be at least 12 months old and must have had a home with the applicant at all times during the preceding 12 months (section 13(2)).
(c) Never have been married (section 16).
(d) Have parental agreement to the adoption (section 16), or, (e) be free for adoption (section 18).

Transracial adoption

According to writers and scholars, and those in the social work profession, transracial adoption is the adoption of children by families who are of a different race to that of the child. For example, Simon and Alstein consider it to be 'the practice of placing infants and children into families who are of a different race than the children's birth family' (Simon and Alstein, 1996: 5). Although this practice can work either way, the most common form of transracial adoption, and the type referred to here, is the adoption of black minority ethnic and mixed-race children by white families: 'transracial adoption is the adoption of black children by white families' (Turner and Taylor, 1996: 262). This definition has been widely accepted as the most accurate by the majority with expertise in the field (Bagley, 1993; Courtney, 1997; Gill and Jackson, 1983; Small, 1986).

The history of such transracial adoption in Britain is particularly difficult to trace, largely due to the lack of early official records about its frequency or pattern. However, many point to the mid-1960s as a mark of the significant change in adoption patterns regarding the increase in the numbers of transracial (white adopters and black minority ethnic and mixed-race adoptees), and intercountry (Western adopters and children from developing countries), adoptions that were occurring. During this period, the numbers of available white babies for adoptions decreased and so the adoption of black children by white families became seen as acceptable, be it as a last resort (Barn, Sinclair and Ferdinand, 1997, in Gupta, 2003: 208). For instance, the British Adoption Project, established in the mid-1960s, saw the majority of its black children being placed into white homes (Raynor, 1970). Kirton notes that the organisation 'established transracial adoption as a 'recognised' phenomenon' (Kirton, 2000: 9). The practice of transracial adoption at this time was defended by the view of racial assimilation and as a way of 'saving' the large numbers of black children, often from what was wrongly perceived to be their own feckless and inadequate black birth families.

Then, in the 1970s, a rise in the recognised opposition to transracial adoption occurred, largely due to attention from movements such as the 1975 Soul Kids Campaign (Soul Kids, 1977). This was followed by more effective opposition in the 1980s with the work of Black and in Care (1984) and, as Gupta (2003: 208) notes, the New Black Families Project and the work of the Association of Black Social Workers and Allied Professionals. Since the 1980s then, transracial adoption began to decrease slowly in some areas, which led to the increase of inracial placements. However, more recently, there has been a swing towards the pro-transracial adoption camp, with calls being made for 'the ending of misguided restrictions' in adoption (BBC News, 1998). This is supported by figures showing it is estimated that in Britain, '20 per cent of children with an adoption plan are from black or minority ethnic backgrounds' and that '89 per cent of adopters are white couples' (Tizard and Phoenix, 2002: 79). It is not surprising then to see transracial adoption occurring on the following scale: 'in 1995, 24 per cent of the adoptions recorded by local authorities and six per cent of those reported by voluntary agencies were "transracial" placements' (BAAF, 1997, referred to in Tizard and Phoenix, 2002: 81).

A number of reasons have been offered in explanation of this trend. This includes the argument about the re-negotiation of the stigma attached to unmarried mothers, the growth in single parent families, widely available contraception and greater access to abortion, which was legalised in the late 1960s with the *1967 Abortion Act* (Kirton, 2000), all of which meant that there was a sharp reduction in the number of available white children for adoption (Gill and Jackson, 1983: 2). In parallel with this situation, the number of black minority ethnic and mixed-race children available for adoption had increased. Reasons for this included the way in which we were witnessing an intensification of the problematising of black and minority ethnic families in terms of their child rearing traditional methods (informal adoption and 'othermothering') and styles ('baby-fathers'), which meant that more and more children were being removed from homes and put into care institutions.

In particular, Barn (1999) examines the high rates of 'mixed-parentage' children, especially regarding children born to one white parent (usually the mother, who had raised them as a single-parent prior to the child's removal), and one Black African Caribbean parent (usually the father), and their over-representation in the care system. In drawing upon findings from her two studies (Barn, 1993; Barn, Sinclair and Ferdinand, 1997), she reported that the reasons for such children entering the care system included family relationship difficulties, physical abuse and neglect, mental health problems of the mother, and claims that the child was troublesome and beyond parental control. However, although these problems are by no means at all exclusive to black minority ethnic or mixed-race children, Barn is also keen to emphasise that questions must be asked about why 'white mothers of mixed-parentage children only receive attention when they reach a crisis point' (Barn, 1999: 282). Nevertheless, a situation emerges which explains high numbers of mixed-race children in care institutions (Barn, 2006).

Opposition to white families' adoption of black children

The campaign in Britain to highlight the high rates of such adoptions was led by opposers of the practice, such as the Association of Black Social Workers and Allied Professionals (ABSWAP). One of its members, John Small, outlined the group's position on transracial adoption. Small argued that the placement of the black child in a white home leads to the adoptee failing to develop a sense of Black identity, failing to develop survival skills, failing to develop cultural and linguistic attributes to function fully in the black community, developing a negative self-image and poor self-esteem, and instead developing a white identity which would lead to problems in the real world (Small, 1991: 66). Similarly, the British Agencies for Adoption and Fostering (BAAF) also emphasised the importance of same-race adoption, and even argued that in some cases, leaving black minority ethnic children in care with appropriately trained and experienced staff is preferred to a transracial placement (BAAF, 1987).

High rates of transracial adoptions were also occurring in the US, and were most passionately highlighted with the campaign led by the ABSWAP's equivalent, the National Association of Black Social Workers (NABSW, 1994). This organisation pointed out that transracial adoption is problematic for both the Black adoptee and the Black community as a whole. This is because it damages the racial identity development of the adoptee by taking away from them knowledge and experience of their African American heritage, and ill-equipping them with the survival strategies necessary for living in a racially discriminatory society. For example, at the NABSW Annual Conference in 1971, Will T. Merritt, the NABSW president said: 'Black children in white homes are cut off from healthy development of themselves as Black people' (Merritt in Simon and Alstein, 2000: 38). Later, he claimed, 'Black children who grow up in white families suffer severe identity problems' (ibid: 38).

On a wider scale, such adoptions are seen as a form of 'cultural genocide' (NABSW,

1972),[4] depriving the black community of their children, and hence their legacy, by having their children act as 'donors' to the white community (Gill and Jackson, 1983: 1–2). Indeed, in highlighting how with genuine efforts black homes can be found for black children, Hayes (1998), notes that in Britain, 'not enough emphasis is placed on finding black families to adopt black children' and asks us to consider 'Why is this? Is it because there are too many white couples waiting for a first or second child? Couples whose needs should be met? What about the needs of the black child? The continuing exercise of transracial placement further perpetuates the myth that black families do not adopt' (Hayes, 1998: 189).

NABSW therefore took a firm position against transracial adoption, which it claimed was necessary in order to:

- *Preserve African American families and culture.*
- *Enable African American children to appreciate their culture of origin through living within a family of the same race and culture.*
- *Enable African American children to learn how to cope with racism through living with families who experience racism daily and have learned to function well in spite of that racism.*
- *Break down the systemic barriers that make it difficult for African American and other families of colour to adopt.*

(Neal, 2003: 1)

It argued that 'all efforts should be made to keep children with their biological relatives via preventive services or return those children who are already in foster care; for those children who cannot return to relatives, adoption by a family of the same race and culture is the next best option to preserve cultural continuity; and transracial adoptions should be a last resort only after a documented failure to find an African-American home . . . and be reviewed and supported by representatives of the African-American community' (NABSW, 1994, in Neal, 2003: 3).

Key aspects of the debate

There are several aspects to the transracial adoption debate, which separates it from any straightforward adoption debate. These are obviously based upon the perceived racialised differences between the black minority ethnic or mixed-race adoptee and their white adopters. Firstly, there is the question of whether it leads to the adoptee suffering from identity development problems, not only because of the obviousness of the adoption, but more so because of the so-called essence of these racialised differences. The second issue follows on from this to question whether it then leads to the adoptee not being able to develop a positive and healthy identity, in particular a positive and healthy black identity. The third issue relates to this last point, and questions whether the adoptee will be able to survive in what

---

[4] The 'cultural genocide' comment was later removed from the organisation's 1994 statement.

is essentially seen as a racist society in which black minority ethnic or mixed-race skin has very little value.

These questions primarily shape the debate about transracial adoption, and have been the focus of most of the literature and research on the topic. Hence, there have been numerous studies and accounts given as to whether white families have the ability to teach black minority ethnic or mixed-race children how to develop a positive Black identity. Here, it is argued that only survivors of racism can teach the coping strategies that are required to tackle the racial discrimination that all black people will face at some time in their lives, and that this is done by them being able to pass on information about the black history of oppression, struggle and racism, and provide experience of the black culture.

Within this debate, there exists division in opinion. Firstly, there are those people who oppose transracial adoption on the grounds that it leads to serious identity development problems for the adoptee who has been denied their blackness. Secondly, there are others who support the practice of transracial adoption by arguing that white parents are capable of teaching black issues, and more importantly, because there are so many white prospective adopters compared to black ones, they are able to meet the child's immediate welfare needs by securing a stable and permanent home sooner rather than later. Thirdly, there are a growing number of people whose opinions rest mid-way between the traditional clear-cut division. This group recognise the significance of the opposition arguments around identity development and racist society survival skills, but also see transracial adoption as a route that can, if carefully managed, have positive outcomes for racial identity development issues.

What the debate unfortunately does is pay inadequate attention to the slight differences in the transracial adoption of mixed-race children, in particular the different ways in which they are racialised, and consequently identify themselves differently. Here, mixed-race children have instead largely been defined as 'black'. This is illustrated by Hayes (1998), who, having worked as a specialist adoption and fostering officer in Britain, argues that 'if the child is of mixed-parentage, that child should not be placed in a white home. That child will at some point in life be viewed as black by the world' (Hayes, 1998: 189). In explaining this, Small argues that the vast majority of African Caribbean people have some white ancestors somewhere in their genealogical history, and they only differ from today's population of mixed-race people in respect of when that mixture occurred. Small then goes on to argue that the inclusion of mixed-race children under the term black is therefore necessary because today's majority (white) society sees and discriminates against anyone who has 'the slightest taint of black' (Small, 1986: 92). This is supported by the comments of the young people in Tizard and Phoenix's (2002) study who, although they had moved away from singular racial definitions such as black, and instead said that they viewed themselves as having a 'mixed' identity, they nevertheless thought that part of that identity still meant that they saw themselves as another racialised group who were still subject to racism (Tizard and Phoenix, 2002: 236).

However, it is recognised here that the transracial adoption experiences of mixed-race children are likely to differ from those transracial adoptees born to two black parents, just as the experiences of mixed-race children living with biological parents are likely to differ from black minority ethnic children living in their biological homes. This is because mixed-race children generally are racialised differently and as such identify themselves differently. For example, Tizard and Phoenix's study (2002), found that although such mixed-race individuals recognised their black heritage, they were reluctant to identify themselves as wholly black because to do so would ignore their white parent and white heritage. The young people therefore emphasised their 'mixed' identity. Similar findings were reported by Alibhai-Brown's sample of mixed-race people (2001). Therefore, it would be fair to argue that although the transracial adoption of mixed-race children and black children both involve a movement across racial boundaries, a distinction remains between them in terms of the types of boundaries that they are moved across. This is similar to the transracial adoption issues and variances experienced by different black minority ethnic groups. For example, Hussain Sumpton's (1999) case study of the Indian Muslim child placed with an Indian Sikh family illustrates how there are different identity, ethnic and cultural issues involved in the consideration of race, ethnicity and religion in adoption placements, and that not all the issues can be classified as having to occur within polarised binary boundaries of black and white as essentialists would argue.

Intercountry adoption

Intercountry adoption is the practice of adopting a child from another country. Due to economic and social inequalities, the main pattern of such adoption usually sees 'the export of children from poor countries to rich ones' (Frost and Stein, 1989: 106). It is a relatively new practice which saw a boost shortly after the end of the World War II. The motivation during this period was largely a charitable one, with 'a desire to provide a home for abandoned and destitute war orphans', although this later shifted to becoming 'a service for childless couples in the West' (Tizard, 1991: 745).

The debates around intercountry adoption share some similarities with those in the transracial adoption debate. Bagley, Young and Scully (1992) provide an outline of these areas of controversy. First is the view that some participating countries may see intercountry adoption as a solution to the problem of 'unwanted' children rather than providing in-country help or family support. The next criticism levelled against intercountry adoption is that it means the removal of 'a potentially productive population who could assist in that country's development' (Bagley, Young and Scully, 1992: 172). In this sense, argues Tizard, it is 'a new form of colonialism, with wealthy Westerners robbing poor countries of their children, and thus their resources' (Tizard, 2001: 746). The third view is that the money spent on intercountry adoption should instead be spent on helping to develop the participating country and assisting its population. A fourth criticism levelled against the practice of intercountry adoption is that it leads to cases of the stealing, kidnapping and selling of babies on the black market, or abuse by profit-making agencies. Finally, there is the view that intercountry adoption leads to identity problems for the children involved. This is because as well as having to adjust to a new, national culture, it is predicted that they will face racial discrimination, marginalisation and identity conflicts as a result of the differences.

Tizard (2001), emphasises that it is this last point on which the strongest objections to the practice of intercountry adoption are based: 'even if the practice is well regulated . . . children from Third World countries will lose access to their own culture and roots, and will have a confused identity. In addition, they will be exposed to racism, an evil which they would not meet in their own country' (Tizard, 2001: 746). Indeed, some of these points are supported by personal documented accounts given by intercountry adoptees themselves, as in Jardine's (2000) reflective piece, in which, having been born in Hong Kong during the 1960s and adopted by a family in the United Kingdom, she discusses issues of loss and her cultural roots, and in doing so concludes: 'while we know how successful adoption can be – and in many respects I would say that of mine – I think we need to constantly remind ourselves in whose interest intercountry adoption is, and not neglect the motivation to keep children in their own country of origin and work in partnership to encourage this' (Jardine, 2000: 491).

Supporters of intercountry adoption practice would argue, however, very much like supporters of in-country transracial adoption, that although these are not ideal solutions, this practice does allow for the child's welfare needs to be met and, for this reason, it should not only be allowed but actively encouraged. One should remember however that the majority of those people taking this stance themselves come from adoption agencies, often privately run, and which specialise in intercountry adoption. Examples of such agencies abound and can readily be found by simple internet searches.

The global adoption market

By its very nature intercountry adoption is, for want of a better description, a global market. A key problem with this, though, lies in how there is no single international law regulating adoption of this type, which means that what happens between the two countries involved depends upon a large degree of 'bilateral agreement' (Triseliotis, Shireman and Hundleby, 1997: 197). In addition, procedures not only vary from one country to another, but also between agencies within the same country (Simon and Alstein, 1991: 25).

However, some fundamental principles on the practice of intercountry adoption were outlined in the Leysin Report (United Nations, 1960). The report was born out of a conference attended by 80 child welfare experts from sixteen European countries, the United Nations, International Social Service,[5] and the International Union for Child Welfare.[6] No representatives

---

[5]This is an international non-governmental organisation established in the 1920s to assist those with problems as a result of the mass migration of peoples to the Americas (Worotynee, 2006: 9).

[6]This began in the 1920s to work on promoting the United Nations Declaration on child rights issues (Worotynee, 2006: 10).

from Third World countries were invited to attend the conference (Bagley, Young and Scully, 1992: 138). Bagley, Young and Scully (1992) provide a summary of the report's 12 principles:

1. *The primary concern on adoption acceptability should be those surrounding the best interests of the child.*
2. *Search for an adoptive family should in the first instance be undertaken in the child's own country.*
3. *To limit time spent in institutionalised care.*
4. *To find homes in the child's own country, when that child has special needs.*
5. *Parents to operate within the boundaries of full informed consent.*
6. *Parents to have some degree of education on what their child's new life is likely to be like.*
7. *Completion of adequate home study.*
8. *Consideration of appropriate matches.*
9. *A trial supervised period upon placement where fit can be determined.*
10. *All documents to be legitimate and scrupulous.*
11. *Legal responsibility for the child to be established immediately when that child arrives in the new country.*
12. *The adoption to be legal in the view of both the sending and receiving countries.*

(Bagley, Young and Scully, 1992: 138–45)

However, they also note that 'it is clear . . . that in a large number of cases of the ICA those twelve principles are not being applied' (Bagley, Young and Scully, 1992: 146). In the most serious of cases, this has led to problems around abuse of this system. For example, 'baby brokers' and the black market where babies are stolen or kidnapped, or where mothers are coerced into giving up their child or even lied to by being told that their child has died after birth. Cases of bribery have also been found, or instances of 'fattening farms' where children are made more presentable in a bid to make them appear more healthy which then allows them to be sold for a much higher price (Bagley, Young and Scully, 1992; Tizard, 1991; Triseliotis, Shireman and Hundleby, 1997). Indeed, adoption on a global scale can now be viewed as having market value. It is a business where profit-making is the key goal. In this sense then, questions around the legitimacy in which it is practised are raised (Triseliotis, 2000).

Due to the lack of formal record keeping on an international scale, any figures on the numbers of children experiencing intercountry adoption are difficult to provide, although it is estimated that on a global scale over 30,000 intercountry adoptions take place every year (Selman, 2001). However, informally estimated figures are much higher than this. For example, in his meticulous investigation of statistics, Selman stated that 'the number of intercountry adoptions is much higher than many recent estimates . . . and is now at its highest ever level in global terms' (Selman, 2001: 18). Selman (2000: 22–3), provides a good atlas of the intercountry adoption scene, in terms of the movement of children from one country to parents in another country:

- *Late 1940s – Europe to US.*
- *Mid 1950s – Korea to US.*
- *1980s – Korea, Colombia and India to the US and Western European countries (Sweden, Norway and Britain).*
- *Early 1990s – Romania to the US and Western European countries (in particular, Sweden, Norway and Britain).*
- *Mid 1990s – China and Russia to the US and Western European countries (in particular, Sweden, Norway and Britain).*
- *Late 1990s – Vietnam to the US and Western European countries (in particular, Sweden, Norway and Britain).*

Selman also provides a fairly recent list, from the last 25 years or so, of the main exporting countries, identifying them as: Korea; India; Colombia; Brazil; Sri-Lanka; Chile; Philippines; Guatemala; Peru; El Salvador; Mexico; Haiti; Poland; Honduras; Thailand; Russia; Vietnam; Romania; Ethiopia; and, Bulgaria (Selman, 2000: 22–3).

Sending countries

The view that some countries may see intercountry adoption as a solution to the problem of 'unwanted' children, as opposed to investing in the provision of in-country family support, has been a view particularly levelled against one of the Asian sending countries, namely Korea (Bagley, Young and Scully, 1992: 173). Korea has developed dramatically within the past 30 years, yet despite this, it still has the reputation of being known as an orphan exporting country. This is largely because 'Korea continues to be a sending country with one of the highest rates of intercountry adoption' (Selman, 2001: 18). The 'export' of Korean babies in this way is still a lucrative business. For example, one estimate is that Korea, in particular South Korea, has since 1955 sent more than 120,000 children out of the country for adoption, with over 70 per cent of these being placed in the United States of America (Selman, 2001). Another estimate claims that Korea is still sending an average of six orphans overseas each day (Hong, 1999).

There are several reasons that can be highlighted to explain the high number of exported Korean adoptees. To start with, in Korea, especially South Korea, the adoption business perpetuates itself, because rather than simply addressing the discrimination against unwed mothers and orphans, intercountry adoption serves as a sort of safety valve for the social problems of unwed mothers and abandoned children (Rothschild, 1988; Selman, 2001). Additionally, Korean adoptees bring in much-needed hard currency. This relieves the government of the costs of caring for the children, which would be a potentially high drain on the budget. It also helps with population control, an obsession of the Korean government (Rothschild, 1988). Another factor is that Korean society's aspirations include being able to go abroad, or to send family members abroad to study, and to have a better life. The political situation of the country also increasingly endorses this view, which permeates the Korean personality. Therefore, in terms of intercountry adoption, the philosophy goes that 'the parent sends the child abroad because they love the child'.

Every year, Korea welcomes back a few of the babies it has sent abroad for adoption ever since the end of the Korean War. However, returning as adults, the adoptees encounter a contradictory reception. They are met by a culture that continues to adopt out children, yet at the same time the Koreans are overcome with guilt for having sent the returning adoptees away and are enthusiastic to educate them about Korea. Some Koreans even urge these foreigners to become Korean – it is, after all, they say, their biological heritage. On the other hand, although Korean society has the view that biological links bind all Koreans in a cultural context, it also views the raising of someone else's baby – even if Korean – as shameful and unacceptable (Baker, 1997). In 1989 the Korean Ministry of Social Affairs outlined their plan to reduce the number of Korean born children sent out to other countries for adoption. However, in 1998, Korea's number of intercountry adoptions was 'still above 2,000 a year and domestic adoptions below 1,500' (Selman, 2001: 18).

Eastern European countries such as Romania, Poland and Bulgaria are also amongst the highest ranking in sending countries (Selman, 2004; Albers, 1997; Ryan, 2004). In this case, poverty, civil wars and the fall of communism throughout the region resulted in huge numbers of children being made available for intercountry adoption, with Romania especially exporting huge numbers of orphaned children: 'Romania, in particular, became notorious in the early 1990s because of media exposure about problems in its child welfare system and the thousands of children languishing in institutions. During this period, several thousand were adopted from Romania' (Ryan, 2004: 53). Many of these children were adopted by parents in the US (Hollinger, 2004).

With a history of famine, drought, civil war, and devastating illnesses, like HIV/AIDS, many children have also been adopted from African countries. For example, Ethiopia sends approximately 800 children per year to be adopted in other countries, such as Norway, so, for instance, from the end of 1991 to the end of 2002, more than 300 Ethiopian children were adopted by families in Norway (Howell, 2006: 204). In terms of the intercountry adoption scene, nations within Africa, such as Ethiopia, are relative newcomers (Howell, 2006: 203). Unlike other sending countries, Ethiopia is also well-known for being a country in which adopting a child can be done with relative ease and the additional 'rapid transaction period' of the adoption process (Howell, 2006: 204). These factors contribute to making it a favourite destination for those seeking to adopt a child from another country.

Receiving countries
Figures show that the US has 'adopted more children internationally than all other countries of the world combined' (Engel, Phillips and Dellacava, 2007: 1). For example, there are an

estimated 22,000 plus intercountry adoptions into the US every year (ibid). A mapping of sending countries shows that most adoptees came from Russia, China, (South) Korea, Vietnam, and Guatemala (Simon and Alstein, 2000). Despite differences in procedures, on a practical level the US requires all intercountry adoption procedures to comply with US Federal and State laws, as well as the Immigration and Naturalisation Service procedures (Simon and Alstein, 1991: 25). Like Britain though, the US also experiences large numbers of unofficial intercountry adoptions.

Hamwi (2006), however, notes that the US is also a sending country, with approximately 300 children in the year 2005 sent to be adopted outside of the US. Many of these children are adopted by parents in Canada (102 children in 2005), the Netherlands (31 children in 2005), Germany, Sweden and New Zealand. A large number of these adoptees are of black minority ethnic or mixed-raced origin, whose birth mothers have often sent them to be adopted outside of the US in the 'hope that they will face less discrimination abroad' (Hamwi, 2006: 17).

Similarly, on a historical level, Britain was an exporter in the intercountry adoption scene, very much viewing it as a means of offering children a better quality of life. Over the last 100 years or so, and especially following World War II, children were sent to countries such as Canada, Australia and New Zealand. Although exact numbers are not recorded, it is thought that Britain was sending children at roughly the same high rate that Korea had since the mid 1950s (Selman, 2000). However, Britain today has fully established itself as a 'receiving' country, although it is difficult to say how many children Britain is responsible for taking in. This is blamed on inaccurate statistics on official intercountry adoptions, and an inability to monitor unofficial ones. However, in attempting to quantify patterns, the Government's Explanatory Notes for the *Adoption (Intercountry Aspects) Act 1999*, claims that: 'there are currently over 300 adoptions each year of children from overseas by adopters living in the United Kingdom . . . there are approximately 100 other cases each year where people avoid the adoption procedures and bring children to the UK without approval' (DoH, 1999, sections 4–5).

It is estimated that the huge number of 30,000 children from Third World countries were adopted by families in Sweden from the 1970s up until 1987, and another 6,000 by families in Norway (Triseliotis, 1993: 121). Intercountry adoption into these Scandinavian countries, commenced largely after the Korean War in the early 1950s. This was particularly the case of Sweden, which in the first instance, pushed ahead with a large, independent intercountry adoption programme, led by voluntary agencies who offered advice, prepared cases and dealt with the adoption process, which was then shortly followed in the mid 1960s by the setting up of a government run application and 'clearing house' for those wishing to adopt from abroad (Selman and White, 1998: 218).

Key arguments in the debate

The foundations of the arguments in the transracial adoption debate are based around notions of racial discrimination and racial identity development difficulties. They can be outlined as follows:

1. *Transracial adoption does not address the serious social and economic power imbalance based on notions of racial superiority that exist in society. This is additionally so in cases where the adoption is also an intercountry one (Tizard, 1991). Indeed, such adoptions reinforce power imbalances by using white middle-class standards, which pathologise black minority ethnic families as problematic and inadequate (Chimezie, 1975), and by having an over-eager willingness to 'rescue' the children in these families. This discrimination is further extended when black minority ethnic families apply to adopt black minority ethnic and mixed-race children.*

2. *It is a form of 'rape' or even 'cultural genocide' (NABSW, 1972), as it removes from the black minority ethnic community its most valuable resources, its children (Gill and Jackson, 1983). Indeed, it is seen as a form of black service to white families – a form of slavery and oppression (Abdullah, 1996).*

3. *Obvious racial and physical differences will make the adoption an ever-present issue, which will always hinder the ability for intimate family relations to develop.*

4. *Obvious differences will also mean that the adoptee will be burdened with constant feelings of 'not belonging' to the adoptive family. This will leave them with a 'deep sense of personal isolation' (Gill and Jackson, 1983: 5).*

5. *Whilst growing up, the adoptees' social contact will primarily be with that of their adoptive family, this being the white community. As a result, the adoptee will be ill-equipped to embark on healthy social relations with non-white people, both as a youngster outside of the family environment and as an adult when he or she has left the adoptive home.*

6. *Because the adoptee would not be able to relate to members of the black minority ethnic community, they will be rejected by them. At some point they will also be rejected by the wider white community, who will always view them as black and in racially discriminatory ways. This will lead to intense feelings of isolation (Small, 1991; Ahmad, 1990; Dutt and Sanyal, 1991). In addition, the child who is also an intercountry adopted child 'will lose access to their own culture and their roots' which subsequently will lead to them having a 'confused identity', which will be worsened by the fact that they 'will be exposed to racism' that they 'would not have met in their own country' (Tizard, 1991: 746).*

7. *Adoptive families are unable to teach vital coping mechanisms and survival skills that are necessary for living and succeeding in a racist society where black skin has very little value.*

8. *The adoptee will not be able to settle key identity issues that are a by-product of living in a racially defined society. As a result, they will experience a sense of racial limbo. This will lead to poor self-concept and low self-esteem (Small, 1991; Ahmad, 1990; Dutt and Sanyal, 1991).*

9. *The adoptee will take on racially discriminatory ideas or notions of racial superiority held by members of their white adoptive family and community. As a result, they will develop a hatred of their own black self. (Small, 1991).*

These arguments have been based around theoretically derived concerns of identity development, in particular, the idea that the black adoptee's 'primary identity' is the black one, which is pre-fixed and determines the experiences of the individual. Here, opposers of transracial adoption maintain that there are two reasons why this true Black identity can be seen as essential and unchanging. It is firstly 'appointed by nature' (Singer, in Weeks, 1993: 15), or based upon a 'genealogical categorisation of race', which is 'concerned with origins and lineages of reproduction' as Dyer (1997: 20), in his discussion about whiteness identifies. Secondly, it is one that is determined by attributes about race and blackness that are socially constructed upon ideas about group preservation or 'historical forces' (Harris, 1995: 7). For anti-transracial adoption groups then, this is interpreted as meaning that the black identity must be lived and realised in order for black people to survive in today's racist society. As Small states: 'the black experience is unique' (Small, 1991: 65), and 'if a healthy personality is to be formed, the psychic image of the child must merge with the reality of what the child actually is. That is to say, if the child is black (reality) they must first recognise and accept that they have a black psychic image' (Small, 1986: 88).

There are a number of problems with these theoretically derived arguments. Firstly, a somewhat narrow view of racial identity development and the experiences of the adoptee is presented. This is because it assumes that *being* black is a primarily genetic and biological *truth* and the basis upon which identity is formed and lived relations in society are based. It also assumes that any societal influences on this black identity development is tied to 'resisting' and 'surviving' stereotypical notions about blackness, which are perpetuated by a racist society. For those opposing transracial adoption, these ties to biology or socially constructed attributes about race mean that only full 'participation in collectivities organised around an essentialist identity' (Ballis-Lal, 1999: 57), in other words an inracial black placement, would lead to a successful, positive and healthy identity development for the black adoptee. By taking such a restrictive view, the full complexities of the debate are not considered, that is, what does blackness as a racial identity actually mean today in a society which contains so many racially mixed individuals? Secondly, these arguments are heavily based on conjecture, assumptions and theory, meaning that they 'do not generally take the form of detailed reference to research findings' (Kirton, 2000: 64). They therefore lack 'empirical confidence' (Cohen, 1994: 60). Thirdly, insufficient consideration is being paid to hybrid racial identities, which today are 'increasingly becoming the cultural norm . . . a new generation in which purified notions of "Englishness" or "blackness" are a standing joke' (Cohen, 1994: 72). Indeed, an outdated notion of blackness is being used and 'privileged above all other identities' (Alibhai-Brown, 2001: 177). These problems are the main concerns of this book.

The research evidence

In addition though, it is worth highlighting that the research evidence also falls short of supporting such arguments. Despite this, however, the findings are worth noting. Of the studies that do exist, problems in the value of birth origins, experiences of racism, feelings of being different and self-rejection have been highlighted. In following up a previous study where the experiences of 24 adopted children were looked at, Tizard interviewed six mixed-race adoptees and their white adoptive parents. Tizard found that four of the families who had transracially adopted had failed to (yet) tell the child about his or her ethnic background. One adoptive mother of a mixed-race child was even concealing the fact that he was 'coloured' and had a West-Indian father (Tizard, 1977: 181).

Dagoo, Burnell, Fitsel and Reich (1993), using data from a series of six focus group meetings for adults who had been transracially adopted, found that those raised in a racially mixed family environment and community did not feel as different and conspicuous as those raised in a white environment. All the adoptees also said that the transracial adoption had led to them being seen as different and meant a problematic childhood, because it drew negative attention in a world where their dark skin was not valued. However for several of those who did have early contact with other black people, this had brought the realisation that they were outsiders as they felt a sense of not belonging, and a sense of isolation. Hence they had neither felt themselves to be a full part of their black birth community nor of their white adoptive community (Dagoo et al. 1993).

Similar results were also found by Shekleton (1990), who carried out group-work with six black transracially adopted adults, and found that although the participants were told at an early age that they were adopted, for most the subject was then never mentioned again by their parents. This sometimes led to adoptees feeling that something was wrong with being different. This was then reinforced by name calling and bullying at school, and the white siblings distancing themselves from adoptees in public. During adolescence, the transracial adoptees had experienced feelings of isolation in their adoptive homes and being trapped in their blackness and difference, which led to either self-rejection or a rejection of their (adoptive) parents. Feelings of 'not being good enough' and of 'being different' also sometimes made socialising difficult for adoptees. As adults, the transracial adoptees had feelings of fear that their fragile black image might be questioned or challenged either by black or white people together with a feeling of shame at recognising racist and stereotypical attitudes in themselves towards other black individuals.

Tizard argued that such attitudes reflect how the adoptees are 'denying a part of themselves' (Tizard, 1991: 753), which Feigelman and Silverman (1984) found was associated with feelings of being ashamed of one's origins. This was due to several reasons, and included the adoptee's feelings of difference and a desire to fit in with the adoptive family, their experiences of racism, their feelings of rejection and the hostile attitudes they had harboured towards their country of birth or towards their birth parents for sanctioning the adoption (Feigelman and Silverman, 1984; Tizard, 1991).

In reviewing the theoretical, policy and practical issues surrounding adoption, Triseliotis, Shireman and Hundleby (1997) make the observation that the research evidence suggests that during early childhood, the adoptee's positive self-esteem and self-concept levels are not based on an essential notion of blackness. Rather they depend upon the quality of the parenting provided by the adoptive parents. For example, the degree to which the adoptee experiences sensitive parenting in childhood and at the same time is prepared for the negative experiences that they are likely to experience into adulthood, helps the adoptee to develop a positive self-esteem. However, Triseliotis et al. found that as the adoptee grows older, they move away from such parental protection and are more influenced by the attitudes of their wider community. If such attitudes are 'hostile and rejecting' they have 'devastating' effects on the adoptee's self (Triseliotis et al., 1997: 193–4). Triseliotis et al. point particularly to the studies of Dalen and Saetersdal (1992, in Triseliotis et al., 1997: 193) and Rorbech (1991, in Triseliotis et al., 1997: 193), which found that although the adoptees were well adjusted in childhood, as adults they were marginalised and felt more discrimination. This emphasises the necessity and the importance of sensitive parenting in childhood and beyond.

Similar observations were made by Thoburn, Norford and Rashid (2000) in their study of 297 children of minority ethnic origin who had been adopted or placed with permanent foster parents between 1979 and 1986, 71 per cent having gone to a white family. Data on the children had been gathered from records obtained ten years after the placement had been made. In-depth interviews were then carried out with 38 sets of parents of 51 young people (at least half of these were in families which had at least one parent of minority ethnic origin) and with 24 of those young people themselves. These interviews were carried out between 12 and 15 years after the placement had been made. Parker (1999) argues that such studies conclude that transracial placements are no more likely than the inracially placed ones to have broken down. However, whilst most black transracial adoptees stated that they had learnt much from their white parents, some argued strongly for inracial placements, which were tied to feelings of having suffered 'additional stress as a result of losing contact with their racial and cultural origins as well as their birth families' (Parker, 1999: 159). Parker therefore notes that 'placement with a family of a different ethnic and cultural background should be unusual and should be based on specific reasons in individual cases' (Parker, 1999: 159).

Research supporting transracial adoption

Other research evidence questions the validity of such essentialised arguments and empirical findings. Evidence has found that although slight differences in identity development do exist between transracially and inracially placed black adoptees, these differences are minor and have very little negative effects. For example, Feigelman and Silverman sent out 1100 questionnaires to adoptive families in an original national survey in 1975, to which 737 responded. In 1981 they carried out a follow-up survey with 372 of these families. In the subsequent analysis, Colombian, Korean and 'Afro-American' transracial adoptees were compared to the same ethnic groups in same-race placements, and also with white children in same-race placements. Feigelman and Silverman found that 'the adolescent and school-aged transracial adoptees were no more poorly adjusted than their inracially adopted counterparts' (Feigelman and Silverman, 1984: 58), and so argued that there is little empirical evidence to show transracial adoption to be damaging to the racial identity, racial awareness and self-esteem of the transracial adoptee. Therefore, transracial adoption was favoured as an effective policy.

Zastrow compared 44 white couples who had adopted a black child with 44 white couples who had adopted a white child. Information was obtained via interviews with adoptive parents and by reading adoption records that were held by the adoption agency about the families. Zastrow found that the transracial adoptive parents 'reported considerably fewer problems' related to the child's race than was expected to be the case (Zastrow, 1977: 81). Similar results were also found by Brooks and Barth (1999) in their longitudinal survey of American transracial adoptees, which led them to conclude that their 'study provides further evidence that transracial adoption is a practical and appropriate placement option for children in need of permanent homes' (Brooks and Barth, 1999: 98).

Simon and Alstein (2000), carried out a 20-year study from 1971 to 1991 of 'Black', Korean, Native American, Eskimo and Vietnamese children adopted by white couples in the mid-western US. In 1971, personal interviews with 4–7-year-olds and their parents, and the use of the Clark doll test found children to have accurate racial self-identifications with no preference for white characteristics, or negative reactions to black identity. In 1979, mail questionnaires and telephone interviews with several parents in the original sample revealed family tensions. In the 1983–84 personal interviews with children and parents, it was found that such behaviour had stopped. The researchers also asked children to complete a self-esteem scale questionnaire. The results showed that no one group of respondents manifested higher or lower self-esteem than the others. In 1990–91, the adult adoptees and their parents were again interviewed. The authors found that there was no difference in levels of family integration. They concluded that in general transracial adoptees grow-up well adjusted and that transracial adoption can serve the child's best interests because, as their results showed, the transracial adoptees felt loved, secure and comfortable with their racial identities.

In a British study, Bagley used several measures of mental health and adjustment questionnaires to measure the adjustment and identity of 27 Afro-Caribbean and mixed-race children adopted by Caucasian parents and 25 Caucasian children adopted by Caucasian parents. Bagley found that 'although the outcomes for the transracially adopted group are likely to be different in identity terms from Afro-Caribbean children brought up in same-race families ... these children seem well prepared by transracial adoption to participate effectively in a multi-cultural, multi-racial society' (Bagley, 1993: 285).

In a previous study, Bagley and Young (1979) examined the adjustment and achievement levels of three black and 27 mixed-race children adopted by white parents. The authors compared this group of transracial adoptees with three other groups. These were:

• 30 non-adopted white school peers of the transracially adopted children.
• 24 mixed-race children who had been in care and who had not been adopted.
• 30 white children who had been adopted by white parents.

The authors found that the transracial adoptees had an excellent adjustment in comparison with the other three groups, and found that the general outcome of transracial adoption is more favourable if families have positive attitudes to, and links with, the black community or if they live in a multi-racial community. Therefore, the authors concluded that transracial adoption should be considered as an option for children who cannot be inracially placed.

Using a standardised questionnaire and semi-structured interviews to measure health, behaviour at school, social adjustment and self-esteem in a study consisting of 36 black, Asian and mixed-race children in white families living in Britain, Gill and Jackson (1983) also found transracial adoption to have positive outcomes. However, unlike Bagley and Young's (1979) findings, Gill and Jackson's black transracial adoptees in fact had little contact with members of the black community. These authors found that 60 per cent of Caucasian adoptive parents with black adolescent children had no black friends, and their children likewise had few contacts with other black adolescents. In fact the adoptees 'saw themselves as white in all but skin colour' (Gill and Jackson, 1983: 81). Yet despite this, they found that the majority of the transracially adopted children had good levels of self-esteem and showed very few signs of behavioural maladjustment and so they concluded by noting that, for the short-term at least, transracial adoption can be successful.

However, despite similar positive findings about the relative success of transracial adoption, some authors have suggested care and caution in its use. For example, in studying the self-concept scores, family relationships and school progress of a sample of 30 black transracial adoptees and 30 black inracial adoptees, McRoy and Zurcher (1993) found transracial adoptees to have strong family bonds and satisfactory school progress. In addition, the authors found there to be no differences between the 30 transracial and the 30 inracial adoptees in self-concept scores. However, the authors also found that only 30 per cent of the transracial adoptees identified themselves as black, and concluded that this was because adoptive parents were failing to 'equip the black transracial adoptee with the necessities that are required to becoming bi-cultural', and the tendency for them to have problems of misidentification due to growing up in white communities (McRoy and Zurcher, 1983: 139). As a result, they emphasised caution in practicing transracial adoption. This again demonstrates values and the power of sensitive parenting in the ways in which adoptive parents prepare the black adoptee for the racism they are likely to face in wider society.

Similarly, in one phase of Johnson, Shireman and Watson's (1987) longitudinal study, where 42 black transracial adoptees and 45 black inracially placed adoptees were studied, it was found that 80 per cent of the inracially placed adoptees identified themselves as black, compared with 73 per cent of the transracial adoptees, whose number contained more children who were mixed-race or fair-skinned. However, despite this positive finding, Johnson et al. saw the seven per cent difference as significant enough to emphasise that the transracial adoptees' racial identity development and self-identification as black was being surpassed by inracial adoptees, and that because of this, together with the fact that the transracial adoptees were being brought up in white communities with little contact with black people, transracial adoption should be approached with care.

Adoption in Britain: policy and practice

In order to understand the state of contemporary adoption policy and practice in Britain, we need to consider four key influential factors: economic and class factors; attitudes towards inheritance; attitudes towards heredity; and attitudes to non-marital children (Triseliotis, 1998: 57–8).

The first law on adoption in England and Wales was introduced in the 1920s with the *1926 Adoption Act*. In formally establishing legislative rulings on the process and meaning of adoption, in brief, this was that: 'all rights, duties, obligations and liabilities of the parent or parents, guardian or guardians of the adopted child, in relation to the future custody, maintenance and education of the adopted child ... shall be extinguished, and all such rights, duties, obligations and liabilities shall vest in and be exercisable by and enforceable against the adopter as though the adopted child was a child born to the adopter in lawful wedlock' (section 5). It followed the long-standing anxiety around informal adoption patterns that had until then been occurring, and in particular reports of abuse and 'baby farming', many of which attracted media attention (Keating, 2001). On a more immediate level, it followed the concern that emerged around the large numbers of war babies' either born illegitimate, or who were children orphaned as a result of the 1914–18 First World War. Here the focus was changed from heir provision for childless individuals to welfare provision for the child. Under this Act, adoptive parents could, and usually did, pass off adoptees as their own biological children. This was largely because of the stigma that surrounded adoption (Howe and Feast, 2000).

The introduction of adoption legislation was a positive step in that it formally recognised, and was able to begin to deal with, abuses in child placement. It introduced regulations to deal with 'financial abuses and inappropriate placements' that were being made and also firmly established the adopted child's status as to now 'equate the position of adopted children for purposes of succession more nearly to that of birth children within a family' (Ball, 1998: 72). Support for these safeguards improved with further amendments to adoption law.

In 1950, the *Adoption of Children Act* was introduced, and this emphasised a 'fresh start' view of adoption in terms of the relationship between the adoptive parents and the adoptees. As such, it still seemed to be surrounded by the stigmas of previous adoption law. The *1958 Adoption of Children Act* followed shortly after. This 'brought an interest in extending adoption to those children previously considered beyond its scope, whether on grounds of their age, disability or racial background . . . (who) became known as 'hard-to-place', simultaneously indicating both the possibility and difficulty of their adoption' (Kirton, 2000: 7). The *1976 Adoption of Children Act*, which outlined the 'freeing' of children waiting to be adopted, was later amended by the *1989 Children Act*, which required a 'due consideration' of 'the child's religious persuasion, racial origin and cultural and linguistic background' (section 22), in respect of child care decisions. The Act seemed to fall in line with the United Nations Convention on the Rights of the Child (United Nations, 1989), of which Britain is a signatory: 'when considering solutions, due regard shall be paid to the desirability of continuity in a child's upbringing and to the child's ethnic, religious, cultural and linguistic background' (article 20).

A contemporary view

When it came into office in May 1997, the New Labour Government vowed to review adoption legislation. In 1998, a Local Authority Circular report *Adoption: Achieving the Right Balance* (DoH, 1998), noted that consideration needs to take account of all the child's needs. It acknowledged that although knowledge of history, culture and language via 'placement with a family of a similar ethnic origin and religion will often most likely meet the child's needs as fully as possible, safeguarding his welfare most effectively and preparing him for a life as a member of a multi-racial society', meeting these 'wishes and feelings may be restrictive or unrealistic', and therefore they should not be regarded as the decisive factors in placement practice (DoH, 1998, sections 12–14). It went on to state that if exact matches could not be identified, then efforts to find alternatives should be made. In referring to the report in November 1998, Paul Boateng, the then Health Minister, said that 'the rules should make it easier for transracial adoptions to take place' and that the time was now right 'to end misguided practices' so although social services should try and match adoptees with adopters of similar backgrounds, they 'should not be the determining factor' (Paul Boateng quoted in BBC News, 18 November 1998). The Health Minister emphasised the report's message that 'it is unacceptable for a child to be denied loving adoptive parents solely on the grounds that the child and adopters do not share the same racial or cultural background' (DoH, 1998: 4).

In 2000, *The Prime Minister's Review of Adoption* document (DoH, 2000a), supported the *Balance* report when it stated the need for a new approach which places all the needs and rights of the child at the centre of the process. Following this, the *Adoption and Children Act* was introduced in 2002. This implemented the proposals of the 2000 White Paper *Adoption: A New Approach* (DoH, 2000b) by calling for the child's overall welfare to be the paramount consideration in issues relating to adoption.

Although not overtly mentioned in UK legislation governing intercountry adoption, this view seems also to be reflected in the UK-wide legislation on intercountry adoption. This can be deduced firstly from the absence of the very mention of the significance of the racial and ethnic background of the adoptee, and secondly, from the requirement of the adoptee to forsake their birth national identity and take on that of his or her adoptive country. For example, the *1999 Adoption (Intercountry Aspects) Act* only notes that the 'minor shall, if the requirements of subsection (5A) are met, be a British citizen as from the date on which the order is made or the Convention adoption is effected, as the case may be.' (*Adoption (Intercountry Aspects) Act 1999*, section 7).

On the whole then, adoption legislation and policy in Britain seems to recognise that although the child's race, ethnicity, culture and language of his or her birth community are important factors for consideration in placements, a greater level of emphasis is placed on the view that they should not exceed the child's welfare rights and needs to be placed in a secure and loving home sooner rather than later.

Views from adoption organisations

However, although national legislation and policy guidance seems fairly clear, this message, which is one that largely supports transracial adoption, has not quite filtered down as such to local child placement agencies. For example, in response to Paul Boateng's comments regarding the *Balance* report, mentioned earlier (DoH, 1998), Felicity Collier, the then Director of the British Agencies for Adoption and Fostering, said that although she welcomed the guidelines, she nevertheless 'warned against taking the section about race and culture out of context, because placement in a family of similar ethnic origin and religion was often most likely to meet a child's needs, (and) many adults who were transracially adopted as children speak of feeling isolated and confused about their racial identity' (Felicity Collier, quoted in BBC News, 18 November 1998).

Indeed, this is illustrated in the practice guidelines offered by BAAF (Prevatt Goldstein and Spencer, 2000). In selective reference to legislation, government circulars and research studies, an argument is made for placement with foster carers or adopters who can:

● *Provide cultural continuity as a daily experience within the home.*
● *Reflect the families' particular religious observance and encourage religious heritage, at a pace and level that meet the individual child's needs.*
● *Continue to communicate with the child in their first language.*

- *Provide protection from, open acknowledgment of and a suitable challenging response to racism, including skills that the child can learn not to perpetuate or collude with it.*

(Prevatt Goldstein and Spencer, 2000: 7–9)

BAAF argues that in order to ensure these needs are met, placement with a black family, especially one that is also a match in terms of culture, religion, language and class, is most appropriate and should be actively pursued. They argue that this is because a black family can offer the child:

- *A positive black attachment figure which the child can internalise.*
- *An environment where the black child is normal rather than exceptional.*
- *A range of black role models coping with everyday life.*
- *A resource for ways of coping with challenging racism.*
- *Continuity with some aspects of the child's heritage.*
- *Access to aspects of culture, not available in the dominant society, which involve ways of being and ways of seeing as well as ways of doing.*
- *Access to some of the symbols which enable the child to fit comfortably, if they so wish, with their ethnic group/class.*
- *A secure and informed framework in which to reject or adapt aspects of their heritage.*

(Taken directly from Goldstein and Spencer, 2000: 16–17)

Varying practices

The resulting interpretations of this guidance means there are widespread variations on the transracial adoption policy, and which vary from region to region, and often depend on the racial make-up of the social workers themselves who take charge of placements. For example, one study found that black students on a course studying for a social work qualification were significantly more likely to support a same-race placement in comparison to their white colleagues (Kirton, 1999). Such feelings are not surprising given black social workers' own experiences of a racially discriminatory institution (Lewis, 1996; Butt and Mirza, 1997). However, Okitikpi (2005) notes that there is also a problem in that the social worker's approach 'has tended to owe more to a simplistic interpretation of the children's racial identity and their cultural affiliations rather than an informed understanding or appreciation of their interracial background and their self perceptions' (Okitikpi, 2005: 1). This has contributed to the disparities across social work practice regarding the placement of black minority ethnic and mixed-race children.

On one level then, transracial adoption in some social work departments in Britain is something of a rarity. A problem with this situation is that children are waiting longer in care whilst a 'same-race' placement is sought (Children First in Adoption and Fostering, 1990). Owusu-Bempah and Hewitt argue that this is also a problem because the ethos around this practice seems to 'pathologise and marginalise these children from mainstream professional provision (because) black children's emotional, educational, social and psychological needs' are simply being defined 'solely in racial terms, irrespective of their true causes' (Owusu-Bempah and Hewitt, 2000: 110). Similarly, Gilroy (1992), who questions the validities of same-race policies and the essentialist thinking underpinning these policies, notes:

> Same-race adoption and fostering for minority ethnics is presented as an unchallenged and seemingly unchallengeable benefit for all concerned . . . the content of the racists' pathology and the material circumstances to which it can be made to correspond are thus left untouched. The tentacles of racism are everywhere, except in the safe haven which a nurturing black family provides for delicate, fledgling racial identities.
>
> (Gilroy, 1992: 58)

Hence there is an assumption that:

* There is a singular black identity.
* The needs of such children are all identical.
* Black families are best placed to serve these needs.

Goldstein and Spencer (2000), who, in line with an essentialist way of thinking believe that racial matching is important and should be actively encouraged, make the point that racial matching is taking longer to implement, admittedly because of the lack of available black families willing to adopt. However, it is suggested here that this is not so much because of the unwillingness of black minority ethnic families who wanted to adopt black minority ethnic children, especially if we consider the work of the *Black and in Care* and the *Islamic Fostering Service*, which has shown that black minority ethnic adopters can be found. Rather, it is because of the institutionally racist nature of the child welfare system, which imposes white middle-class standards, or what Park and Green call 'a euro-centric standard of measurement' (Park and Green, 2000: 15), and which pathologises black minority ethnic families as problematic and inadequate and so discriminates against them when they apply to adopt black minority ethnic and mixed-race children (Ahmad, 1989; Chimezie, 1975). It is also argued that the 'traditional methods of long term and informal fostering' prominent in African communities,[7] are not recognised as successful methods of child-care (Sunmonu, 2000).

Indeed, specialist interest organisations highlighted the discriminatory nature of the system and responded with a series of initiatives aimed at recruiting adopters from black minority ethnic communities, such as the work undertaken by one British organisation, *New Black Families*. This organisation demonstrated that with targeted efforts and fairness in recruitment, black families can be found for black children (Small, 1982). The success of similar attempts has also been provided by the *British Adoption Project* (Raynor, 1970), *Black and in Care* (1984) and the *Islamic Fostering Service* (2004) in Britain.

---

[7]Hill (1977) revealed that 90 per cent of African American children born out of wedlock are informally adopted within the African American community.

CHAPTER 3

Racialised biographies

This chapter presents the narratives of a sample of six individuals. They were all united by the common experience of having been transracially adopted, and agreed that this had been a primary influential role in their construction of racial identity. In addition, though, they had other racialised biographies, such as intercountry adoption, mixed-race, offspring of immigrants, and which had also been significant in how they had constructed a racial identity. The sample consisted of the following respondents:[1]

1. Alison, 40 years old, female, mixed-race, offspring of immigrants.
2. Hee Yun, 26 years old, female, intercountry adoptee, mixed-race.
3. Julie, 43 years old, female, offspring of immigrants.
4. Natasha, 22 years old, female, intercountry adoptee, mixed-race.
5. Robert, 41 years old, male, mixed-race, offspring of immigrants.
6. Will, 21 years old, male, offspring of immigrants.

Each of the adoptees were interviewed in depth in 2002. They were asked to talk in their own voices to express their views, feelings and experiences about having been a transracial adoptee, and in relevant cases also, an intercountry adoptee, a child of mixed (interracial) parentage, or the offspring of immigrants. For more details on the method of data collection used, see appendices. In particular, adoptees were asked to comment on the following:

* How the adoptive family had approached issues of race.
* Feelings of sameness and difference in the adoptive home.
* Knowledge, experience and significance of birth heritage.
* Searching for one's own birth family.
* Role of birth family and/or birth heritage on perceptions of self.
* Working through difficulties associated with racial difference.
* Views on the practice of transracial adoption.

The adoptees narratives proved insightful. They not only offered qualitative data, but were also considered an appropriate way to allow multi-dimensional and multi-layered meanings to emerge. Hence the reader will notice that at times a number of different points are drawn from the same narrative. Here, along with some sociological commentary, are the adoptees' narratives.

---

[1] Pseudonyms have been used to protect identities.

The place of race in the adoptive home

In looking at the ways in which adoptive families approach issues tied to race and racial differences between themselves and the adoptee, the existing body of literature has found that although adoptees are told about their adoption from a young age by their adoptive parents, further information and actual experience of the adoptees' racial background has often been neglected. It is suggested that such neglect is due to a variety of reasons, which swing from being unintentional or naïve, that is, a lack of knowledge or a view that 'love is enough' (Hayes, 1988), to the more dangerous reasons, such as the adoptive parent's own racist attitudes or negative stereotypes about black minority ethnic people (Small, 1986; Tizard, 1977).

Parental approaches to racial difference

Alison, Julie, Will, Robert and Hee Yun had all been raised in white adoptive homes. Natasha, however, had been raised in an adoptive home in which there were some biological children who were also of mixed-race heritage (white European and black African Caribbean). Despite this, Natasha's adoptive parents had not made any efforts to provide her with information or experience of her own black African Caribbean birth heritage whilst she was growing up.

With Natasha's adoptive family not having talked to her about her birth heritage, Natasha began to make a number of attempts on her own to learn more about some of the black African Caribbean communities in her city:

> *I once went with somebody to a gospel night and to be honest it was like completely, you know, 'wow', over my head sort of thing, and I really just sat there and I laughed all the way through, I thought it was embarrassing, it was like you know 'la, la, la' and I thought 'ok, well it's not me' you know it probably would not have been in my (birth) culture, if you like, and you know it was probably the Jamaican thing, but still it's quite close to obviously what I might have been doing.*

> (Natasha)

Natasha's self-directed attempts to learn more about some of the black African Caribbean communities in her city, and to integrate herself into those communities, failed. This was because she felt so different to them and their practices. She later added:

> *It was really weird, because I wasn't used to that . . . it was really different.*

> (Natasha)

For Will, Robert, Alison, Julie and Hee Yun, who had all been raised in white adoptive homes, there had also been no real information or experience provided by their adoptive parents about their birth heritage. For example, when asked whether his adoptive family accommodated for his racial background, Will replied:

> *They didn't do anything like that no.*

> (Will)

In fact, the only time that any of the adoptees could recall their adoptive parents showing obvious concern about their birth heritage and the racial difference was when Alison recalled an incident with her adoptive father:

> When I went off to Australia, you know my dad was quite concerned that Australia is quite racist, I don't know why he comes out with these things but he does, and you know he spoke to a couple of girlfriends who were white and Australian, and said 'Alison's not going to face any racism is she?'

> (Alison)

However, such demonstrated awareness was a rarity. As a consequence, all the adoptees were in one way or another critical of their adoptive family's approach in providing information about birth parents and experience of birth culture. For instance, Hee Yun, was quite angry and upset with her adoptive parents:

> I would say it's not accepted, you know it's not acknowledged, yes acknowledged that's the word, that I am Korean in that family. They knew I come from there but that is not acknowledging that I come from there.

> (Hee Yun)

Will was also quite angry with his adoptive parents, but more so because they had not understood his feelings of difference and didn't support him when he sought information about his birth background:

> I think they should have helped me.

> (Will)

In particular, the adoptees highlighted the inadequacy of their adoptive parents' tactics in reducing their negative perceptions of racialised differences. There were a number of reasons given for the adoptive families' insufficient approach. The first was that although not realising it themselves, the adoptive parents held negative views about black minority ethnic people. For example, Will had said about his adoptive mother:

> Me hanging around with the black kids at college and school and not doing what she said . . . she still thinks that I'm hanging round with bad people . . . I don't understand why she does because she knows who they are and stuff but she still thinks that and sees me as bad.

> (Will)

However, of greater concern was that adoptees picked up on these negative views. For example, when I later asked Will about his upbringing he began his narrative with the following comment:

> (I've had) a white upbringing. I mean I haven't been brought up badly or anything . . . I was brought up with certain things like, always do the right thing and go to church and that, and to go to school, and to keep yourself out of trouble and that.

> (Will)

Upon being asked whether Will thought he would have been brought up differently and not taught those things if he had been brought up in a black African Caribbean home, he replied:

> Yeah . . . I would not have cared as much . . . when I think about the situation they (black people) could maybe do the same as me.

(Will)

Will clearly picked up some of his adoptive mother's negative stereotypes about black minority ethnic people, especially, it was later revealed, about black African Caribbean people. Although Will had a broad network of black minority ethnic friends, as well as white friends, in a subtle way his comment supports Chimezie's claim that some black children reared in white families and communities 'will develop anti-black psychological and social characteristics' (Chimezie, 1985, in Simon and Alstein, 2000: 41).

Similarly, Julie and Alison also harboured some rather negative views about black minority ethnic people, in particular black African Caribbean people. However, this could not directly be attributed to the negative attitudes of their adoptive parents. Rather, it seemed that their negative views had emerged from their own encounters with other black minority ethnic people, as well as them having been used to being a racial 'novelty' in their white social environments. For example, Julie said:

> I can only describe it as kind of engrossed in blackness with a capital B, you know and (she) became a Rasta and had locks and the works and some succession of black baby-fathers which I had not approved of at all and I used to say things like 'why have you bought into this particular bit'? You know the hair and stuff I can understand, but why the baby-fathers, you know how does that make your life better . . . it was something you know I was kind of interested in because when I became aware of the phenomenon I think I learnt about it through the media you know, it's not something that's impacted on my life at all. I was just very, very curious as to how we, as to what was in it for the women, you know having quite often quite a few children by a wide range of men some of whom didn't seem to be a lot of use and whose main role appeared to be to bounce in occasionally and you know, be daddy as opposed to being anything useful . . . I can understand why people might you know they have a choice of serial relationships but it does appear to be a particular thing with this acceptance of the fact that men go round spreading their seed and women bring up the children . . . and what I also find bizarre is that she certainly wasn't prepared to talk to me about it.

(Julie)

On a similar level, Alison made the following comment:

> It was a mixed place, but it was mainly black as well, and you know, I could not cope with that either, well yeah, I felt oppressed by it, it was in your face. And black people tend to be quite loud and 'look at me, aren't I great' sort of thing, and I just thought

'oh my God' type of thing, you know . . . and they talk in a different way, you know they talk in that way . . . that funny talk that black people do.

(Alison)

Another reason given by adoptees for the adoptive parents' inadequate approach was that adoptive parents de-valued the birth heritage, or in their naivety and ignorance did not consider it important. This could be either with respect to providing knowledge or experience of it to the adoptee, or making the effort to learn about it themselves so that they could pass that on to the adoptee. This view was also partially due to them having viewed their own white heritage as the 'norm'.

They (adoptive parents) knew I come from there (Korea) but that is not acknowledging that I come from there. So, maybe it's the fact that they did not know better. I was the first child for them of this experience, so that's maybe it.

(Hee Yun)

A third reason for the adoptive parents' inadequate approach was due to a lack of information and resources, that is, either a lack of access to resources, or a lack of take-up of available resources. In particular, Julie, Alison and Natasha felt their adoptive parents essentially disregarded, out of innocence and naivety, their birth heritage and the racialised differences that existed, not only in not providing information about birth heritage, but also in terms of day-to-day practicalities. For example, Julie said:

I think that people didn't think about those kinds of things in those days . . . the hair thing I think my mum would have been intensely grateful if anything was explained to her with what to do with the hair . . . and I used to have this terribly dry skin and I'd always assumed that it was me . . . I was an adult before somebody said to me you do realise that very dry skin is not uncommon in black people.

(Julie)

A fourth reason as to why adoptees viewed their adoptive parents' approach as inadequate was that it was also underlined by a rather naïve approach. This was that the adoptive parents had taken the view that 'love is enough' to raise the adoptee. For example, Robert, Hee Yun and Will felt that their adoptive parents ignored the racial differences or the adoptees' birth heritage out of a naive and ignorant assumption that there was no serious problem. In other words, there had been a sort of 'love is all you need' or 'love is enough' view held by some of these adoptive parents. This is illustrated by the following comment that was made by Robert:

It just wasn't talked about very often at all, I think maybe, yeah, once or twice I remember my mum telling me what little she knew about my parents, and that was about it really, it wasn't a kind of an ongoing thing because they felt, you know in their sort of naivety about the whole thing, I think they sort of just thought that it's probably better not to keep on addressing those issues and just sort of get on with just treating me like the rest of their children.

(Robert)

The adoptees felt that despite these problems, there had not been any intentional animosity or 'hidden agendas' with the adoptive parents' approaches to birth heritage, both in terms of the lack of information and experience they provided to the adoptees. However, there does seem to be an echo of some of the arguments made by those opposers of transracial adoption, these being that black minority ethnic children raised in white homes are, with a few exceptions, denied their blackness by 'meaningful – but nevertheless ignorant – white substitute parents' who are unable and fail to provide 'knowledge, understanding, sensitivity, intelligence and the ability to empathise and to recognise racism' (Hayes, 1988: 14). In this sense then, the adoptees were denied recognition, either through lack of information or experience, of their birth heritage. This is despite the fact that such denial was presented in subtle and less overt ways. For example, although none of the adoptees had experienced being directly told by their adoptive parents that 'they can choose to be white if they wish' (Hayes, 1988: 14), or that 'colour in this society does not really matter', it is argued that the lack of recognition given by adoptive parents could be interpreted as 'the denial of the reality of the visibility of the black child in a white family' and how this creates 'the pre-conditions for the phenomenon of identity confusion' (Small, 1986: 82).

Although all the adoptees were in some way critical about their adoptive parents' approach, the effects of inadequate approaches had varied. Some of the adoptees experienced particular problems, whereas others did not.

Robert felt that his adoptive family had been unable to understand his experiences of racism as a child and later his feelings as a young black African Caribbean adult, which then led to a boundary being formed between him and his adoptive family.

I'm pretty sure that I didn't talk to my family or parents or siblings about it, I suppose I didn't really see it as a need to because . . . it would just be the odd little incidents now and then that just got dealt with at school, also a bit of me kind of felt that they would not understand . . . (because) the kind of issue of race of my father being Nigerian, it just wasn't talked about very often at all . . . I think gradually over the years I think I would have maybe liked to know a little bit more about my parents, but it wasn't sort of like a deep yearning need.

(Robert)

However, although having very little information about, and no experience of their birth heritage, Julie and Alison did not see this as a cause for concern. For example, Julie said:

I suppose there's a definite sense that as I say 'yes I don't have a black consciousness' . . . it doesn't bother me.

(Julie)

Feeling different

Following this discussion, I asked each of the adoptees to reflect upon what being transracially adopted meant for them, in particular whether they felt as if the transracial aspects of their adoption brought about any unique differences in their experiences within the adoptive family, that, say, inracial adoptees would not have faced.

All six individuals felt they experienced no particular differences, in that they were treated as a biological child or a fully integrated member of the adoptive family. As a child growing up in the late 1960s and 1970s, Robert recalled:

> *We used to go off on holidays and things together . . . I was never excluded from the rest of the family in terms of that, you know when we'd go off together I certainly wasn't treated any differently from the rest of the family or anything like that.*
>
> (Robert)

Although Hee Yun suggested that being an intercountry adoptee, as well as a transracial adoptee, further deepened her feelings of difference from the adoptive family, Hee Yun did not feel as if her adoptive parents treated her any different to their biological child. In specifically talking about her adoptive mother, Hee Yun said:

> *(There was) no difference to how she treated me because I was adopted.*
>
> (Hee Yun)

However, despite admitting not being treated differently by their adoptive families, the adoptees felt that the obvious racial differences that were ever-present and feeling that they were alone in their non-whiteness was significant in their experiences. This is so even for those who are mixed-race by birth. This is therefore something distinctive to the experiences of transracial adoptees, including those who are mixed-race. For example, Will and Hee Yun felt as if the transracial status of the adoption brought about experiences that were rooted in the racialised differences and thus made them feel different:

> *At Christmas as well, I felt different . . . because I'm the only one of this colour.*
>
> (Will)

Hee Yun similarly said:

> *Something about not being well in your own skin and um, trying to be someone else . . . it's difficult to say, but you try to find your identity . . . 'cos you lie about yourself. You have to find yourself and more than anything else you want to know where you belong and what makes you.*
>
> (Hee Yun)

For Hee Yun and Will, these feelings of difference were apparent outside of the adoptive home. In particular, school was a common site where such feelings of difference emerged. As a Korean-born child growing up in 1980s Germany, Hee Yun said:

I very quickly became an outsider at that school because I was so different and they asked me questions, I mean people, kids want to know questions about yourself you cannot answer . . . They ask me 'why are your parents not look like this?' 'what is adopted?' . . . sometimes I would answer them as . . . but I got quite fed up because it was quite often . . . at least fifty to sixty kids want to know 'why you look like this?' and 'why is your eyes like this?' and 'why don't you have right, real parents?' . . . I found out that kids started talking about me behind my back, so like 'she's that way' and 'she's so stupid . . . it was because of your eyes, because of you being small, because of you being stupid you know . . . and that's what they mean, you are stranger, different from me.

(Hee Yun)

In late 1980s England, Will had similar experiences:

It was you know, people saying things and then I would tell myself that I wasn't the same . . . and every time it was parents evening . . . all the kids at school, no some of the kids at school, not bullied me, but every time they saw it, it made it difficult being adopted, how can I put it? I used to get not embarrassed but I could not really talk about it. I was feeling really sad about it and asking 'why?' I think yeah, it did make them take the mickey out of me, you know because I was different really. Other people, I would not say staring, but would ask me questions over and over again, like 'why are you adopted?' and 'why do you have white parents?

(Will)

As a result of their differences being negatively perceived, Hee Yun and Will felt a strong grievance at having been transracially adopted which exhibited itself in the adoptees' feelings towards their birth parents and their country of birth. For example, Will felt angry at having been denied the opportunity to be raised by his birth family:

I wasn't supposed to be there and I didn't choose to be there, in a white home instead of my real home.

(Will)

Hee Yun was also particularly upset and angry at her lack of choice and the denial of an opportunity to be raised in her country of birth:

They (the Korean government) just thought that 'we have so many children' and you know, 'what are we doing with it', they didn't think about the child wanting to know about their history later when they had grown up . . .

(Hee Yun)

Hee Yun's comments support the study of young people in care by Fisher, Marsh and Phillips, who reported a sense of powerlessness felt by the young people in terms of how decisions were being taken about them without their consultation. The authors point out that 'the young person's sense of being uninvolved in discussions was an important forerunner of a broader theme of powerlessness' (Fisher, Marsh and Phillips, 1986: 69).

Hee Yun had contradictory feelings about her adoption. On the one hand she was angry, primarily towards the Korean government for the intercountry adoption programme, at the adoption agency for treating her as a commodity, and also at her adoptive parents for taking part in the crime of her adoption. However, on the other hand, Hee Yun was reluctant to criminalise her adoptive parents and instead tried to rationalise, and almost excuse, their actions. She spoke about her adoptive mother:

> It is an emotional thing to accuse her of being involved. You cannot call her a criminal, but she was involved in this crime. Not that she knew it though. So in the end of the day I can not accuse her of the crime, because she did not know.

> (Hee Yun)

Similarly, Will was also reluctant to criminalise his adoptive mother, in that he had some understanding, gratefulness and respect for her in choosing to adopt him and then to keep him when circumstances within the adoptive family had changed. When Will's adoptive parents separated, Will seemed to be grateful to his adoptive mother for her decision to keep him:

> She was kind of fair to be honest, I mean she could have said to my adopted dad 'take him back', because they both adopted me.

> (Will)

These two last examples suggest that Hee Yun and Will saw their own adoptions as 'a form of deviance' (Bagley, Young and Scully, 1992: 72). This is because they saw it as morally wrong. However, despite their feelings, both adoptees also demonstrated gratitude and respect towards their adoptive families.

In reflecting upon what being transracially adopted meant for each of the adoptees, it was also evident that opinions were not always negative. Some adoptees had seen their adoption as having provided them with a 'second chance' and this was particularly so for Natasha, Alison, Julie and Hee Yun. Natasha, who was also an intercountry adoptee, said:

> I think I've sort of learnt that I've been given a second chance, and to me that's really quite important because if I hadn't been adopted I probably would have . . . you know, had a much, much harder type of life, you know, not had this good life or the good clothes or the good job.

> (Natasha)

Despite having earlier spoken about her anger at the denial of choice in having been transracially adopted out of Korea, Hee Yun also spoke about her adoption as another chance. In talking about the day she was brought into the adoptive home, Hee Yun said:

> I just walked through. I just remember I just thought at one stage 'oh it's nice here', and I just lay down and slept . . . I always describe it as my birth really because that's

the first memory that I've got from my life, so that's how I've been born really . . . that was my first experience and it was a very warm and welcoming experience.

(Hee Yun)

It was also evident that perceptions of racialised differences between the adoptee and their adoptive family were not always negative. This was particularly so if the differences were perceived by the adoptee as having its advantages. For example, Julie, Natasha and Alison felt as if they were 'chosen', and therefore had a special quality that led to them being wanted:

My parents always used to say 'we chose you', and that makes you feel very special . . . I just felt like I mattered in the house.

(Julie)

I always felt as if I was different, but . . . that turned me into a bit of a novelty, so I played on that . . . I just felt almost like the most important person . . . when I arrived they (social services) gave me an allowance, so I was walking around in all these new clothes and they (adoptive brothers) were walking in the hand-me-downs.

(Alison)

Alison's 'novelty status' in being the only '*non-white*' (her words) person in a white social environment, is something that is clearly rooted in the transracial aspects of the adoption. This had profound effects on Alison's behaviour and perception of self in relation to others. As an adult Alison developed an attitude whereby she felt being around other black people would affect her 'novelty status':

It could be competition you know, it could carry on from when I was younger, you know, I'm still the novelty if I'm different to everybody else, so I'll be remembered.

(Alison)

Even those adoptees harbouring negative perceptions of racialised differences acknowledged that the differences also had its benefits. Will felt that being adopted had led to special treatment:

To be honest the only person who got special treatment was myself really, yeah, out of the three of us, I think I got away with more . . . just because I was adopted really, I think, no other reason . . . I still get shouted at, don't get me wrong, you know but it was just stuff like if I'd come home late and I would not get a big shouted at, but she'd still shout.

(Will)

Tactics for reducing feelings of difference

In light of disclosing their awareness of racialised differences, and their positive and negative perceptions of these differences, the adoptees talked about the tactics used by their adoptive parents to reduce negative perceptions of racialised difference.

All of the adoptees in this research study recalled that from a very early age their adoptive parents were fairly open about the adoption. Similar findings were reported by Howe and Feast (2000), who looked at the searching experiences of 159 adoptees, 30 of whom were transracial adoptees. However, the adoptees in this study suggested that their parents were forced to be open about the adoption because of the obvious racial differences. For example:

> From the word go mum, well I mean people said to me when did your parents tell you that you were adopted and I'd say well quite soon because it was apparent, you know, so they kind of did it from the word go.

> (Alison)

> I mean they always talked about it openly I think in their own way, of course with transracial adoption there's no option of pretending that a child's not adopted . . . so you have no option but to talk about it openly.

> (Julie)

The adoptive parents' openness was therefore largely something that was beyond their control. This is because the transracial aspect of the adoption and the racial composition of the adoptive family forced this openness. This was also the case for those who were mixed-race. This degree of early openness, then, seems to be something that is unique to transracial adoptees. However, in saying this, Tizard found that such obvious racial differences do not always bring openness. In her study of mixed-race transracial adoptees, Tizard found that some adoptive parents of transracial adoptees were concealing the fact that their adoptive child was mixed-race as '(one) child whom the parents were 'passing' as white was in fact dark-skinned and obviously of Indian parentage . . . (another) child had not been told that his father was West Indian, although it had been pointed out to him that his skin was darker than that of his adoptive parents' (Tizard, 1977: 181).

In this study the adoptive parents' portrayal of birth families was largely positive. Hee Yun said:

> My mum explained really that my birth mum had to give me up for adoption and she always tried to put a positive view on my birth mother, so she tried to explain to me that it's not her fault.

> (Hee Yun)

Many of the parents were also open about the adoption and answered the adoptees' questions with little hesitation:

> I think they'd answered any questions I had. And I don't think I ever asked about the practicalities . . . you know, it was more from the point of view of the things that they told me.

> (Julie)

For Hee Yun, a book about a young boy's adoption was also used by her adoptive mother to explain the adoption:

> I had this book, it's a Swedish book, very hippy like, flowers and things, very cute . . . 'Booblan' was coming from a different country and 'Booblan' was a child . . . from a poorer country, their parents for what ever reason . . . could not keep 'Booblan', it said they were upset they could not and . . . so 'Booblan' gets to be adopted to this parents because it's really basically the book saying, because one parent could not get, could not keep, you know for that reason had to give up 'Booblan' and they gave it to the other parent who could take the child and wanted a child. And then they just describe about the bit that they do with the planes, pictures with planes, it's flying over and 'hooray' and they have a massive party, and it stops there with 'Booblan' having his first birthday with his friends in that new area with new parents.
>
> (Hee Yun)

This particular story made Hee Yun feel wanted. It also reduced her feelings of difference because she was able to normalise the adoption experience, and the intercountry aspect of the adoption, in that others in the story were also adopted in this way.

However, this type of openness only existed during the adoptees' childhood years, primarily because the adoptee stopped asking questions, either because they were no longer interested or, as in Natasha's case, because they sensed that the questions were upsetting their adoptive parents:

> They haven't talked much about it. I've not really asked them questions. Mainly because I don't really want to hurt them . . . I think my (adoptive) mum would be 'ooh she's getting to that stage now where she wants to find out' and she may be a bit worried that I'd run off and find her (birth mother).
>
> (Natasha)

After having initially volunteered information and answered questions about the adoption, the adoptive parents used a number of tactics aimed at reducing the adoptees' sense of difference. A common tactic was to make the adoptee feel 'special', loved and wanted. This was the case for Hee Yun, Alison, Natasha and Julie. Natasha said:

> It made me feel really quite special, and my mum used to say you know 'you're special'. . . I think it's the words you know, 'oh wow I'm adopted'.
>
> (Natasha)

Additionally for Julie, the adoption had even been romanticised:

> They met me at a christening and my dad danced with me all day because he thought I was so wonderful. There's this kind of image you know . . . in falling for this little two-year-old and wanting to dance with me.
>
> (Julie)

However, some adoptive parents felt that ignoring or underplaying racialised differences would help to limit the adoptees' negative perceptions of these differences, and in effect make them feel like a wholly integrated (or 'real') member of the family. Hence a second parental tactic was to withhold, limit or edit information about birth parents. Natasha talked about discovering information when she carried out a secret search of her adoptive parents' possessions:

> I mean I have found out a few things. I mean there are a couple of things that I found out through dare I say being really nosey, because I mean my mum's got a study upstairs in her house and I was just looking around one day and I found this letter that my real mum had written to my mum now.
>
> (Natasha)

A third parental tactic is one that is unique to the experiences of transracial adoptees. This was to not push the adoptee into experiencing the culture of their birth parents. For example, Hee Yun's adoptive parents had not encouraged her to learn about Korean culture or the Korean language:

> She (adoptive mother) did not make me Korean . . . she waited for me. It was me who had to go and say 'can I learn?'
>
> (Hee Yun)

Interestingly, none of the mixed-race adoptees reported their adoptive parents attempting to reduce feelings of difference by emphasising the partial racial commonality shared between them, i.e. the fact that these adoptees were born to one white parent.

Having discussed the tactics used by adoptive parents to reduce the adoptees' negative perceptions of racialised differences, the adoptees then went on to talk about the success or failures of these tactics.

Although Hee Yun's adoptive parents' portrayal of her birth family had largely been positive, such a positive view was insufficient:

> However it was theoretical, you could maybe say 'ok, I understand that', but emotionally it took me a long time, I think up until about now, to work with the hate feelings. I was a person who was beaten up, because you know that although it's not a rejection, it feels like a rejection to you. And you always have to reason between your emotions and the facts. You have to negotiate between the emotions and the logical bit.
>
> (Hee Yun)

Robert also thought that the lack of information was insufficient. Even though he admitted that he was not initially too concerned about the adoptive family not talking about the adoption, this later changed when he became aware of 'the black politics of 1980s Britain' (Robert) and wanted to learn more about his birth parents and his birth heritage:

> It wasn't a kind of an ongoing thing because . . . I think they sort of just thought that it's probably better . . . to just sort of get on with just treating me like the rest of their

children, so you know there are some benefits in that and some problems in that attitude. It was kind of more later on, probably after when I was about eighteen that I got as if I felt that I needed to know a bit more.

(Robert)

Similarly, Natasha, Will and Hee Yun grew eager to be told more about their adoption and birth family whilst growing up. Natasha explained why:

It's things that you pass on as well, really, isn't it. To be honest, it's something that's going to settle me as well though because to be honest, sometimes I wonder if I am actually settled in myself, and I don't think I am, I think once I do know what happened, everything is going to go ooohh, and I am going to feel normal . . . I mean my life is normal, but sometimes I just feel really angry in myself . . . because there are various things that have happened in the past . . . but if I can find out answers to this I will be happy, a lot happier than I have been . . . it's the not knowing that's the problem . . . Inside, I just feel a little muddled. I do feel a little hurt sometimes . . . I think it's just a problem in myself, within me . . . I think once I've found out I will be settled, a lot settled.

(Natasha)

For Hee Yun, Will and Natasha, not being able to talk more freely about their adoption or being unsatisfied with the adoptive parents' approach also led to feelings of isolation or guilt about seeking further information:

It is very difficult for a child, to cope with this and to cope with their emotions if they did not get encouragement from their parents.

(Hee Yun)

I think that's why there's a barrier up between me and them . . . because they don't know or understand.

(Will)

I started to suddenly think you know, I would not mind finding out a few things. But . . . I don't want to hurt my parents by doing it . . . it's just my mum. It's the fact that I don't want to hurt her which makes me step back and re-think that 'oh I'll say nothing' and reconsider if I want to ask her stuff, but like I said I will definitely one day ask her.

(Natasha)

Indeed, Natasha was so afraid of upsetting her adoptive mother that she resorted to secret searches:

Like I said, I know me asking might upset her (adoptive mother) so I don't want to do that . . . I just, well sometimes I have a quick look around her study on my own, when she's not about.

(Natasha)

However, Natasha was not angry with her adoptive parents for not telling her more about her adoption:

> I don't feel angry, no. I just feel that . . . it would have been quite nice to have a little bit more extra info . . . about my roots I suppose.
>
> (Natasha)

Hee Yun on the other hand had been particularly upset with her adoptive mother for not having made her learn Korean as a child:

> That is not respecting the culture. And I am saying if you have another child from another background try as much as possible to learn about it and get into it as much as possible. I am saying to actually learn it is another thing, but to even attempt and try to learn is also good, and she did not. She waited for me. It was me who had to go and say 'can I learn?' I was the only Korean person in a German family and it's me that has to go and do this, it's me that has to say 'hello yeah I'm Korean, but I have other needs as well'. You know I said to my mum 'why did you not go and learn Korean with me . . . together?' And she says she asked me when I was a child and I say 'no I do not want to learn Korean'. But I was a child, I did not know. Why did she not take me by the hand and say 'come we go learn Korean, you are Korean and I support that'? It is no good just me learn Korean. I have no one to talk Korean to. But she waited for me to come with my hand up and say 'I want to learn Korean'. Me, as a child who does not know anything.
>
> (Hee Yun)

The adoptees' feelings of difference in the adoptive home, along with the inadequacy of parental tactics, had profound consequences on adoptees. In particular, it deepened their already negative perceptions of difference. For example, Hee Yun and Will both talked in some detail and depth about their experiences of constantly feeling different to their adopters, as highlighted by a comment made by Will:

> I don't feel as if I fit in because I'm the only one of this colour . . . (I was) paranoid, that everyone was different . . . and that I wasn't the same.
>
> (Will)

For Will, who talked quite negatively about feeling different within his family, most specifically on the grounds that he was of a different colour, this difference had meant barriers between him and his adoptive family being erected, which were also strengthened by his views that his adoptive family were unable to understand his feelings:

> (My adoptive mother) always brings it up in an argument anyway, that I went to find my real mum and that she didn't want me to, she said that she didn't want me to find them, and then I told her that I was and just went on my own to do it. I think . . . it's just something you have to do, even if you've had a good upbringing . . . surely though

*she should realise, and she should help me and want me to know. But obviously not
. . . I think (my adoptive siblings) feel the same as her. She's thinking that and so are
they, but I don't really know, I can't talk to her about it really or them.*

(Will)

As a result of the problems resulting from perceptions of difference, and the adoptive parents'
inadequate tactics for reducing feelings of difference, the adoptees were forced to develop
their own coping strategies.

Hee Yun and Will dealt with the differences in various ways. As a child, Will would cry
and get upset:

*I would tell myself that I wasn't the same, and on very special occasions, like on my
birthdays and that, and at Christmas, I'd say to myself that I wanted my real parents
there. Then . . . I would cry.*

(Will)

Whereas a young Hee Yun would constantly ask her adoptive mother if she loved her:

*I mean I have an older brother, five years older, and he is the natural child . . . and it
was a question of 'who do you love more?' I say to my mother 'do you love him more
or me?'*

(Hee Yun)

In contrast, Alison as a child dealt with the differences by inventing dramatic stories and
using humour:

*I remember the first parent's evening and I thought 'oh my God' . . . and so then I
started making up these stories about what had happened to my real mum and dad,
you know, how my real parents had been killed in a plane crash and stuff like that . . .
there was an incident at school when we were asked to write down for a project . . .
called 'who am I?' and we had to write down who we'd got our eyes from and our
brown hair from . . . and I was sat there thinking 'well I look nothing like my mum or
dad' so . . . wrote 'I've got green hair and . . . four legs'.*

(Alison)

The manner in the way that Hee Yun, Will and Alison dealt with the differences, however,
was that Alison strongly felt that her difference within the family made her the focus of
positive special attention, as opposed to the negative attention that was experienced by Will
and Hee Yun. Again, it is interesting that like the adoptive parents, none of the adoptees
attempted to reduce feelings of difference by using the white parts of their biological
parentage to base commonality upon.

Two important findings emerge from this. Firstly, how adoptive parents used a number of
tactics aimed at reducing the adoptees' negative feelings of racialised difference. These
tactics included making the adoptee feel special, underplaying the racialised differences by

withholding information, and not pushing the adoptees to learn about and experience their birth culture. Secondly, although some of the adoptees revealed that the adoptive parents' tactic of making them feel 'special' helped to reduce some negative feelings around racialised differences, most of the adoptees' were critical of parental tactics. The adoptees' main criticism was how they actually did very little to reduce negative perceptions of difference, and how they instead deepened adoptees' feelings of difference, which they were left alone to deal with.

Searching for birth roots

Adoptees were also asked to talk about their birth heritage. In doing so, the adoptees revealed that they all had some level of knowledge about the circumstances surrounding their birth, based on information that was passed on to them by their adoptive parents.

Knowledge of birth and reasons for adoption

The adoptees' knowledge of these circumstances varied, and for some, race had been significant. For example, racialised controversy surrounded Alison's birth because one of the reasons behind Alison's white birth mother abandoning her was due to the mother's fear of her own family rejecting her partially black baby:

> He, the granddad was very racist, very racist, and so he was completely against her (birth mother) having all these black men, well not all these, these two relationships with black men, you know because she had the one and then she had Lionel (birth father) and he (grandfather) never . . . they (grandparents) would never entertain him at all and what was worse than black was having these . . . well . . . half-caste children, as they called them then, you know these kids who were neither one or the other, you know he was 'I don't want these brought into my house' and whatever . . . so my mother abandoned me and left me on the train . . . she got home and thought you know 'oh God, what have I done? I want her back'. But in the sixties she was treated as criminal, you know, it was a criminal offence to abandon a baby, so she'd actually lost me from that point.
>
> (Alison)

However, for other adoptees, race was not seen as a contributory factor in their birth parent's decision to put them forward for adoption. For example, Natasha's birth mother had not planned to have a baby, and upon finding herself pregnant, without a partner or supporting family, and financially unable to raise a child on her own, she had no option but opt for adoption:

> I found this letter that my real mum had written to my mum now, saying that basically these are the circumstances. My dad was apparently a seaman that travelled a lot of miles and all over the place, you know he just sailed, I think he was a transporter of

some sort, and my mum was quite young and that I was basically a mistake and that I should not have happened, and that she's 'thankful', in the letter she said, because at least it's gone to a family that's wanted to love and care for me really. She said she didn't really want to let me go but she had no choice because she could not afford to keep me.

(Natasha)

Similar circumstances occurred for Will, whose birth mother had abandoned him in a hospital:
She (birth mother) said that she gave me away because she could not keep me, that she was too young . . . so she had me, left me in hospital and I was took away.

(Will)

Evidence shows that regardless of their own racial heritage, birth parents, and in particular birth mothers, put their child into care or forward for adoption for reasons of stigma, inadequate financial income, and lack of support from the family and the birth father (Holman, 1975; Maza, 1983; Mech, 1983; Schor, 1982; Shyne and Schroeder, 1978). However, it is also argued that because members of the black minority ethnic population 'suffer disproportionately in terms of poor housing and unemployment', have less access to statutory resources and preventative work, and are more susceptible to institutional racism (Barn, 2001: 20), the cumulative result is a greater number of black African Caribbean and mixed-race children, especially those who are of a black African Caribbean and white European 'mix', are entering care (Barn, 1993; Barn, 2001; Bebbington and Miles, 1989).

In the study reported here, the type and focus of the knowledge that all the transracial adoptees possessed about their birth heritage related to factual points around the circumstances surrounding their birth. These covered where they were born, why they were adopted, if their birth mother loved them and only reluctantly put them forward for adoption, their birth parents' racial origin, what the birth parents looked like, and so on. In other words, the knowledge base of transracial adoptees was similar to that of those who are black minority ethnic and inracially placed, and even those who are white and inracially placed (Howe and Feast, 2000).

However, some of the transracial adoptees' knowledge base was more detailed, reflecting the significance of the racial and cultural birth heritage in the adoptees' sense of self and racial identity development. The knowledge was firstly related to their birth culture, and in particular traditions, religious beliefs, customary practices, celebratory holidays, and historical figures, etc., and secondly about the community of those who were of the same birth racial origin, and the practices and homogeneity existing within the boundaries of the black minority ethnic community. For example:
I got to meet other Korean adoptees . . . I got more information about the history and people . . . it helped me quite a lot in finding myself in developing me myself.

(Hee Yun)

You know being aware of things going on internationally and in London about how black people, the black community were treated, you know, just being aware of being black . . . so it was just sort of a gradual process from my teens that I gradually took more interest in race issues and the apartheid and mainly then meeting more black friends.

(Robert)

An important point emerges here, and this is that most transracial adoptees require more detailed information about their birth heritage, because they hold negative perceptions about their adoption and the racialised differences between them and their adoptive parents, and therefore (as the next section will show) search to resolve specific racialised issues around identity and belonging.

Experiencing the birth heritage

In various ways and to different extents, all the adoptees had experiences around their birth heritage, some of which were positive and others negative. Consequently, relationships bore different meanings and were of different importance in each of the adoptees' racial identity development.

In talking about his experiences of birth heritage, Robert recalled having a number of experiences, which were largely positive, in terms of his birth family and others of the same birth racial origin:

He's (birth father) got four daughters, you know he got married and had four daughters with his Nigerian wife, and I get on ok with them. Again, I've only been over to Nigeria about four times and I'm not I regular contact with them, but when I do see them I'm ok with them. I just, you know, I suppose I feel better and more comfortable with other black people.

(Robert)

These experiences made Robert feel a positive sense of sameness and belonging, in particular with his birth father's black Nigerian heritage. These positive feelings in turn gave Robert a deeper sense of his own black self:

It was definitely here about my birth identity. Definitely more about that. [So then did you think that becoming closer to your birth father especially, that that would bring you closer to your birth identity and experiences of being black?] Definitely, yeah.

(Robert)

On the other hand, Julie had no contact with these elements of her birth heritage, and this made her feel like an outsider from the black community:

I became aware of the fact that the existence of the NF, National Front, and that was all quite frightening. You know as I became kind of older I became more aware of boot boys and skin heads . . . and that I found was all inhibiting. I felt I didn't have skills to deal with that or understand it so I stayed well clear . . . I think that because of, I think there wasn't an awful lot that impacted on a teenager who was fairly sheltered and lived in a village . . . and of course, you know, as far, if there is such a thing, as far as your average black person goes I'm not particularly black at all you know my skin colour and my hair and that's as far as about it goes.

(Julie)

However, despite these factors, Julie felt confident with her sense of self:
I'm not a stereotypical black person, but it doesn't bother me personally . . . I have a lot of strengths. I'm grounded and have a strong sense of self and am successful in what I do.

(Julie)

Being raised in a predominantly white environment and having failed in her attempts to negotiate herself a position within the black community and gain experience of black African Caribbean culture, Natasha similarly talked about having felt like an outsider from the black community. However, like Julie, Natasha had insisted that this was not a concern for her, because she felt confident enough in her sense of self:
I think I'm just me, an individual, the original me.

(Natasha)

The majority of the adoptees though, recalled a complex set of experiences in that they had a more balanced set of both positive and negative encounters. For example, making contact with some aspects of her birth heritage, in terms of Korean culture and others of the same birth racial origin, was important to Hee Yun and helped her to deal with some of the difficulties as a result of her adoption:
I think it brought me quite a step forward . . . I think that that many of these hate feelings when I was an outsider has influenced my way of how to interact with people. I still sometimes feel like this, but I think I have learnt some ways of how to deal with this.

(Hee Yun)

However, because Hee Yun was unable to access specific information about her actual birth and her birth parents, she also continually felt angry, rejected and powerless, which had problematic consequences on her identity development:
I've tried to deal with it but I think there's something I still need to go on thinking about . . . it makes me feeling sometimes very bitter about it. Although it's a situation thing, it's very difficult to say because you know you can reason with it and you can say ok, Korea has been in a very difficult situation, however, does it give it the right for a person to decide over other children's lives, to give them the wrong history or none at all.

(Hee Yun)

Alison also had a contradictory and difficult set of experiences. This was because although Alison felt that her experiences with some of her birth sisters helped her feel a sense of sameness and belonging, in particular by bringing her physical similarities, she also had some negative experiences with some of her other birth sisters:

> When they would come, they would make me feel that they would draw attention to me, which I didn't want. If we went into town and there was three of us, and they may have brought a couple of mates down as well, they'd draw attention to the fact that, I mean looking back I suppose we were you know it (town of residence) is not very multi-cultural, and I don't know, they were drawing attention to me and I didn't want them to and I was happy enough on my own, but I didn't want all the negative attention that they were creating, you know by saying, well they've all gone through loads of racism, they've had loads of issues you know, they said that they'd be walking down the street and somebody would spit at them, you know and when I said that that has not happened to me, they can't believe it, and I might have said stuff like 'oh maybe you're looking for it' . . . I just think that they went looking for it, like I said going to the bar and saying 'we're not getting served because were black', and I'm saying 'well ok maybe they are racist, but why can't you look at it the other way, that white person is not getting served either'. . . and I just said 'look at it from other angles', and they would not, you know.

> (Alison)

Alison also recalled negative experiences with others from the same birth racial origin:

> I mean I've never had a black boyfriend. I've had rows with them . . . I had an argument with a black guy because I didn't want to dance with him, and he went you know 'oh do you only dance with white guys?' and I went 'oh my God!' you know.

> (Alison)

These negative experiences with members of the birth family and others of the same black African Caribbean racial origin illustrates Alison's sense of difference from the black part of her birth heritage. This sense of difference is due to the mixed-race nature of Alison's birth heritage, as well as the transracial aspect of her adoption and being raised in a white environment:

> I just can't cope, you know I haven't had any black friends or any mixed-race friends at all throughout the whole of my life and I just could not cope with these sisters of mine who were like taking over and portraying me in this way and putting me in their category . . . I didn't see myself as being black, so that was part of it all as well. I mean they may have had a more multi-cultural upbringing, you know more black friends and more Asian friends, I mean and I haven't.

> (Alison)

Reporting on mixed-race people and their experiences with black[2] people, Tizard and Phoenix found slightly more than one-third of their sample 'said they felt uncomfortable with black people than those who said they felt uncomfortable with white' (Tizard and Phoenix, 2002: 116). This was partially due to the young people's unfamiliarity with black people, and feeling more at ease with white people, whom they saw as primarily accepting them more as individuals. Similarly, when asked about their feelings concerning black people, 13 per cent of the sample gave negative answers. Tizard and Phoenix pointed out that only 'a minority of our sample had met hostility, exclusion and verbal abuse from black children' (ibid: 225), and as for negative encounters with black people, an equal number was reported for encounters with white people. Therefore, Tizard and Phoenix concluded that mixed-race people are no more likely to have negative experiences with black people than with white people.

Reasons for searching

From the little empirical data concerning adoptees that do research their origins or backgrounds, it is possible to identify two broad categories. Feast and Howe (1997) identify these as:

- Information seekers – those adoptees who seek information about their birth or background.
- Contact seekers – those who seek contact with birth relatives, and for the transracial adoptees, those who seek contact with others of the same birth racial origin or cultural background.

In the study reported here, the adoptees' searches fell into both these categories. For example, Will searched for members of his birth family. In doing so, he not only wanted information about them, but to also meet them and establish a long-term relationship with them:

> I wanted to be with my real family . . . because I'm a different colour. I would prefer to be like that in a proper way, with my real family and that, to be honest.

(Will)

In seeking to fill the noticeable gaps in the literature about transracial adoptees' experiences of searching, the adoptees were questioned about this subject. All but one of the interviewees had searched. Julie had not made any attempts to search, nor did she have any plans to do so:

> I suppose largely because I've been very happy where I am . . . I guess if I'd been one of these people who felt that they'd been given away by their parents and their adoption was proof that they weren't loved and possibly weren't wanted in the first place, and

---

[2]Tizard and Phoenix (2002) use the term 'black' to refer to all people with two African or African Caribbean parents.

all that other stuff, I guess it might have been more of an issue for me. But because as I say I was loved and happy . . . it's not really been an issue for me at all. And I think because of the ease with which I could find out also. I'm looking through these letters, it's amazing there are clues all over the place . . . It's all just there all I have to do is pick up the phone and ring Preeya (birth mother's friend who dealt with the adoption) and say, you know, 'tell me about Beverley' (birth mother) and it would all be there. So it's almost the ease of which, the ease of it that has perhaps in some ways left me free not have to think about it. You know children, particularly if they are not happy with their adoption build all these fantasies around it, you know. I suspect I never had to for those two reasons.

(Julie)

However, it seemed that Julie's apparent lack of desire to search was largely due to a fear in what she may find. Therefore, she felt the need to protect herself by exercising control and power over her own life. When I asked Julie whether she thought about her birth parents, she said:

No . . . I think it's more about wanting to know that if I do anything it will be on my own terms 'cos . . . what if I don't actually like these people, you know, what does it actually mean for a relationship, do I need yet another relationship with an elderly person . . . This way round is fine. I suppose the only thing that is a very real factor is, should I decide I wanted to initiate something, then discover that Beverley's dead or whatever . . . you know, I don't know how I would feel about that then, you know, if at the same time I made the decision, that the rug is then pulled out from under my feet . . . I can imagine that that would kind of rock anyone's kind of universe. It's not the usual stuff about a secret love child coming out of the woodwork . . . I mean I had two reasons for being remarkably uncurious. One is fearful of what you will find and the other one is not having a sense of needing to know. I've always assumed for me it was the latter.

(Julie)

When asked about searching for details about her birth culture, Julie expressed a similar view point:

Well I don't really know about the racial mix either, and again it's been something I've been depressingly uncurious about . . . I've never had the curiosity to find out, I've always felt that you know you're so clearly a product of the people who bring you up, you know, I am so much like my (adoptive) mum.

(Julie)

The idea that adoptees who choose not to search are more likely to have had a positive experience in the adoptive home is a common argument. For example, Thompson (2000), in discussing Howe and Feast's (2000) report, *Adoption, Search and Reunion*, which studied

472 adoptees, 394 of whom had searched for birth family members, highlighted how 'adopted people who were active searchers were less likely to describe their adoption experience as very positive or positive (53 per cent) than those non-searchers (74 per cent)' (Thompson, 2000: 29).

The original authors of the report mentioned above, Feast and Howe (1997), and again as Howe and Feast (2000), and later as Kirton, Feast and Howe (2000) wrote that adoptees begin to search because of two distinct factors. These are firstly 'particular triggers', and secondly 'motives' (Kirton et al., 2000: 8). They referred to the latter as being 'concerns of longer standing' (ibid: 11). The 'particular triggers' were identified as key events which prompt an adoptee to want to search, such as the death of an adoptive parent, where the adoptee seeks a 'substitute' or 'somewhere to run', a difficulty for the adoptee in holding onto a relationship or other problem, with a current relationship; or the birth of their own child. These authors later added the two events, of health problems and receiving support and encouragement from other adoptees, to this list of triggers. These motives and concerns of longer standing were identified as thoughts and feelings that would have pre-occupied the adoptee throughout childhood, adolescence and into adulthood, although at different times, in various ways and with different levels of intensity. Such concerns include an adoptee's wish to contact a birth relative, a desire for background information, a curiosity about their origins, or, some concerns around personal identity, culture or racial origin.

Although the authors of the report found that transracial adoptees were just as likely as inracial adoptees to have 'similar motives for searching', they also observed significant differences, in that 'people who had been transracially placed were much more likely to have felt different to their adoptive families when growing up' and have more 'intense' issues around identity and belonging. As a result, the transracial adoptees 'began their search at a younger age' compared to inracially placed adoptees. It was found that the mean age of transracial adoptees who first started their search, by, say, contacting the Children's Society, was 25.8 years compared to the mean age of those inracially placed, which was 31.2 years (Howe and Feast, 2000: 150–4).

Alison's comment illustrates how concerns of longer standing worked in her case:

> I said (to my adoptive brothers) 'can you imagine going through the whole of your life and people saying you, where do you come from?' and I never took that as being racist, I just took that as them being interested about where the colour had come from, I mean this is probably in my naivety throughout my whole life, and you know I'd say 'I was adopted, and my dad was black and my mum was white', and I said to them, my brothers, 'everywhere I had gone that's one of the first questions people ask within the first ten minutes ... but I never minded', but it always drew attention to the fact that I didn't really know where I came from, you know my identity and who I looked like, and so every time that came up, those thoughts were in my head.

(Alison)

As mentioned above, transracial adoptees also began searching at a much younger age, usually upon turning eighteen,[3] which was when they were legally permitted to do so. This was despite the differences in how much adoptees thought about their birth heritage. For example, if we remind ourselves of Robert's earlier comment:

> It was kind of more later on, probably after when I was about eighteen that I got as if I felt that I needed to know a bit more.

(Robert)

And,

> When I was eighteen I found my real brother . . . and then when I tried to find my real mum through social services they would not let me . . . social services were saying that there were no details for her, that she left none, that she just left me in the hospital. But then there was one of her friends I knew, who happened to know another of mine, and she went back to her and said this about me.

(Will)

Hee Yun, whose legal documents about her birth and adoption had not been kept by any of the parties involved in these matters, had, however, during her teens, began researching the history of Korean intercountry adoption and information about Korean culture. At eighteen, Hee Yun then made her first contact with other Korean people and embarked on her first visit to Korea, where she also visited the orphanage where she had spent the first two years of her life:

> When I was eighteen I started . . . In Germany I got to know a few Korean adoptees . . . then my grandfather died and left me money so . . . I went to Korea . . . I saw the orphanage, where I was, it was still there.

(Hee Yun)

An important finding, then, is that transracial adoptees start searching at a much younger age than those who are inracially placed. Another key finding is that the transracial adoptees' birth heritage, in terms of their racial background, is a significant factor in their searches. This is because, despite whether they had positive or negative experiences, the adoptees racialised distinctions had led them to feel constantly different within their white adoptive home and predominantly white adoptive social environments. This led to them having difficulties in developing for themselves a racial identity that they were comfortable with. For example, Robert said:

> Just that sort of feeling of not feeling as a whole integrated person . . . I suppose I was in a bit of a limbo. So though, I had a crude sense of identity as just being black, there

---

[3] In England, section 26 of the Children Act 1975 (later part of the Adoption of Children Act 1976, section 51) gave adoptees aged 18 years and above the legal right to access information about their adoption.

was kind of no substance, there was nothing to support that really in terms of family ties or relationships, or parents, or that whole sort of social fabric.

(Robert)

In order to ease this difficulty of 'substance', the adoptees sought details of various aspects of their birth heritage. These details were perceived by the adoptees as providing them with answers to their questions about their birth heritage, such as where they are from, what their racial origin is, and so on, which would then give them a sense of completeness. As Natasha said:

I want to feel more settled in myself . . . to feel less angry and more happier . . . to feel complete . . . knowing would be a big patch to cover the big gap . . . to feel more normal.

(Natasha)

Additionally, some of the adoptees felt that searching for certain aspects of their birth heritage, such as their birth family, would also provide them with a particular sense of belonging, which was associated with biological familial ties, as well as racial ties. For example, searching for and making contact with members of the birth family, in particular the birth father who was black African Caribbean, was viewed by Robert as bringing him closer to his racial identity:

I met up with my dad and his family, so that gave me more of a sense of feeling more of a whole and a complete person.

(Robert)

However, the study reported here found that there are no differences in reasons for searches between mixed-race transracial adoptees, and those born to two black African Caribbean parents. This finding is supported by Howe and Feast (2000), whose sample of searching transracial adoptees also included those who were mixed-race by birth.

The adoptees' searches were also used as a means of answering the racialised questions of others. This is an important finding. For example, adoptees talked about being bullied, teased and questioned at school by the other children about their adoption, in particular about the transracial aspects of their adoption. Hee Yun explains:

. . . strangers come up and ask him who is that and (my adoptive brother) says 'it's my sister' and they sometimes make a joke out of it 'cos they find it really funny because of people cannot grasp an idea of being adopted . . . if you get to hear it so many times it's like somebody is hammering it into you, 'you are not who you seem to be'.

(Hee Yun)

Some adoptees were questioned in a similar manner about their mixed-race background by both black and white others:

It really used to upset me, name calling . . . but it was white kids calling me names and black kids calling me names, because I wasn't black and I wasn't white, I was mixed, which made it even worse, for them obviously . . . the adoption wasn't an issue until people made it an issue, like calling me names . . . I think it was mainly, like I say, the colour issue rather than the adoption issue . . . they'd see that they (adoptive parents) were white and they'd say 'ughhh your parents are white, that's really weird' and stuff, and then say nasty words and stuff . . . but what they saw is what they picked on, and at that stage it was the colour thing.

(Natasha)

This means that the answers sought by adoptees through searching were not necessarily entirely related to identity development problems, but rather it was a reflection of them living in a racialised society where race has meaning in everyday social relationships. Hence, the questions about the adoptees' racialised differences, compared to the others in their adoptive environment, led the adoptees to seek out commonality and acceptance with others of the same racial background. This commonality was primarily sought from members of the birth family:

I want to know who I look like . . . I would just love to know and that's why I would just look at her if I did see her, you know to compare and say oh yes, I have her skin colour, or I have her hair, or nose . . . I suppose it's like oh there's a little bit of me there that's with her and vice-versa.

(Natasha)

Alison searched for her birth siblings only because they were also of mixed-race background, like herself:

That's all I wanted, to find my sisters, not my birth parents . . . I kind of decided that I don't look like my mum and I don't look like my dad, because my mum's white and he's black, which is a silly thing to say, but one's white and the other's black and I'm not, so I won't look like either of them, so I look like nobody. But then I did know that I had a sister. So that's that really.

(Alison)

The desire for an adoptee to seek out physical similarity has also been noted by Kirton et al. (2000). These authors found that five of the 13 transracial adoptees who searched and experienced reunion with at least one member of their birth family, 'had a significant interest, which tended to focus, though not exclusively, on looks and physical similarity' (Kirton et al., 2000: 11). The adoptees' desire for physical commonality with a birth parent was also found in studies carried out by Campbell, Silverman and Patti (1991), Hollingsworth (1998), and Kowal and Schilling (1985).

Some adoptees additionally sought commonality from others of the same birth heritage, in terms of racial origin and cultural background, as opposed to solely from birth family members. This meant that their searches were not just about seeking physical commonality, but also about finding people who could share similar experiences of being from a black African Caribbean heritage living in a racialised society. As Robert says:

> *I see it as maybe more specifically applying to African Caribbean people, and yeah, I sort of see it as important to me, but more because I do feel that there is a lot of racism in society . . . it's sort of a cultural and social thing, you know . . . it's kind of a feeling that as time goes on you feel as if you have more of a natural affinity with that people.*
>
> (Robert)

In talking about their views of their birth heritage, the transracial adoptees also revealed feelings of anger towards the birth family in particular for having put them forward for adoption, together with a sense of loss at having missed out on a life with their birth family. Hence, the desire for 'a full and coherent birth story' (Schechter and Bertocci, 1990: 64), had guided their search. For Will especially this sense of anger and loss was very strong:

> *I did feel that I wanted to be with my real family . . . at the end of the day I should not have been adopted by them people, cos we're a different colour ain't it . . . I do think I've had a white up-bringing . . . but then I just wanted to get back at her (birth mother) really . . . I want revenge . . . I just want her to, at the end of the day, I want her to be sorry for what she's done.*
>
> (Will)

Intercountry adoptees also spoke of feeling angry at their country of birth. For example, in talking about her anger with her birth mother, Hee Yun also spoke of the equal anger that she had towards Korea:

> *In former times of Korea, in the sixties and the seventies, where some records were kept and some were destroyed, some were wrongly kept and extra stories were made up, and sometimes, because there was a pressure on mothers in that time, on single mothers . . . so it could be that I am an orphan or it could be that I'm just an orphan on letters . . . You have to negotiate between the emotions and the logical bit . . . I think what happened in Korea with the adoption, was a kind of crime in the sense that everything was not properly dealt with, you know that is a crime.*
>
> (Hee Yun)

This study's transracial adoptees additionally reported feelings of anger and loss at having missed out on a life with others of the same birth heritage. In talking about his birth family and members of their local black minority ethnic community, Will said:

> *She (birth mother) had my brother, kept him for a bit and then put him into foster care, and then she had me, left me in hospital and I was took away. Yeah, and after that she then goes and has three kids . . . there's no sense in getting rid of two and keeping three . . . she just used to make me angry as well, upset and angry, because I used*

to think that it's not really fair that I'm in this situation, and I got angry about that as well . . . I should be with them people at the end of the day.

(Will)

These additional feelings are particular to transracial adoptees, because they are directly borne out of them being transracially adopted by white adoptive parents and raised in a predominantly white social environment. For example, in providing an account of her feelings about her own transracial and intercountry adoption, Sue Jardine, who was born in Hong Kong and then adopted from China to England, discussed how she had felt a 'loss of connection with Chinese people' (Jardine, 2000: 488). When there is a re-connection between adoptees and their birth heritage, some of the adoptees reported a feeling of completeness. For example, Robert said:

With black people, it's kind of a feeling that as time goes on you feel as if you have more of a natural affinity with (black) people.

(Robert)

On the other hand, some of the transracial adoptees in this study also reported intense feelings of difference in relation to their birth heritage, the birth family and others of the same birth racial origin. These adoptees viewed their birth cultural background as one that they were not associated with:

They (adoptive parents) never really said anything about the culture or anything . . . but some of my other sisters, they go over to Barbados, because they feel as if that's the culture that they need . . . Claire and Lucy definitely do take after their dad and that culture . . .

(Alison)

Having no association with their birth cultural background and being raised in a white home was also viewed as having no real culture. In other words, the adoptive white culture was viewed as being 'cultureless':

I think she (birth sister) is trying to put some culture into my life by giving me salt-fish and stuff like that . . . I think she likes to hang on to that bit of culture, but I haven't got any of it and I think that she thinks I'm a bit white like that.

(Alison)

Maybe because they were more cultured than I was, roots type of thing, because a lot of them were Jamaican or Afro-Caribbean that went in there, and then there was me.

(Natasha)

Many transracial adoptees, like inracial adoptees, report contradictory feelings about all aspects of their birth heritage (Howe and Feast, 2000). For example, as documented earlier, although feeling angry at her birth mother and Korean society in general for putting her up for a transracial and intercountry adoption, so much so that she criminalised their actions, Hee Yun also talked about longing to belong to Korean society:

> They had just thought you know the best way for us, the government and the people who made the decisions is that we adopt some out . . . They just thought that we'd do that and maybe even get some money out of it. And that what is the bitter taste in this. It makes me feeling sometimes very bitter about it . . . but I want to go back there . . . I was born there . . . so it's also part of me.

(Hee Yun)

However, for transracial adoptees these contradictory views and feelings are deepened by the paradox between their physical racialised differences, especially, their black skin colour, and their white set of experiences. This meant that adoptees were often criticised for their black looks and white behaviour:

> In the end they (birth sisters) called me stuff like 'coconut' and 'bounty bar', meaning black on the outside and white on the inside, and you know I could not cope with it.

(Alison)

Negotiating difference

Adoptees were then asked to talk about the variety of ways in which they negotiated and re-negotiated the feelings of difference that they experienced between the adoptive heritage and the birth heritage.

In considering the effects of the search on the perception of self, the extent to which one's birth heritage will always act as an important link to the development of identity was explored. The literature on the effects of searching has largely focused on adoptees who search for birth relatives only. Here experiences have varied. Kirton et al., and Shekleton found that some of their transracial adoptees felt as if they had lost out on a life with either their birth family (Kirton et al., 2000: 16), or with a black family (Shekleton, 1990: 4), whilst other adoptees saw the contact as bringing the bonus of a second family or delight in finding others who had similar physical features (ibid: 16).

In the study reported here, the adoptees' experiences of searching for birth heritage also revealed significant effects on their perceptions of self. Like the adoptees in Kirton et al.'s study, the adoptees also saw their search as bringing them a second family and similarities in physical features. Alison said:

> I've got (birth) sisters and I've never had sisters and it's great, and not only have I got sisters but I've got sisters that look like me, you know and so, my (birth) sisters have become almost closer than my (adoptive) brothers.

(Alison)

However, for some adoptees, the search did little to resolve their racialised feelings of difference. This was because, contrary to hopes and expectations, the adoptees did not feel any bond or commonality with birth parents or others of the same birth racial origin or birth cultural background. Indeed, in talking about the experiences and identity development of transracial adoptees, Shekleton found that the majority of transracial adoptees in her study had a 'vague generalised identification with other black people' which had been 'insufficient to meet the intense need for defining 'self'' (Shekleton, 1990: 4). This was so for adoptees in this study. In particular, Will was not only rejected (again) by his birth family, but was also criticised for having a white upbringing. As Will said about his search for his birth parents:

> It was a waste of time to be honest . . . I think my (birth) parents thought I was too, you know, white . . . so it wasn't worth it, we're different . . . I've had a white upbringing.

(Will)

Feelings of loss

Like Kirton et al.'s (2000) sample, some of the adoptees felt as if they had lost out on their birth heritage, in particular, on a life with their birth family or with others of the same birth racial origin and birth cultural background. This is another important finding.

Thus, let us consider a narrative presented earlier by Robert:

> I've missed out on those sort of years where I was, I suppose I was in a bit of a limbo. So though, I had a crude sense of identity as just being black, there was kind of no substance, there was nothing to support that really in terms of family ties or relationships, or parents, or that whole sort of social fabric.

(Robert)

The current body of literature on mixed-race people who are raised by their white biological parent, usually the mother and sometimes with a white step-parent, does not seem to support this idea of missing out on the black minority ethnic birth heritage. In the study reported here, however, Robert was keen to recompense this sense of loss and non-belonging by choosing to identify himself as having a black minority ethnic racial identity, even though he was of mixed-race background. In explaining why this was so, let us consider Robert's earlier comment:

> I just feel more comfortable with black people on a whole.

(Robert)

Natasha, too, felt a sense of loss, as when she spoke about the Seychelles, her country of birth:

> I feel like I've missed out, because all I have is three photographs, I mean I don't even have them personally, my (adoptive) mum and dad have them, and that's why I thought 'oh that looks nice', but that's all I've got. It is a bit sad . . . I would like to know more about the place I was born in.

(Natasha)

However, Natasha did not feel as if she missed out on a life with any aspects of her birth heritage, and in fact even felt that she had been saved from what might have otherwise been a more difficult upbringing:

If I had not been adopted I probably would have been the cliché of working in somebody's house over there, but it's true. I probably would not have been working, I probably would have been on the street, probably picking coconuts for somebody or something and selling them at the side of the road ... I've been given a very good chance compared to over there in the Seychelles because that's how they make their living, that's what they do.

(Natasha)

Alison was also pleased that she had been adopted, and in meeting her birth sisters and hearing about their life, she was especially pleased that she did not grow up in her birth family, birth culture and with others of the same racial origin:

From when I met my older sister I thought I'm glad, because knowing what she went through, you know because she had a hard time, so I was glad, but I never met him (birth father) ... everything I've heard is not particularly very nice ... I mean he used to beat the living daylights out of them if they ... well, Amy said that there was an incident where it was really hot and sunny and they came back from school and saw all the other children in the streets in their bikinis playing with water and stuff, so they put their bikinis on, he got home and went ballistic, because as far as he was concerned they were running around half-naked, they were ten years old, so he took them inside and he hit them with a belt ... because the relationship between the (birth) mum and the (birth) dad was so off and on, off and on, off and on, the children will tend to take sides ... and some of the children would go with mum, with Maureen, that's her name, and some would go with him, and sometimes they'd actually be together, you know, but she was in and out of refuges and stuff ... but I just don't think that it's right to say that it's in your culture because if you're in a country where it is not right, and it's wrong, you should not do it, regardless of your culture, you know and I always think that if you do come to a country you then have to abide by their rules, you know no matter what religion or race you are, you can't bring your own in and say this is what I do in my country ... I mean if it's alright for a West Indian guy to beat his wife up in Barbados, then that's fine, but if you come over to England, it's not ok, just because it's ok in your culture does not mean that you can do it here.

(Alison)

In hearing about this aspect of the birth family's problems, Alison forms a negative stereotype of black African Caribbean culture as a whole, that is, the idea of West Indian men 'disciplining' their wives through physical violence. This is interesting, because it is actually a negative view borne out of a lack of experience and knowledge of West Indian culture. One must also wonder whether Alison is justifying her own transracial adoption to herself by rationalising it as having saved her from what she considers to be a culture tolerating '*violent disciplinarian West Indian men*'?

In looking at the effects of the search on the adoptees' perception of self in other ways, the search was positive for adoptees in that it was beneficial and useful to their racial identity development. This was because the search provided them with a sense of completeness and belonging. For example, let us recall Robert's earlier comment which highlighted how he especially enjoyed the way in which his contact with his birth family, in particular his birth father, helped to bring him closer to his racial identity:

> *I met up with my dad and his family, so that gave me more of a sense of feeling more of a whole and a complete person [Do you think becoming closer to your birth father had brought you closer to your racial identity, or was it the other way round?] Definitely yeah. It was definitely about getting closer to my birth identity. Definitely more about that.*

(Robert)

Similarly, Hee Yun said about her search for contact with others of the same birth racial origin and of the same birth cultural background:

> *I think it brought me quite a step forward . . . I went to Korea first for a few months then went travelling round the world for the rest of the year . . . I think it helped me quite a lot in developing and understanding myself better.*

(Hee Yun)

However, for other adoptees, the search presented feelings of racialised difference to that of the birth heritage. For example, Alison took the view that her birth father's black African Caribbean racial heritage and cultural background had no significance in her life:

> *That culture is not mine. It's not the culture that I know, so it doesn't mean anything to me really.*

(Alison)

This was also the case for Natasha, who felt out of place in her attempts to learn more about the local black African Caribbean community. As mentioned earlier, Natasha's testimony to this was her experiences at a funeral and then at a church event:

> *I just carried on, did what I had to do and got out of there. It was really weird, because I wasn't used to that. It was really different [Did you talk to your (black African Caribbean) boyfriend about it?] Not really no, because it was, well I suppose he'd thought it was something that I should already know, you know, I can't explain it.*

(Natasha)

From these accounts, it seems that transracial adoptees do search in an attempt to resolve identity issues, and in some cases these are resolved. However, Lifton's comment that 'it is not that simple' (1988: 73), is also of significance. Lifton discusses the work of Reynolds who found that 'those who were happy in their adoptive homes might search because they felt confident in themselves, while those who were unhappy might be restrained from searching through any guilt' (Reynolds, 1976, in Lifton, 1988: 73). Therefore, according to this, it is not necessarily only the adoptees who are psychologically disturbed, less satisfied with their adoption, or those who have identity development issues who search, but also the psychologically healthy, the confident, and those who are happy in their adoptive homes. Some may just want to search because they are curious or because they want to let their birth parents know that they made a sound choice with the adoption. For instance, although Robert searched to primarily resolve identity issues, he also commented on how he wanted to let his birth mother know that he was okay:

> *My adoptive mum said that my birth mother would have been thinking about me at times like my birthday and I just thought that I felt that I wanted to get in contact with her just to sort of let her know that I was ok. So getting in contact with my mum was more felt for her benefit.*

(Robert)

Although Julie chose not to search because she partly feared what she may find, she was also adamant that she did not search largely because:

> *I've been very happy where I am . . . I was loved and happy . . . it's not really been an issue for me at all.*

(Julie)

Regardless of search motivations and outcomes, it is clear that as a result of having been transracially adopted, the adoptees faced a number of difficulties, and found themselves entering an important negotiation process concerning these difficulties. One of these is the adoptees' constant feeling of difference within the family and the inability of the adoptive family to fully understand this. This gives rise to a second difficulty, which is the erection of barriers between the adoptee and the adoptive family, which acts as a constant marker of their difference and non-biological tie. A third difficulty occurs in childhood and adolescence, and concerns being questioned, bullied, and picked on by other youngsters about their racialised differences, the transracial aspect of the adoption, and the adoption itself, which is made evident by the obvious racial differences. Another difficulty experienced by the adoptees is that they are left to contend with not knowing about their birth parents, and for some, about their birth culture. A fifth difficulty is the contradiction between the adoptees' black minority ethnic appearance, as in their skin colour, and their lived experience as a white person.

These difficulties are clearly unique to the experiences of transracial adoptees because they are rooted in the transracial adoptees' feelings of racialised difference, in particular the difference and isolation of not completely fitting in anywhere, either with their black minority ethnic birth heritage or with their white adoptive heritage.

Re-negotiating experiences of isolation

Some of the adoptees felt as if they did not fit in with people of the same birth heritage, and this was because they were criticised by black minority ethnic others for having been transracially adopted:

> The black people that I was hanging round with, they either didn't like white people or they didn't think I should have been adopted by white people . . . well I think that's what my (birth) parents thought too.
>
> (Will)

Julie also felt that she did not fit in with people of the same birth heritage because of her white upbringing and limited contact with black minority ethnic people. She described an incident that made her feel very uncomfortable:

> I got cornered by what I think must have been a truly eccentric woman in a bookshop when I was like fourteen. She had obviously decided that I was somebody that she could talk to and I felt like telling her to bog off, and she told me at great length all about the problems with the word 'wog' and how insulting the word used to be and it used to be a traders compliment for a rich oriental gentlemen and why she gave me all this stuff I have no idea at all . . . and one of the staff came and rescued me in the end. I felt uncomfortable, I felt deeply uncomfortable, because whilst I suppose the closest thing you could say was that my upbringing was colour blind, at the point where anybody else who I didn't feel safe with made reference to it, I felt really uncomfortable, 'cos I didn't know what, you know, all this was going to be about'
>
> (Julie)

Adoptees also recalled being conditionally accepted by white people, because they were seen as largely being 'black'. As Robert said:

> I don't feel entirely accepted in society or with a kind of attitude where, you know, where white people say that 'I don't like black people, but you're ok'. I mean I don't want to be sucked into that sort of acceptance.
>
> (Robert)

Robert also talked about dealing with the racism that he experienced largely in 1980s Britain which he received (only) from white people at this time. He said:

> I think a lot of the racist stereotypes that used to make me a lot more angry, I think maybe these days I'm not confronted with it in my face so much, so maybe I don't feel as angry as I used to with a lot of the racism in society . . . so, you know, nothing particularly towards me, but you hear people on the bus with stereotypes . . . well I don't come across it as much as I used to, but at various times I have kind of gotten into arguments with people and then feeling after a while too burnt out really, I mean,

I'm burnt out enough through my job without having to confront every racist comment that I come across.

(Robert)

However, Robert later found that by becoming more involved with a black minority ethnic community, and by particularly taking on a black African identity, he was able to access acceptance and support from members of his birth community:

I feel that I have a certain amount of respect from white people who know me . . . but maybe kind of more so from the black community.

(Robert)

The basis of adoptees' feelings of not belonging derived from them not fitting in with either their birth or their adoptive communities. Such feelings of not belonging to either communities supports the arguments of opposers of transracial adoption who maintain that not only will transracial adoptees face racism from white members of society, but also by black minority ethnic members with whom they would be unable to relate to because they would be seen as 'not black enough . . . in culture and attitude' (Small, 1986: 93). For example, Natasha experienced criticism from both white society members and black minority ethnic society members:

But it was white kids calling me names and black kids calling me names, because I wasn't black and I wasn't white, I was mixed, which made it even worse for them obviously. A black girl said 'oh you should not have mixes in this world, you should not have half-castes' and nasty sort of things like that.

(Natasha)

I must have been about eleven or twelve or something, and I was out with some white friends, and this black woman said something to me about, you know, just completely out of the blue, that 'you're neither black or white' sort of thing, so that kind of upset me more than the odd kind of racist remarks about being black.

(Robert)

Therefore, it seems that some transracial adoptees at times felt different and rejected because of their mixed-race status. This is supported by the literature on the experiences of mixed-race people raised by their biological parents. For example, although the 'negative orientation' towards these people has shifted in the last century (Tizard and Phoenix, 2002: 39), they continue to experience feelings of difference, which is often reinforced by rejection from both the black community and the white community (Small, 1981).

Another important finding therefore, is that adoptees felt isolated through not completely fitting in anywhere, either with black minority ethnic people of their birth community, or with white people of their adoptive community. This was linked to their transracial adoptive status, and a pressure to wholly identify themselves as either black or white. In response to these feelings of isolation, the adoptees negotiated their transracial experience and their birth heritage in order to emerge with a racial identity that they felt comfortable with and considered best represented who they were. This is explored in greater depth in the next chapter.

Views on transracial adoption

Being aware that a complex and flexible negotiation process of racial identity development was occurring, in which adoptees used their own ambivalent and ambiguous experiences of racial integration and racial isolation to emerge with individual ways with which to racially identify themselves, allows us to understand their views on the practice of transracial adoption in how the adoptees were not straightforwardly for or against the practice.

Quite surprisingly, very few studies have asked transracial adoptees about their views on transracial adoption. This is disappointing if we consider that they are best placed to inform the transracial adoption debate. Of those studies that have sought the direct views of adoptees, there has been a tendency to gather opinions from personal anecdotes and group discussions, and from adoptees who have the same opinions about transracial adoption, as opposed to sociologically based research. Illustrations of this approach can be found in the studies of Dagoo et al. (1993), and Shekleton (1990), who collected opinions about transracial adoption from adoptees gathered from a post-adoption support group, where the majority of members had negative experiences of adoption. Few studies therefore, unlike this one, seek to obtain transracial adoptees' views about transracial adoption from a sample of randomly selected adoptees with different sets of experiences.

Adoptees here were asked to talk about their views on transracial adoption and not surprisingly, their views were largely shaped by their own ambivalent experiences, as highlighted by the following comments from Will. Having talked a great deal about the negative aspects of his life as a transracial adoptee, he moved on to transracial adoption:

> It's a bad thing because if parents don't help him find his real parents, then that kid's going to go away and find them himself and end up hating the adopted parents as well . . . so I don't think it should happen.
>
> (Will)

When asked whether this view might change if the adoptive parents gave their adoptive child support to find their real parents, he replied:

> It's still not a good idea because by then the real parents might not want to know about the child. (Will)

Although Will appeared to be talking in third-party terms, his views were clearly shaped by his own ambiguous experiences, in that on the one hand he was angry at his adoptive family for not understanding and helping him resolve his feelings about the racialised difference, and yet on the other hand he was grateful to his adoptive parents for having looked after him.

As a result of such ambivalence and ambiguity, adoptees' views were not straightforwardly for or against the practice of transracial adoption. Rather, the adoptees highlighted the value of transracial adoption as a means of finding permanent homes for black minority ethnic children in care, sooner rather than later. Julie, although having previously talked about her 'lack of black awareness' and her susceptibility to be open to attack from black minority ethnic people, argued that despite the difficulties brought about by the transracial aspects of her adoption, was nevertheless content with her developed racial self:

> I see myself as being sort of grounded and have a strong sense of self. I don't think I'm the kind of person to go off and have an identity crisis you know, other than in the sense of who I am and a sense that I'm fairly successful in what I do and who I am. I mean, I have a reasonably well-paid professional job that I like, a reasonable education, I have all this, pensions, investments, all this and quite the opposite of living on the street, and unless something goes wrong, I'll continue to have all that stuff, so there's a sense that from the worldview of having made it, I think I have. Damaged? Adoption might have set back my development, in which case this is the failure version, which I can live with, you know.
>
> (Julie)

Her experiences consequently made Julie in favour of the practice of transracial adoption:

> The most important thing is that the child would want to be loved . . . I mean that is definitely imperative in my own experience . . . it's not as if, you know, race and colour are the only thing, I don't see it being as important . . . a whole host of things other things need to be taken into account which are far more important than what appears to be colour matching.
>
> (Julie)

Despite having experienced some difficulties, Natasha also spoke positively about the practice of transracial adoption as a means of providing children with permanent homes. In calling for a greater use of transracial adoption, she said:

> I think it's a good idea. I think it's nice. I think it should be an easy thing for people to do, because I know that even now it's hard to go through. I just feel there should be more of it, there should be more adoption full stop . . . If somebody wants a child, then I think they should have every right to have a child, regardless of what they look like or where they are from, I really think that, because there's enough kids in this world without parents, you know. I mean, sometimes I think 'oh God people don't need to make more kids, you know, come on, what about us lot'. . . I mean it's worked for me.
>
> (Natasha)

Other adoptees emphasised the necessity for the effects of racialised differences to be carefully considered when placing a black minority ethnic child for adoption. In doing so, they made the point that placing a child with an adoptive family of the same racial background would be a much preferable and beneficial option. Robert said that although he had concerns about some of the arguments used by those opposing transracial adoption, he was very aware of 'how badly black people are treated', especially after living through the race riots and black politics of 1980s Britain. As such, he was '90 per cent anti (transracial adoption)' (Robert).

Although Alison recalled largely positive experiences as a transracial adoptee, her views about the practice of transracial adoption was a little more complex. She used her own positive experiences to argue that both transracial adoption and adoption in general should be utilised more often. Alison stated that she was applying to 'long-term foster a child of dual heritage' because there are 'more black and mixed heritage children that aren't being fostered'. Clearly then, Alison's views were more complex than, but not contradictory to, just making a decision on the basis of her own experiences, since her reasons for seeking to long-term foster a 'black' child included the fact that there are more children from these backgrounds spending longer periods of time in care; a fact supported by the findings of Children First in Adoption and Fostering (1990).

Adoptees highlighted that if racial matching was not possible, there must be an awareness of the need for adopters to provide transracial adoptees with continuous knowledge and experience of their birth heritage. Hee Yun's contradictory views about transracial adoption clearly reflected her own experiences in that although she felt she was given a 'second chance', and thought that transracial adoption and intercountry adoption should continue to happen, she argued that it should be slowly reduced to only take place after certain conditions were met. For Hee Yun, such conditions were that the adoptive parents needed to be involved in the 'other side' of the adoptee through active and genuine efforts:

> If you take responsibility of getting the kid from somewhere else . . . a different culture, then you have to be prepared . . . to get into this yourself . . . learn the language, learn the culture.

(Hee Yun)

CHAPTER 4

Conceptualising a multi-racialised identity

The debate surrounding transracial adoptees' development of a racial identity is dominated by the arguments of those groups opposing transracial adoption, such as NABSW and ABSWAP, who maintain that it damages the racial identity of black minority ethnic children (Tizard and Phoenix, 2002). This, they say, is because the adoptee will fail to develop a true sense of their own black self when raised by the racially naïve white adoptive family, and which means that they will grow up not knowing who they are, face identity conflict and confusion, be unable to positively relate to their own racial background, and develop a low self-esteem or even a hatred for their own black self. Hence, they will face serious difficulties both personally and socially (Small, 1986). This chapter seeks to examine in more detail key influential factors and the negotiation process involved in the racial identity development of transracial adoptees.

In attempting to understand the ways in which transracial adoptees developed a racial identity that they felt comfortable with and felt best represented who they were, the adoptees in the study were asked to talk about the key influences in their negotiation of a racial identity, and whether they thought that having a transracial or mixed-racial identity brought with it a series of problems.

In particular, adoptees discussed the following:

- Notions of a transracial identity.
- Global politics and national identity.
- Re-negotiating a more fitting multi-racial identity.
- The role of physical features in racial identity development.
- Negotiating socially and culturally constructed ideas about race.
- The importance of birth heritage in one's life.
- Using experiences of racism to shape self-definitions.
- Feeling proud, self-esteem and confidence.
- Racial belonging and feeling confused.

Here, along with some sociological commentary, are their narratives.

Allocation of a transracial identity

All of the adoptees in this study themselves recognised the inevitability of being racialised in certain ways, largely because they were of a black minority ethnic group, and living in a predominantly white society. Hence, being racialised and developing a racial identity is an inevitable outcome of living in a society where race has meaning. However, these adoptees' experiences of being racialised were largely influenced by their status as a transracial adoptee. This meant that whether adoptees settled more towards having the racial identity of their birth parents, or one more towards that of their adoptive parents' racial identity, or on an identity that equally encompassed both roles, they all tackled very much the same issues developing that racial identity. These issues emanated from being of black minority ethnic origin or mixed-race by birth, yet being raised by a white family in a predominantly white social environment. In addition, because each of the adoptees could not fully ignore either the birth or adoptive parts of their heritage, they developed a transracial identity which took into account their experiences of the degree to which they were accepted by some groups and rejected by others. Such acceptance (sameness) and rejection (difference) is seen as 'the dynamic principles' of identity (Jenkins, 1996: 4), and are important in how individuals negotiate their sense of self in society. This means that the adoptees' trans-racial identity largely represented where they felt they belonged in relation to these two parts. The transracial identity then, is the racialised identity that an adoptee negotiates when they are adopted by a family who are of a different racial background. This is an important point.

In seeking to understand what factors constitute a transracial identity, a number of important influences were identified. These are:

1. The nature of experiences in the adoptive home, in particular if they were positive or negative.
2. Levels of acceptance into and commonality with the birth heritage, this being the family, culture, and others of same racial group.
3. Levels of acceptance into and commonality with the adopted heritage.
4. How others classified the adoptees' physical features and their own negotiation of these classifications. For example, whether they agreed or disagreed with them, found them beneficial or a limitation, and if they chose to challenge or conform to them.
5. How others categorised adoptees in social relations and their own negotiations of these categorisations.

The significance of each of the adoptees' influences varied in form and intensity. This meant that there were different approaches to the transracial identity with each of the adoptees, in that although all were mixed, some identified more with the white role than the black role, or vice versa.

As mentioned at the beginning of this chapter, both the debate and the literature on the racial identity development of transracial adoptees is dominated by certain groups. They contest that 'Black children in white homes are cut off from healthy development of themselves as black people' (Merritt, 1971, in Simon and Alstein, 2000: 38). Stonequist

(1937) used the theory of 'the marginal man' to argue that people raised between two cultural groups face serious psychological difficulties, as a result of being rejected by the dominant white group and looked upon as different by the black minority ethnic group. The basis of these arguments is that being born in the margins of two different and conflictual cultures, inevitably leads the transracial adoptee to feel as if they belong to neither, as opposed to both, and to then develop racial identity development difficulties.

However, the adoptees' negotiation of a transracial identity contradicted this belief. This is because their identities clearly incorporated both parts of their black minority ethnic birth heritage and white adoptive heritage. Despite this though, all the adoptees talked about how they were constantly being forced to choose between their white side and their black side and it was this that they found problematic. They also made it clear that their feelings of being made to choose were not tied to the adoption issue per se, i.e. to choose between birth heritage and adoptive heritage, but more so the racialised aspects of the adoption issue, i.e. black minority ethnic birth heritage and white adoptive heritage. This left the adoptees feeling as if they were being denied the right to identify their own self in the multiple, complex and diverse ways in which they actually saw themselves. This is something that was also identified by Tizard who argued that 'most studies do not explore the extent to which the young people assign themselves a mixed cultural identity, but ask them to choose between their adopted and original identity' (Tizard, 1991: 754).

Resisting inaccurate labels

In terms of race, the adoptees were regularly being mis-identified, and talked about their annoyance at constantly having to correct these inaccurate labels. For example, in talking about an adoption reunion programme set up by the Korean Government, Hee Yun said:

> *Now the Korean government or some provinces are feeling a bit guilty or something, so they started doing projects like 'come and get to know our culture' and you get a really negative view of you because if you don't speak Korean language or if you don't want to speak Korean, you are looked down upon. That is much more worse if you don't want to speak Korean. They don't give you the option if you want to speak Korean. They say 'oh you are Korean', well I am German, I'm not Korean really anymore. They say 'you are Korean, you should know our culture, you should get to know and learn the language', and that is what is happening. It's not the right way that they should react to this. They should give us the choice, they didn't give us the choice before. So they should give us the choice now . . . they still seem to think that we are Korean and it's really difficult to say that we are just Korean because we are not just Korean anymore. We are Germans who have maybe had a Korean background.*

(Hee Yun)

In discussing how society through racialisation processes allocated such a transracial identity, though telling the adoptee that they can only be either black or white, the adoptees talked about their understanding of the meaning of race in society. Adoptees talked about their own experiences which led them to recognise that in a society where race has significant meaning, it is inevitable that identities are racialised. In doing so, all the adoptees talked about their experiences of being involved in social relations whereby their identity was defined and shaped by others on the basis of race, in particular their assumed 'blackness'. The adoptees went on to discuss how they conceived their own racialised identities, and in particular the extent to which they chose to embrace a positive black identity. However, it emerged that not all of the adoptees chose to identify themselves as being entirely black. Rather, each of the adoptees' choice of racial identity varied according to space, time and context of experiences and the meanings that they had attached to these experiences.

Only one of the adoptees had presented themselves as having a majority black racial identity. They saw this as being necessary in enabling them to develop a positive racial identity. Here, in particularly having largely had negative experiences of having been transracially adopted had led to a firm and passionate understanding of being black. This was interesting, given that this adoptee was actually mixed-race by birth. For example, Robert who had already talked about how he based his racial identity around physical, cultural, political and social meanings, also said:

> I acknowledge I have a mixed cultural heritage, but I see myself as Black, black African, Black African-Igbo-Irish to be precise . . . I'm not very politically active now, but for a long time I was, so yeah, I would kind of take it (Black) as a political term of you know, all people of colour or non-white people.
>
> (Robert)

In contrast though, another mixed-race adoptee talked about the 'special status' which she had in her white social world and her negative experiences with some members of the black community. These experiences had left Alison with a desire to largely assert her white identity. However, due to the mixed-race aspect of her birth Alison settled on choosing to describe herself as having a *mixed* racial identity, which tended to lean more towards the white parts of her biological and social heritage. For Alison, this equalled a positive racial identity:

> I think a lot of people see me as my sisters described me, as being black on the outside and white on the inside . . . but I suppose really I'm mixed, 'cos of my birth parents, although more white 'cos of my upbringing.
>
> (Alison)

Although another adoptee discussed her difficulties with both sides of her birth and adoptive heritages, she also talked about having a strong sense of attachment with parts of her Korean birth heritage and her white adoptive heritage. Therefore, Hee Yun chose to present her racial identity as one that is *mixed*, and this incorporated elements from both parts. In speaking with a sense of firmness about the significance of this choice, Hee Yun said:

I am a born Korean with German nationality . . . sometimes I am Korean, sometimes German . . . I cannot live as if I am just a German . . . I am also a Korean . . . I know that my identity is made up of loads of different parts of my life . . .

(Hee Yun)

In talking about their negative experiences with both black and white individuals, another adoptee who was born to two parents of black African Caribbean origin highlighted how their negative perceptions of difference led to a choice of not completely attaching themselves to a particular racial identity. This is because they currently did not equate doing so with having a racial identity that they felt comfortable with or best reflected the way in which they saw themselves. This can be viewed as a direct, damaging result of their negative experiences with both black and white individuals. As a result, this adoptee was in the process of negotiating themselves a '*mixed*' racial identity that they felt secure with. This meant at the time of interviewing, this adoptee had chosen to assert identification with various racial groups, and in addition emphasised a belief in the notion of 'common peoplehood', i.e. the idea of belonging to the human race as opposed to a particular racial group. Will said:

I would just describe myself as black because of the fact that my birth parents were black and nothing else. That's just the way it is really . . . I'm black (but) I know I have white elements in me. I can't explain it really, it's just things in me. I suppose that makes me mixed, I don't know . . . I never thought about having a racial identity though. I just never really thought about it. It means nothing to me . . . I'm just human at the end of the day . . . if I like people I hang out with them, I don't say 'oh he's black, so I'll have him as a friend' or anything, it just depends if I like them.

(Will)

Similarly, Natasha claimed to have no racial identity, but an attachment to such 'common peoplehood' as discussed by Will. This suggests that Natasha was also in the process of negotiating herself a *mixed* racial identity that she felt comfortable with. For example, Natasha said:

I don't have black or white skin, but brown (skin) . . . I have no racial identity, I'm not black and I don't see myself as white either. But I think I'm just me, an individual, the original me . . . I'm human, yeah a human person at the end of the day.

(Natasha)

Another adoptee also talked about her racial identity in a vague way and claimed that she had not really thought about the type of racial identity that she had. Julie's absence of in-depth thought was, she claimed, due to her lack of curiosity and a belief in a 'nurtured' view of identity development. However, Julie emphasised that she was aware that she had some sort of racial identity, although she could not be sure what this was. This suggested that she was also in the process of negotiating herself a *mixed* racial identity that she felt comfortable with:

I've never had the curiosity to find out, I've always felt that you know you're so clearly a product of the people who bring you up . . . I tick 'black mixed'. . . on these forms . . . (but) I mean to all intent and purposes I suppose that I can't honestly say that I feel a great deal different from white people who have been born and brought up and have had my set of experiences. I don't have a sense of anything that's particular of a black consciousness you know . . . yes, I clearly have a cultural and racial identity, but it's not perhaps a stereotypical black one.

(Julie)

What is interesting here, though, is the way in which in response to the pressure to choose between a black racial identity and a white racial identity, some adoptees respond by rejecting this limitation. In doing so, they often move away from the idea of having a specific racial identity by emphasising instead of belonging to a notion of 'common peoplehood', or claiming to have not given the question much consideration. This may support the arguments of identity confusion. It may, however, also indicate that the adoptees in this study were still in the process of negotiating themselves a racial identity that they were comfortable and happy with.

The racialisation of national identity

In considering the place and shape of race in one's life, adoptees also talked about national identities, in particular racialised notions around Britishness. All but two of the adoptees were born and raised in Britain. Of the other two adoptees, one was born in the Seychelles and raised in Britain, and the other born in Korea and raised in Germany. The global politics of race, struggle and nationhood was particularly significant for those adoptees who had also been intercountry placed adoptees, such as Hee Yun or those adoptees whose birth parents had come from another country, such as Robert.

As one would expect, all the adoptees had spent most of their lives in their adopted country. Most of the adoptees had not visited their birth parents' or birth grandparents' country of origin, nor did they have any desires to do so. The reason for this was that the adoptees felt that they had no ties with these countries. This is so for Alison, who, in talking about Barbados, her birth father's country, demonstrated her disassociation from it, by referring to Barbados as *'his country'*. For example, in a section of her narrative referred to in the previous chapter, Alison said:

I mean if it's alright for a West Indian guy to beat his wife up in Barbados, then that's fine, but if you come over to England, it's not ok, just because it's ok in his country does not mean that you can do it here.

(Alison)

The lack of any ties with the birth parents' or grandparents' country of origin and the adoptees' disinterest to develop any links was largely due to them viewing their adoptive parents' country as their own. This was also particularly the case for adoptees who identified themselves as having a racial identity that was more white than black. Hence these adoptees tended to identify themselves as having an English or British national identity.[1] As one adoptee said:

> The English society . . . I mean it's where I'm from . . . I hate to say it, but probably a white society. Yeah, because you know mainly due to my (adoptive) mum and dad because they've been here and I've been brought up here . . . I've ended up here and that's how I've grown up to be really . . . I think it's very influential, mainly because it's how I live. I feel as if I've kind of slotted in here, you know like in this place I think I've fitted in quite well.

> > (Natasha)

However, two of the adoptees had visited their birth parents and grandparents' country of origin. They did so in an attempt to obtain information about their birth heritage in order to develop their sense of self, in particular their racialised sense of self. Thus, Hee Yun and Robert both visited their birth parents or grandparents' country of origin in order to resolve identity issues and to develop their birth racial identity:

> Getting in contact with that side was definitely more about developing my racial identity, yeah, definitely more about that.

> > (Robert)

> In my teens, when I got older my most precious wish was to once stand in Korea in the crowd and not to be recognised, that I am somebody else. When I was a teen it didn't look like my parents were rich enough to send me to do this in Korea, but then my (adoptive) grandfather died and left me money so I went . . . it was good . . . I think it helped me quite a lot in developing and understanding myself better.

> > (Hee Yun)

These two adoptees refused to identify their national identity solely in terms of their white adoptive side. Rather, Hee Yun chose to highlight her national allegiance to both Germany and Korea:

> I grew up in Germany and that's where I spent most time . . . but a thing is that I'm not just only German, I am Korean.

> > (Hee Yun)

On the other hand though as we saw earlier with his narrative, Robert, who despite being of mixed-race birth, had identified himself primarily as black, and also in particular emphasised

---

[1] Contrary to recent research (CRE, 2002) most of the adoptees in this study spoke about the English identity and British identity in inter-changeable ways, making no real distinctions between the two.

his African (Nigerian) national identity. At the same time, Robert also illustrated his lack of patriotism to the notion of being English/British:

> I feel more affinity to the Irish than the English, you know . . . I'm in contact with my own (Irish birth) mum who's in Australia . . . and as I say I've been over to Ireland and got a strong affinity with the Irish, but in terms of actually how I perceive my sort of cultural identity, I would not sort of see myself as, I don't see myself as mixed really . . . I see myself as Black, Black African, Black African – Igbo-Irish to be precise . . . I enjoy a lot of the English life, but I suppose through the years I feel I've become very focused on the sort of negative aspects of British culture, you know the sort of racism . . . I do think that white racism is a major factor which has made me see British society very negatively . . . I don't see myself as British. Administratively I happen to have a British passport, although I would value a Nigerian one much more.

> (Robert)

It is interesting that those adoptees who identified themselves as English or British also identified themselves as being more white than black. Similarly, it is significant that Robert, who identified himself as black chose to primarily identify with his birth father's Nigerian identity, and to a lesser extent with his birth mother's Irish heritage, as opposed to his adoptive family's English or British identity. This suggests that associations with national identity are also racialised.

The adoptees' perception of this is not surprising, considering how such views are constantly being advocated and reinforced. For example, the following is part of a speech that was made in 1989, during calls to allow British passport holders from Hong Kong to settle in Britain. The Conservative MP John Townend gave the speech:

> The fact that the Hong Kong Chinese are very hardworking and hold British passports does not make them British. If millions of Chinese come to the UK, they would not integrate and become yellow Englishmen . . . this possibility should make us consider what has already happened to this green and pleasant land – first as a result of waves of coloured immigrants and then by the pernicious doctrine of multi-culturalism . . . the British people were never consulted as to whether they would change from being a homogeneous society to a multi-racial society. If they had been, I am sure that a resounding majority would have voted to keep Britain an English-speaking white country.

> (Townend, 1989, in Miles, 1990: 148)

Clearly, according to the political speech, dominant notions of *true* Britishness and Englishness are still based on racial terms. Hence, being English or British is still associated with a notion of 'whiteness'. This point is also argued by Alibhai-Brown who, in calling for a more inclusive British identity, noted that 'British society is still racially divided' and to be British is still regarded by many as being 'white' (Alibhai-Brown, 1999: 15). This is also reported by Modood, Beishon, and Virdee (1994). Although Modood et al. found that many

Caribbean youth take pride in their 'Blackness',[2] and at the same time recognise that in a variety of ways they are also British, these young people also recognise that their colour is an 'obstacle to their being accepted as British' (Modood et al., 1994: 108).

However, the notion of Britishness being closely associated with whiteness is questioned by others who argue that the British identity is today a more multi-racial one and that many of the country's black minority ethnic groups who were born and raised in this country to parents and grandparents who arrived in Britain from elsewhere, now consider themselves as having an English, or in particular a British identity. For example, in a recent survey of attitudes around the British identity,[3] it was found that in terms of race and ethnicity 'all groups feel comfortable using the label 'British' (CRE, 2002: 8). The survey also found that 'being British is not about being white: 86 per cent of the British public disagree that to be truly British you have to be white. This is fairly consistent among all sections of the population' (CRE, 2002: 4).

However, for the transracial adoptees in this study, national identities were still racialised, in that being English or British was viewed as being closely tied to being white. This was so whether views on Britishness were positive or negative. Those adoptees who identified themselves as being English or British had also negotiated themselves a position that was more towards the white side of a racial identity.

Developing a multi-racial identity

The adoptees clearly understood that their identity development had been influenced by their race. This is because they had all been involved, although in different ways and to different degrees, in social relations whereby physical, cultural, social and political definitions and meanings about race had been attached to the social context.

In exploring the ways in which adoptees had been racialised and their own negotiations of these definitions, and how these then led to settlement on a racial identity that they felt comfortable with and best reflected who they were, the idea of a racial continuum can be utilised.[4] In the reported study, adoptees had been placed on a black-white continuum, on which there are two polarised ends, the black identity and the white identity. The individual's positioning on the continuum is determined by the categorisations of others and the individual's negotiations of these categorisations, which then determine how the individual is placed at different locations upon the continuum, whether more towards the black end, the white end, or somewhere in a space that contains elements of both. The adoptees' negotiated choice of position, in whether they saw themselves as more black than white or vice versa, meant that all of them negotiated a transracial identity that incorporated both their black and

---

[2]Modood et al.'s (1994) use of a capital letter to reflect political status of term.
[3]This survey was carried out by the MORI Social Research Institute for the Commission for Racial Equality in 2002.
[4]The use of a 'black/white continuum' to examine racial identity was highlighted by Barn (1999: 278).

white parts, in other words a mixed identity. This is consistent with the idea that racialised identities are not all fixed, but open to interpretation and modification.

Factors influencing shift were partially dependent on how other people classified the adoptees in certain ways, on the basis of physical features, and socially and culturally constructed ideas about race. Often these categorisations were not of the adoptees' choosing. This meant that in developing their racialised identity, the adoptees challenged and negotiated the racialised labels of others in order to determine where and how they identified themselves. Four areas emerged as significant in how adoptees were classified and positioned on the black-white continuum. These are according to their physical features; existing socially and culturally constructed ideas about race, experiences of birth heritage, and experiences of racism. Each of these factors and the adoptees negotiation of them in the racial identity development process is now considered in more detail.

Physical features

The adoptees' position on the black-white continuum was primarily influenced by their physical features, where adoptees were largely categorised more as being black. Being identified on the basis of one's human body, i.e. biology, is argued by Jenkins (1996) as being significant to the development and negotiation of one's identity. This is because 'the human body is simultaneously a referent of individual continuity, and index of collective similarity and differentiation, and a canvas upon which identification can play. Social identification in isolation from embodiment is unimaginable' (Jenkins, 1996: 21). Hence the ways in which the adoptees in this study were racialised on the basis of their physical features, is understood as significant in their positioning in the continuum. The most common features for the adoptees in this research study had been those of skin colour, hair texture, facial profiles such as the eyes and nose, and body shape. Both black and white people used such physical features as a tool of identification when categorising the adoptees.

Most of the times, definitions were negative. For example, Hee Yun was often labelled as an outsider by white people on the basis of her having a different skin colour:

> We had quite a mixed class, but the majority of them were still white people . . . I very quickly became an outsider at that school because I was so different and they asked me questions . . . They keep asking me questions, 'how you look this colour'.

(Hee Yun)

Hee Yun's facial profiles, in particular her eyes and nose, were also used as a negative point of focus by others in her predominantly white social environment. This meant that her 'very Korean looking face' not only being used as a marker of difference, but additionally led to her being labelled as being flawed:

> Having such eyes, small nose . . . they say it's stupid.

(Hee Yun)

As mentioned earlier, Hee Yun's East Asian body shape had added to this categorisation of difference:

> *I was too small for my age in German terms, and so I was kept back a year because the doctor decided, and I was then too old for the class. So I was older then everyone else in this class.*

(Hee Yun)

Another adoptee, Natasha, was also labelled negatively on the basis of her skin colour. However, this had been done by both white others and black others:

> *They (black children and white children) would both call me names because I wasn't really one or the other but had a bit of both, which really made it worse in the sense of them teasing me . . . you know, though it was their problem really.*

(Natasha)

However, some adoptees felt that although they were labelled on their basic physical features, in particular their skin colour, such labels were not necessarily viewed as negative or as a problem. Despite this though, they still found themselves being placed on a continuum whereby they were being identified in certain ways. For example, during childhood where she was a minority in terms of race, Julie found herself being positioned by others towards the black end of the continuum:

> *I mean in terms of kind of racism and stuff, you know perhaps I was particularly naive. I mean kids are not nice to each other anyway, kids are brutal, kids are honest, kids are incredibly rude so when it comes to any name calling that goes on, the fact that the rude names that I was called are now, you know, you'd call racist abuse. I don't, I mean some of it no doubt was, you know, but I think a lot of the rest of it was simply the same kind of name calling that goes on with children full stop. So, you know they made reference to my blackness as they made reference to somebody else's freckles or fatness. You know, in some ways there are worse things then being called black if you are a child . . . I don't remember anything that I found particularly distressing or offensive.*

(Julie)

Similarly, Alison talked about being positioned by others according to her physical features. She said:

> *On one occasion I do remember, and Duncan would tell you, my youngest brother, he had a boy in his class who was very racist. I think they were fifteen at the time, fifteen years old, Alistair his name was, don't ask me how I remember, I just do, and I think his parents had the kind of attitude of you know 'they should all go back to where they came from, back on the banana boat' and all this rubbish, anyway this Alistair came round one night, and I didn't know what it was all about, you know what was going*

on, and Duncan said to me 'oh Alison answer the door' and I answered the door, and I don't even know his reaction and he said 'Oh God have I got the wrong house?' and I said 'well who are you looking for?' and he said 'Duncan' and I said 'no, he's my brother', and his face just fell to the floor.

(Alison)

However, it seems that as long as Alison is labelled as having a particular type of difference and as being a minority in this difference, she feels she is accepted to a better degree amongst the white others in her social environment. This is because, as long as Alison is seen as 'more white than black', she has no problem with her being labelled on the basis of her skin colour. For example, Alison added to her last comment:

But even he had a sort of attitude that was like 'well you're different, you're not like the others', you know what I mean, which is a bit like how people have always been to me.

(Alison)

This is also illustrated in Alison's later comments about how she welcomed her facial profiles that were more '*white European*' looking. This was because they had not only made her more accepted in her predominantly white social environment, but had given her just the right amount of difference in order to make her a novelty in her white social environment:

I mean they've (birth sisters) got a big mix of friends that are Asian, black, white, mixed-race, but that's because of where they live, you know if I lived in London and didn't have that mix then I would think that there was something wrong with me, but, you know, bearing in mind that I left (name of town) when I was sixteen, I've never lived in a place like that again, so I mean I might say that maybe part of me is racist to a certain degree of not wanting people like that in my life, but, maybe there is a bit of that . . . I don't know, it could be competition you know, it could carry on from when I was younger, you know, I'm still the novelty if I'm different to everybody else, so I'll be remembered.

(Alison)

However, when Alison is labelled as black, she becomes upset and annoyed at being racially tied to her physical features. In response to this, Alison negotiates herself a new position on the continuum by rejecting and challenging these definitions, and moving towards the white end of the continuum. This means that she not only chooses to position herself towards the white end of the continuum, but also negotiates the definition of others so they now too acknowledge this position. This illustrates how racialised identities are open to interpretation and modification. She said:

I work for social services now and my colour has become a rip-roar issue, but you know unbelievably so, and to the point of being quite oppressive . . . it was never an issue,

I mean I didn't think I wasn't black, I've never thought that I wasn't a different colour, but my friends will say to me you know 'oh I don't look at you and see you as black, I see you as you', or whatever . . . The issue at work that I've now got is that society tells me that I'm black and I don't want that label.

(Alison)

Some adoptees took more direct action in using their physical features to negotiate their position on the continuum. For example, Robert used his hairstyle as a strong assertion and representation of his black self:

When I was becoming more aware of my identity, it (four-inch Afro hairstyle) was a sort of strong statement of who I thought I was.

(Robert)

However, other adoptees were not able to confidently exert so much control in this self-defining process. Instead, they found themselves being labelled by others when they wore their hair in certain ways. For example, Julie talked about when she had once worn her hair in what is usually perceived as a '*black style*' almost out of ignorance or naivety:

After my hair got to a certain length I stopped combing. I mean what I would find was that when I tried to brush or comb my hair in the morning I would get these little knots and the harder they were to get out the more likely I was to leave one or two just 'cos I could not and I'd think I'd sort that out later and eventually realised that actually this is something that is going to turn into a little dreadlock and they just kind of, I just didn't do anything at all I just left it and once they'd formed they'd continued to grow in that way.

(Julie)

In her naivety, Julie found that she offended black people, in particular black African Caribbean men. This is because they had viewed her naivety and used it to place her more towards the white end of the continuum, a position that Julie herself accepted. She said:

It was mostly not particularly polite comments you know, I think they were making a set of assumptions and I can also remember and heaven knows why this happened I was walking through the streets one night having been at a pub with some friends and this chap on a bicycle pulled them (dreadlocks) and then cycled off, and it was a black guy and he had locks too, so I ran after him shouting and went to pull his locks and of course you know touching people's locks is not a particular courteous thing to do but I thought since he'd been particularly rude I would be rude to him but he went absolutely ape . . . but I was upset. I was pissed off I mean it's no different from somebody cycling past and you know hitting you on the head or on the back, you know, it was just felt like some minor assault which required redress so I belted after him and tried to pull his hair.

(Julie)

Similarly, Alison talked about her hair in terms of the way in which it impacted on how others defined her and how she negotiated these categorisations by using it to self-define and locate herself towards the white end of the continuum. For example, in choosing to wear her hair in her 'natural style', Alison felt it most accurately represented who she was, an offspring of a black African Caribbean father and white European mother, who happened to have inherited more of her birth mother's white racial features. For example, Alison said:

> *(My birth sister) straightens her hair all the time and I think it makes her look more black, but I don't go there . . . I'm the only one who's got curly hair now because they (birth sisters) all straighten their hair, and I think it makes them look more black, than mixed-race . . . I mean if you line me up with my sisters, we all look like sisters, we've got different features, and I mean some of my sisters look more black than white, our skin colours are all different, and I think some have picked up more features from their Dad than their Mum, whereas I think that Vanessa and me have picked up more features from my Mum, because . . . the features are more white than black.*
>
> (Alison)

Alison was pleased to self-define in this way, and is annoyed when she is considered beyond (towards the black side of) this marker. This is because Alison saw this as an inaccurate reflection of who she was. For example, her annoyance at being categorised as anything else is illustrated when she talked about her birth sister's attempts to straighten her hair and send her hair styling products designed for African Caribbean hair:

> *I mean Amy got me loads of products for my hair and it went awful you know I said 'oh Amy my hairs gone all greasy and it's all oily and it's horrible, so thank you very much but no', and she took me in to this hairdressers in London, and they straightened my hair, they blow-dried it straight, and it took ages . . . and that was a bloody whole experience, they got these hot rods that they put onto your hair, you know and you've got all these big black mamas in there with their straightened hair, and oh God, we were there for about four hours and they straightened my hair and I hated it, absolutely hated it, and I thought 'oh God I've got to go out in this tonight', you know because Amy wasn't going to let me wash it and leave it to go curly like I normally do, and I had to go out and I felt really black, black, black that night, I didn't like it at all.*
>
> (Alison)

Socially and culturally constructed ideas about race

The adoptees' position on the black-white continuum also depended on the socially and culturally constructed racialised ideas about race that others used to categorise them.

Some of the labels placed upon adoptees were done so by white people, who socially and culturally categorised the adoptees as being of black or of another minority ethnic origin. They had done this on the basis of their own constructed ideas about race, i.e. racialised stereotypes. For example, Alison talked about feeling as if she was on the receiving end of categorisations, which had assumed that she was black and had certain needs. In particular, Alison recalled being offered a black interviewer when at a job interview and then again a black tutor when at college. Alison's response in both these instances was of shock and annoyance that she had been categorised in this way:

> *I mean when I went to college I was offered a black tutor . . . when I went to the interview for the social work course, a letter came and it said 'would you like a black interviewer?' and I thought 'what?' . . . I mean I could not believe it and I said 'I could not care less who interviewed me as long as they are nice'.*

(Alison)

Julie also found that white others held expectations about her and what they saw as her black African Caribbean personality. These too were clearly based on socially and culturally constructed ideas about race, and at odds with how Julie considered herself:

> *Something I've learnt in adult life is that people always have an expectation of mouthiness from black people. Either mouthiness or sort of an obedience depending on whether you're African Caribbean or Asian you know.*

(Julie)

However, Robert encountered racism and stereotyping by some white people in relation to both his mixed-race and transracial adoption status, which he was clearly annoyed with, largely because it was at odds with how he viewed himself and status in that given society. He said:

> *A kind of attitude where white people say that 'I don't like black people but you're ok'.*

(Robert)

Some of the assumptions and stereotypes placed upon the adoptees were also made by black minority ethnic people, who viewed the adoptee to be black or of another minority ethnic origin. For example, Natasha talked about her experience of being labelled as black and having a particular black African Caribbean culture, by another black African Caribbean individual:

> *You know it was like 'yeah but she's black' and a lot of people were like 'yeah boo-yak-a-shah' to me (Natasha clicks her fingers together and swings her arm outwards), and I'd just say back 'yeah, hi, my name's Natasha, what's yours?' and they'd be expecting me to be called some sort of, I don't know 'Chanelle' or something like that, and I'd say 'my name is Natasha'. So I think they had a lot of pre-conceived ideas.*

(Natasha)

Some adoptees also found that they were labelled as white or non-black or not black enough, by black people. For example, Julie talked about her experience of labels being placed upon her by a black African Caribbean man:

One of the unsuccessful applicants took out a grievance on the basis of race because he felt that he'd been discriminated against, a Mauritian guy, and when I, I think not completely naïve, pointed out that actually the person who got the post was also not white, I got this tirade of stuff about being the wrong kind of black which is the first time I think I actually came up against that . . . you know it had not occurred to me that this kind of hostility would be coming at me from a black person . . . that's what I pick up you know, it's an exclusion thing . . . I suspect that for some black people I am not black enough you know. I kind of sold out in some way or form.

(Julie)

Similarly, Alison said:

In the end they (birth sisters) called me stuff like 'coconut' and 'bounty bar', meaning black on the outside and white on the inside . . . I know I'm more white I suppose, and that's what black people see too, that in my attitude and actions that I'm more white, but they think that because of it, I'm just white, but I'm both, although yes, more white . . . but not all white.

(Alison)

This idea of transracial adoptees not being seen as 'black enough' was discussed by Small (1986) in an account outlining the negative effects of transracial adoption. In discussing the envisaged problems faced by black transracial adoptees, Small argued that 'the majority of these children have not been given the tools to function as a black person' which means that as well as being rejected by white society, 'they are likely to be equally rejected by some black people who may say that they are not black enough, not in the colour sense of the term but in culture and attitude' (Small, 1986: 93).

Experiences of birth heritage

The adoptees' experiences with their birth heritage had also influenced their positioning on the continuum. Although not all adoptees had contacted their birth family, they all, in different ways and to different degrees, experienced part of their birth heritage, in terms of culture or social relations with others of the same birth racial group.

If the adoptees had positive experiences with their birth heritage, they identified more closely with that identity. For example, after her positive experiences with other Korean people and going to Korea to resolve identity issues, Hee Yun felt more confident and assertive in being able to identify herself as 'part Korean and part German'.

Similarly, some adoptees had largely negative experiences with the adoptive white heritage, and very positive experiences with the birth heritage. As a result they significantly identified more with the birth heritage. This was so for Robert who decided to seek out some experiences of his birth heritage, after his largely negative experiences with the white others of his adopted heritage. In doing so, Robert redefined the allocated label given to him by members of his white adoptive community, and instead replaced it with one that moved him towards the black end of the continuum. This is because, as noted earlier, when Robert said:

> *I don't feel entirely accepted in society or a kind of attitude where white people say that 'I don't like black people but you're ok'. . . . I don't want that type of acceptance.*

(Robert)

If adoptees' experiences with their birth heritage were largely negative, they tended to identify away from that identity, and move more towards the white end of the continuum, especially if experiences with the white adoptive heritage were positive. For example, when Alison contacted her birth sisters, she began to have her first real set of experiences of her birth heritage. In doing so, Alison found herself amongst black minority ethnic people, where her 'special status' became threatened and consequently distressed her. This then influenced how she viewed and interacted with black minority ethnic people. In addition to this, it also led to Alison feeling concerned that she was being viewed as another black person, with a particular set of characteristics:

> *I'm still the novelty if I'm different to everybody else, so I'll be remembered . . . (but) they'd (birth sisters) only talk to people who were black, you know the black bouncers outside the door, and they'd talk to them, and you know I just can't cope, you know I haven't had any black friends or any mixed-race friends at all throughout the whole of my life and I just could not cope with these sisters of mine who were like taking over and portraying me in this way and putting me in their category.*

(Alison)

Experiences of racism

The adoptees' positioning on the continuum was also determined by how they had internalised their own experiences of racism. This particularly included the bullying that adoptees faced as young people, which was targeted at their physical features, their social and cultural differences and the transracial aspect of their adoption.

The empirical evidence on transracial adoptees' experiences of racism and racist bullying is thin. Of the very little that does exist, claims about why transracial adoptees are bullied clearly argue that racial differences are a contributory factor. For example, in reporting the findings of a focus group consisting of six transracial adoptees who all had negative experiences, Shekleton (1990) found that the physical and colour differences of the transracial adoptees in comparison to other adolescents meant that they were the 'object of bullying and ridicule' by other children (Shekleton, 1990: 2). In addition, in looking at the literature on the bullying of black children at the hands of white children, Valerie Besag found there to be a 'quiet erosion of identity and self-esteem' of the black children (Besag, 1989: 47). Similarly, in interviewing 58 15–16-year-olds who were of 'mixed-parentage' (white and 'Afro-Caribbean' or 'African parentage') Tizard and Phoenix found that 'the great majority' of their sample of 'mixed-parentage' children had experienced racism in the form of name-calling 'which had been deeply wounding' (Tizard and Phoenix, 1994: 20). Shekleton (1990) also found that the adoptees had felt something was wrong with being different, which had been reinforced by name-calling and bullying at school, and which for some had then led to self-rejection.

The adoptees recalled numerous occasions where they were discriminated against on the basis of race and this had come from both black minority ethnic people and white people. When Robert talked about his experiences of racism from some white people, he said:

> It was a white working class area of South London, which at that time was a predominantly white area . . . I was a black kid growing up in a white family and area, and that's just how it was really . . . I sort of got on with the kids I knew . . . occasionally they'd be racist taunts from other kids in the area . . . I'd be called you know 'nigger' and 'black bastard'.
>
> (Robert)

However, Robert also recalled being labelled by one black African Caribbean person about his mixed-race status:

> The first time it did really actually bother me was when I was . . . I don't know I must have been about eleven or twelve or something and I was out with some white friends, and this black woman said something to me about, you know, just completely out of the blue, that 'you're neither black or white' sort of thing. So that kind of upset me more than the odd kind of racist remarks about being black . . . I was taken aback by it because it was just out of the blue and I didn't know whether she just knew me or what.
>
> (Robert)

Natasha also recalled being bullied by both black minority ethnic and white people about her mixed-race status:

> The bullying first started when I went to boarding school . . . it was just silly things, but then it really used to upset me, the name calling . . . it was white kids calling me names and black kids calling me names . . . I used to have some fights about it. It should not have been about it, but they were, and it was upsetting.
>
> (Natasha)

Other adoptees, who were also mixed-race by birth, recalled being racially bullied because they were transracially adopted. For example, let us recall a comment made in the previous chapter by Will:

> Some of the kids at school, not bullied me, but every time they saw it, it made it difficult being adopted . . . and other people, I would not say staring, but would ask me questions over and over again, like 'why are you adopted?' and 'why do you have white parents?' and all that . . . I think yeah, it did make them take the mickey out of me,

you know because I was different really . . . and every time me and my parents were together and we had to go to parent's evening or something, they (other children) just wanted to know why my parents were white.

(Will)

Being negatively labelled in these inaccurate and often offensive ways, had made the adoptees feel different. Several responses to this feeling of difference were observed. Some adoptees responded by seeking to reduce the racism by identifying themselves more with their perpetrators' racialised identity, in an attempt to gain inclusive status. In doing so, they therefore negotiated themselves a new position on the continuum. For example, in response to being teased about her black African Caribbean features, Alison rejected and challenged the black categorisation, by underplaying the black parts of her heritage and instead choosing to locate herself closer to the white end of the continuum:

I would have been eight or nine, or ten, and this Chinese girl came to the school and immediately she was picked on and bullied and had a lot of racism. And the teacher came to me and said 'will you look after her?' And I'm like 'why, why should I?' . . . What happened is that as soon as I started looking after her they started picking on me as well, and I thought 'oh no I don't want this' so to her face I was nice, but behind her back I was the same as everyone else, you know because I was being singled out and I didn't want to be singled out . . . they'd say 'oh if you hang out with her you'll get like her', because they didn't see me as being anything different because they were so used to me I suppose, you know having been there from the beginning, I don't know really'.

(Alison)

In doing so, Alison felt that she had accessed a certain amount of protection from racial discrimination:

I think that when you've got lots of cultures together, that's when racism comes in, because like they say, there's hardly any racism in Scotland because there aren't many Asian or black or dual heritage people, and the ones that are there just get on with it and they are accepted, and that's the same as going to these little villages, you know as soon as you're in and they know you're fine that's it, and I think that's what it is. I mean if I was to go and live in Birmingham, I might face loads.

(Alison)

Alison felt that being fortunate enough to have inherited more of her birth mother's white European features helped her to do this with relative ease. This view was also held by Julie, who felt that she was more 'cocooned' and protected from racial discrimination because of her physical features, which were more white than black, and also because of her social status, with its middle-class, socio-economic background. She said:

I think black men have a really hard time, it is actually easier as a female. Then there's all those other sort of hidden hierarchy sort of things like having light skin and being well spoken and educated. That tends to, I mean ok you still get the odd kind of lightish thing, but you know the more so cocooned you are by all these things, the more covert things become don't they? [And do you think you've been protected more by this?] I think I am probably protected, yeah.

(Julie)

Other adoptees had responded to the discrimination and bullying by choosing to identify more with the black minority ethnic part of their birth heritage. For example, Robert used the racist name calling to re-negotiate his sense of self and to positively assert his black identity, because he felt that this was something that was attacked the most and hence should be defended:

I suppose the racist name calling was one thing that gave me, well a sort of sense of identity about who I was really, and there wasn't really anything else that was asserting that I was black, so in a funny sort of way it was actually quite positive in a sense.

(Robert)

Other adoptees responded by underplaying the significance of race in their identity development. For example, Will said:

I never thought about it, like I said, I would say I'm black but only cos my (birth) mum and dad are, nothing else really . . . I like being with mixed people now though, cos I got both parts I think, I don't know.

(Will)

The adoptees responses demonstrated that they neither wholly identified with their black or white parts, but with certain elements from each and this made them want to locate themselves somewhere in the middle of the continuum. This was despite the fact that they were constantly faced with a social pressure to be placed at either the white end or the black end of the continuum.

Clearly, the adoptees' physical features, encounters with existing socially constructed ideas, experiences of their birth heritage, and experiences of racism, all combined to play important roles in how they were positioned on the black-white continuum. In addition, adoptees used these very factors to negotiate allocated labels and instead self-define identities that they perceived were more accurately fitting. In doing so, they also negotiated their positioning on the continuum.

From the adoptees' narratives, it is clear that although some adoptees saw themselves as more black than white and vice versa, all of the adoptees self-defined themselves in ways that illustrated that they were neither wholly black nor wholly white, but as having some elements from both parts, meaning that they had a mixed racial identity. This is not only because many of them were mixed-race by birth, but also because of their experiences due to the transracial aspects of the adoption. This showed that racialised identities are not fixed, but open to ongoing interpretation and modification. Similarly, there is no essential blackness or whiteness.

Having a positive or problematic racialised identity

One of the main arguments against the practice of transracial adoption is that it leads to serious identity development problems for the adoptee, specifically, that the adoptee will grow up facing identity conflict and confusion. And, because they will be unable to positively relate to their own racial background, they will develop a low self-esteem and even a hatred for their own black self (Small, 1986). In examining the racial identity development of transracial adoptees, this study sought to test these arguments.[5] It does so by contesting the literature that focuses on all transracial adoptees as having a negative racial identity, and instead argues that all the adoptees' negotiated a transracial identity that incorporated elements from both their black and white parts, that is, a mixed identity. Developing a transracial identity in this way meant that the adoptees were able to negotiate themselves a positive racial identity that they felt comfortable with, and could best be used as an avenue to assert pride, self-esteem and confidence.

Although the adoptees talked about their difficulties involved in the process of developing a positive racial identity that they felt comfortable with, they overwhelmingly talked about their achievement of settlement on a positive racial identity. In the process of developing this positive transracial identity, three main components emerged as significant. These are feeling proud, self-esteem and confidence, and, identity confusion.

Feeling proud

Some of the general literature on adoption has reported adoptees' positive feelings of self. However, the literature on transracial adoption has not done the same. The main reason for this is that debates have been dominated by arguments around the so-called negative perceptions of self that transracial adoptees supposedly suffer from. However, an overriding theme of the adoptees' accounts in this study, of their racialised identity development, was how they felt proud of who they had become due to the transracial nature of their circumstances, that is, people who are neither wholly black nor wholly white, but as individuals who in having a mixed racial identity, encompass elements from both parts. As Hee Yun says:

---

[5]Although adoptees' narratives were used to examine whether they had a positive or problematic racialised identity, no specific measurement tools or assessment criteria were used. Rather, the extent to which adoptees' racialised identity development was perceived as positive or problematic was primarily determined by the adoptees' own assessment, and to a lesser degree by this author's sociological analysis of presented identities.

I have an idea of what it's like on both sides, so I am both in that way, I like it . . . I am a born Korean with a German parentage, sometimes I am more German and sometimes more Korean, it depends . . . I am not just one . . . and that is me, it is what I am now.

(Hee Yun)

Such feelings of pride were tied to the adoptees having survived the difficulties that they faced from both black minority ethnic and white people because of their racialised differences. Will said:

I do feel proud that I can carry on and do stuff, not let things or those people get in the way.

(Will)

On a similar point, the adoptees also reported having a good awareness of one's (racialised) self. To quote Hee Yun:

I choose, I know that it is, that I am Korean and I am German, I am both, see? That is important to me . . . to be both, I cannot just be German, 'cos I am also part Korean . . . I feel more comfortable in myself when I went to Korea and learnt about Korean things, so I was able to be more happier with my German part too . . . it just helped me become a rounded person.

(Hee Yun)

This contradicts some of the arguments of the opposers of transracial adoption. Another finding, contradictory of existing literature, was that none of the adoptees had a hatred for their black self, in the sense that Small (1986) and Maximé (1986) claim. For example, although it is true that one adoptee, Alison, 'underplayed' her birth father's black African Caribbean heritage, and was happy in having inherited more of her birth mother's white European features, it did not mean that she had a supposed hatred for the black part of her heritage. It does suggest, however, that Alison felt uncomfortable amongst black people and instead preferred to be amongst white people, as discussed earlier. However, discomfort and hatred are not the same thing.

Self-esteem and confidence

The adoptees had recalled times when their self-esteem and confidence was low. The main time that adoptees felt this way was when they were younger and had thought about their 'abandonment' by the birth family. For example, for a short while Alison felt rejected as a child when her birth parents had, in her view, given her up:

I remember saying to my (adoptive) mum and dad 'how can he (birth father) not like me, he doesn't know me, I'm his baby, how can he not want me?

(Alison)

However, although Alison felt this way, she did not allow it to seriously damage her levels of self-esteem and confidence. This was because of her positive experiences with her adoptive family who constantly emphasised her 'special status' and how she was 'chosen':

> We'd go to the supermarket and she'd pick the nicest thing and say that's how we chose you and brought you home, sort of thing . . . I just felt special . . . I mean when I arrived, mum brought a kitten for me from the RSPCA . . . mum said I'm going to get a new kitten and that's what I wanted, a kitten, and she got this little ginger cat from the RSPCA and she lived until she was eighteen and my other (adoptive) brothers never had a pet . . . I think part of it is mum giving me this status because I was a girl . . . but part of it I think was probably due to the fact that I wasn't white and she'd (adoptive mother) taken in everything that social services had said and she didn't want me to be left out, but I think it went a bit overboard . . . but it all made me feel special in that family.
>
> (Alison)

Similarly, Julie spoke about her self-esteem and confidence in positive ways, both when she was a child and now as an adult. Although she described herself as being very 'bright, chatty and sociable' before her adoption, Julie was very clear that her adoptive parents nourished these characteristics and helped her develop into an adult who is 'grounded and has a complete and strong sense of self'. Although Julie herself recognised that she did 'not have a strong black consciousness', she also stated that this was only in the sense that her black consciousness was 'not a stereotypical one'. This meant that she was able to develop a strong sense of self, as well as a strong sense of a racialised self that she felt happy with.

However, to say that none of the transracial adoptees suffered seriously from low self-esteem and poor confidence would be misleading, since some of them, in this study, did experience these difficulties. However, they only did so as youngsters. One adoptee suffered from low self-esteem and poor confidence as a result of having been bullied about the transracial aspects of his adoption. This led him to feel different, rejected and imperfect, and as Will says:

> I would tell myself that I wasn't the same . . . everybody else was perfect, in a way, and that their life was better than mine because I was adopted and they weren't, therefore I was thinking that automatically, they were living a better life, I think that's what I thought.
>
> (Will)

In analysing the experiences of adoptees in her study, Shekleton argued that feelings of 'not being good enough' and 'being different' also sometimes made socialising difficult for transracial adoptees. This was because the adoptees feared that their 'fragile black image' would be questioned or challenged either by black or white people (Shekleton, 1990: 5). This was so for Will, who spent much of his youth alone in an attempt to reduce the amount of questioning he received from others about his situation. Will added to his last comment:

I just liked keeping myself to myself and being on my own.

(Will)

Another adoptee also experienced low self-esteem as a result of being a transracial adoptee, but more so as a result of being seen as different to the white others in her social world. Hee Yun said:

They come up and say 'you don't look like (adoptive brother's) sister', so you feel a strange, you feel a bit distant.

(Hee Yun)

For both Will and Hee Yun then, low self-esteem was a direct outcome of the circumstances surrounding the transracial, and for Hee Yun the intercountry, adoption, in that they had been made to feel different and imperfect in comparison to others. Such feelings of difference were rooted in the racialised differences between them and others in their social environment.

However, despite having suffered from these difficulties in the areas of self-esteem and confidence, both Will and Hee Yun stated that they felt they were able to think about themselves positively as adults. This was because of the other achievements they had made in life. For instance, Hee Yun talked about her academic success and Will about his music career:

I study hard, and I come here to do that too . . . I concentrate on doing that, to make a good life for me, to have a good education . . . I am trying to get on a Masters course now as well.

(Hee Yun)

I've been hooked on music ever since I was about fifteen, well, sixteen, seventeen. It's the main thing at the moment, but I'm just in the studio at the moment, but it's money [How much of your time does the DJ'ing take up?] In total probably about, well, a lot longer than I think, probably, going to get and buy records, either once a week or I'd be on the phone to someone buying records or trying to find out the latest tunes that are about or whatever, really. So, it takes up a lot of my time really. [And do you do a lot of gigs and stuff?] Sometimes yeah . . . gigs, and sometimes on pirate radio stations . . . and I'd be travelling up to Birmingham or London or whatever to do like guest shows up there and stuff like you know and then I'd DJ up in clubs and that. [I've heard that you're pretty good, can you do me a disc?] Yeah, ok. I suppose I'm alright, yeah. I work hard at it I suppose. I'm doing a college course as well to learn about the studio side of it, you know the technical stuff as well.

(Will)

Identity confusion

As stated earlier, some of the adoptees did feel that they would not have had such difficult and painful experiences if they had been placed with an adoptive family of the same racial background. Whilst expressing this view, however, none of the adoptees said that they wished to be another colour, i.e. the same colour as their white adoptive parents. Similarly, although the adoptees talked about their racialised identities in different and sometimes vague ways, they were not perceived as being confused. That is not confused in the sense that Small believed when he stated that 'transracial adoption encourages the phenomenon of racial-identity confusion . . . [which] often leads black children to deny the reality of their skin colour' (Small, 1986: 83–4).

Rather, the adoptees felt secure in defining themselves and their racialised identities in the given ways. Such security came through acknowledging that they each had a number of identities, and not just one essential identity. This security also related to the adoptees' acknowledgement that their racialised identity was something that was open to modification because it was flexible and ever changing. Hee Yun said:

> *I could not choose because in every different situation I am a different person. I refuse to choose. You cannot choose, there is no option, because no person is mainly one person, you know with that character. You always change in every situation . . . It is really something where I refuse to say that I am mainly that person. I think it's unfair to say that and choose.*

(Hee Yun)

Clearly, adoptees at times suffered particular difficulties in their negotiation of a racialised identity. However, in different ways and to different extents, they all developed a positive racialised identity. This is because they firstly overcame difficulties by using other achievements as measures of success, and secondly, asserted their own sense of pride as transracial adoptees with a mixed racial identity which allowed them to cater for a sense of belonging that they felt to both their black minority ethnic birth heritage and white adoptive heritage.

CHAPTER 5

Possessing a multi-racialised identity

Although it can be argued that there are no real biological foundations to race we continue to organise our lives and behave as if there are (Mason, 2000). Race is socially constructed, and therefore remains 'a social fact' (Best, 2005: 150). Indeed, as Knowles notes: 'intricately woven into the social landscapes in which we live, race is all around us; a part of who we are and how we operate . . . it is part of the way the world operates' (Knowles, 2003: 1). We use ideas and assumptions about race to predict the behaviour of others, to label people and to allocate privilege or disadvantage. It is used in overt and covert ways to determine the life experiences of individuals. In Western society whiteness is not only the majority, but also considered to be the norm, and racial disadvantage is faced by members of the various black minority ethnic communities. To investigate the operation of race and racialisation processes is vital. Indeed, as Donald and Rattansi note: 'reiterating that there's no such thing as 'race' offers only the frail reassurance that there *shouldn't* be a problem. It cannot deal with the problems that do exist, because it fails to see them for what they are' (Donald and Rattansi, 1992: 1).

Despite the focus of the book the author has a quiet distaste of talking about mixed-race identities. This is because when we speak of such types of identities they all too often are used to refer to those whose parentage is of two visibly different races. This is a problem, because really we all have a biologically mixed-race and socially multi-racial background. Somewhere along our genealogical family tree, some sort of mixing has occurred. A world that has seen vast movements of people through migration, invasion and Imperialism has inevitably ensured this. Similarly, consider the creation of hybrid racial identities. To use terms such as 'mixed-race', is actually 'misleading since it implies that a 'pure race' exists' (Spencer, 2006: 222). The very foundations of this are in themselves 'problematic' (Barn, 1999: 278). It suggests a world of binary blackness and whiteness.

However, individuals continue to use 'race' in real ways, and certainly as markers of difference. Indeed, some argue that it is used as *the* overriding key marker of difference in comparison to other variables, such as gender, age and so on (Barn, 2001: 61). Racialised ideas are used to draw boundaries between racial groups, and to create in-group belonging as well as out-group otherness. Whilst such boundaries continue to be drawn and behaviour organised accordingly, every effort should be made to ensure that the thinking about race and racial identities is progressive and as reflective of reality as is possible. It is this belief that guides the following consideration of multi-racial identities as racial identities in their own right, and the call for their recognition as such in order to move away from racialised notions of binary black and white polar opposites. In particular, the essentialised idea of a fixed black identity is questioned. In doing so, support is given to Gilroy, who in his critique of black essentialism, recognises that they 'deny that the growing order of intracommunal differences visible around money and class, gender and sexuality, status and authority are anything other than minor appendages to the grand inscription of racial purity' (Gilroy, 1995: 16).

Elements of a multi-racialised identity

A number of key factors are important in the development of a racial identity. In considering and theorising about their significance, attention is drawn to the largely socially constructed nature of an individual's racial identity, in terms of the ways in which both biological and cultural elements are constantly being defined, negotiated and renegotiated. It is argued here that for transracial adoptees and other groups of individuals in society, conformity to an essentialised view of racial identity, i.e. blackness or whiteness, is not possible, and therefore should not be demanded. A multi-racial identity is developed as a racial identity in its own right, for a growing body of people who do not see themselves as wholly black or wholly white.

Those having such a multi-racial identity can be viewed as a valid racial group because there is a shared sense of connectedness and a sameness of experiences. Boundaries can be drawn between them and other racialised groups. This remains so even though there are differences between them in terms of the degree to which they view their multi-racial status, as in whether it is more towards a black one than white one, or vice versa.

In using the idea of a black-white continuum to theorise about the development of such a multi-racialised identity, a more contemporary and sophisticated level of thinking emerges. This can be applied to the cases of others in society who are often defined as being of a singular essentialised black racial identity, but who actually consider themselves as owning a more flexible, diverse multi-racial identity, such as children of mixed parentage and settled immigrant children. These groups, like the transracial adoptees, also negotiate themselves a flexible multi-racial identity that is not just a black *or* a white one, but, in different ways and to different degrees, a combination of both. Furthermore, this multi-racial identity is a healthy and positive one that has emerged from a negotiation process in order to produce a label that the individual considers best represents who they are.

So, what is this multi-racial identity? And, how is it developed? In the existing body of literature and the evidence from the study on which this book is based, in which the racial identity development of transracial adoptees was examined, a number of variables can be identified as playing key roles in the development of this identity. These are:

* physical features
* gender
* age
* immediate family

- friends
- immediate and wider social networks
- religion
- history
- geographical location

Physical features, gender and age

One of the most evident signifiers of racial identity is that of physical features. The way an individual looks, in terms of their biology, whether 'alleged or real' (Pilkington, 2003: 16), contributes to the development of their racial identity because they are defined by others according to their appearance. Furthermore, the ways in which they choose to dress, perhaps by downplaying certain features, illustrates that to some degree they are able to alter their ascribed labels and modify their presentation. Common biological or genetic features which play important roles in racial identity include those of skin pigmentation, hair texture, facial profiles such as eyes and nose, and body shape. Pre-existing racial stereotypes, many of which are often inaccurate and crude, are used by others in their interactions with and expectations of the individual. The racialised individual responds by either conforming to pre-existing racial stereotypes or defining new ones.

Similarly, one's biology in terms of gender, and socially constructed ideas about gender, play an important role in the construction of our identities, which consciously and unconsciously develop from the moment we are born. For example, consider the selection of pink coloured items for baby girls and blue coloured items for baby boys. These gendered ideas continue throughout childhood and well into adulthood and are then repeated with a whole new generation. Although these gendered ideas can be questioned and challenged, they continue to influence the allocation of male and female roles, rights and responsibilities in society.

In considering the ways in which gendered and sexualised ideas about particular individuals from certain racial groups are presented, it is fair to argue that these are labels that can be successfully challenged and re-negotiated. However, because of the dominance and power of such gendered ideas, challenges are difficult. This is particularly so for women from a black minority ethnic background, who are forced to work, firstly, within the wider framework of a white male dominated society, and secondly within the sub-framework of a black male dominated society. Indeed within this category there is yet another category, the dark-skinned black woman, who, in comparison to her light-skinned black counterpart, is seen as having even less power, as she is less sexually desirable and is considered to be more extreme and dangerous (Hooks, 1992, in Ali, 2005: 160). However, these ideas go beyond that of sexual desire, as the American sociologist Margaret L. Hunter notes: 'on average, women earn less money than men; people of color earn less than whites, and dark-skinned people of color earn less than lighter-skinned people of color' (Hunter, 2005: 6).

It is important to note that age, like other biologically based features, is something that is socially constructed, certainly in terms of the meanings assigned to different ages. Although its boundaries are often considered to have a 'genuinely universal social criteria', these boundaries are not strictly fixed, although demographers and legislators may contend that they are (Vincent, 2000: 133–5). Rather, the construct of age is differentiated by cultural variances, as well as differences in space and time. These constructions create age norms that place us in categories that, in turn, inhibit us from doing some things, whilst releasing us to do others. Age is therefore like most social constructs that inform the shaping of identity, both enabling and constraining.

In Western societies, it can be suggested that identity development occurs at several key stages during the life course. These are the infant years, during adolescence, and then in the twenties and thirties. These are the stages at which an individual is more susceptible to being influenced by the attitudes of others and the social environment in which they find themselves because they engage in significant and particularly meaningful encounters with others. This then impacts on how they view their own racial self and also how confidently they feel in being able to negotiate labels in order to define their own racial identity.

Immediate family, friends and social network

The members of an individual's immediate family, biological or otherwise, also play a huge role in assisting the development of racial identity. For example, in her study of second generation British-Sikhs, Hall noted how:

> Sikh parents stimulate their children's imaginations by recounting memories that bring life to the past. Stories of lives in India or East Africa transmit a second-order nostalgia for a place the children hardly know. Family legends are formed, relatives' names become attached to personalities, and expectations for future travels are nourished.

(Hall, 2002: 174)

This is supported by the work of Harris and Sim (2000). Indeed, the family is often seen as one of the most rich and emotionally nourishing sources of influence in not only assisting the development of a racial identity, but in addition frequently helps the development of an identity that is positive, healthy and comfortably reflective of how an individual views their racial self. It is argued that the family, amongst other social institutions, is able to do this because families are a prosperous source of social capital: 'social capital refers to connections among individuals – social networks and the norms of reciprocity and trustworthiness that arise from them' (Putnam, 2000: 19). Hence, close familial relationships and interaction enable its members to commit themselves to each other, to knit a strong social fabric, and to create a sense of self, part of which includes a strong sense of racial identity that they feel able to comfortably develop in a fairly safe, accommodating and supportive environment. However, it is important to note that this is not always the case and that sometimes individuals move towards a particular racial identity that may not be one that is supported by the family. Despite this, what is clear is that the family plays an important role in terms of how the individual defines and negotiates their racial identity.

An individual's network of friends (not the same as acquaintances) also play a significant role in that they act as a reflection of how individuals view themselves. This network also acts as an important source of social capital, which contributes significantly to the racial identity development process. Here, friendships are seen as bringing with them a degree of intimacy based on a shared sense of commonality, and hence a fairly safe environment in which the individual is able to reflect on how they are viewed by others. These sites and relationships also then offer the opportunity for racial labels to be negotiated and a more accurately representative label to be tested and presented. Feedback and support from the friendship network is viewed as assisting successful negotiations of a more fitting racial identity that suits the individual at that given space, time and context.

Very much like friendship networks, both an individual's immediate social network, including acquaintances, work colleagues, neighbours, etc., and their wider social network, such as social others that they interact with in their daily lives, also contributes to the shaping of their racial identity. Although these sites may not initially be of the individual's own choosing, they nevertheless act as important network sites which provide a social setting in which individuals interact with others and are able to embark on meaningful and significant interaction processes with other social beings. In this interaction process, racialised ideas are used as a basis for views, attitudes and exhibited behaviour. In receiving these racialised ideas, and working within the boundaries of those given sites, the individual then negotiates labels in order to present one that is more accurately fitting and more suited to how they view themselves in that given space, time and context. Often, the individual may choose to adjust membership of their social networks, especially their immediate site, so as to include others of a similar racial identity as their own.

Religion, history and geographical location

Religion also guides and influences an individual's identity, depending upon whether an individual views religion as having any meaningful significance in their lives. If so, religious spirituality or involvement in a particular religious community can offer space, guidance and support for identity to be comfortably negotiated. Often, race and religion are associated with one another; the assumption being that individuals of certain racial backgrounds are more likely to belong to particular religions. Although such assumptions can be safely made, it is important to recognise that this is not always the case, largely due to the flexible status of both race and religion. In some ways, however, religion can play a role in the way in which individuals choose to racially identify themselves. This is largely due to the racialised ideas that are often bound up with religion, which in turn often relates to nationhood, history and ethnicity.

In talking about the historical knowledge used by people in self-defining themselves and their identity, Harris and Sim note that there are two types of history, that of real history or imagined history (Harris and Sim, 2000: 7). Whether it is real or imagined, the ethnic, cultural and racialised history of the individual also shapes the way in which they view themselves, their place in society and how they settle on a racial identity.

The content of such historical material could include knowledge and experience of migration, oppression and struggle, war and conflict, economic development, traditional customs, religious beliefs and folklore, political government, and eminent figures. Elements of one's history are selectively drawn upon and utilised by the individual in the negotiation of a racial identity. However, certain elements of the individual's history are also used by social others as a basis for their creation of assumptions, ideas and stereotypes, which they use in their racialising of the individual. The individual in turn takes these labels on board in their negotiation process, re-defines them, and will often present more accurately fitting labels in their place.

The place and space in which the individual exists is also important in the development of a racial identity. Here, geographical location (i.e. nationhood), is relevant in terms of the cultural composition and racial make-up of the environment. In particular though, geographical location and the politicised chains binding that space influence the way in which individuals negotiate themselves a racial identity that is, to a degree, reflective of the racial identity issues and struggles that exist in their location.

In this situation, ideas about nationhood, power and politics, as well as more concrete representations, such as flags, anthems, food, dress, monuments, rituals and customs, etc., all intertwine with one another to create boundaries which the racialised individual works within, in their negotiation of a fitting racial identity. This is a difficult task for some individuals, especially the black minority ethnic person living in a geographical location where there is a white majority, such as in Britain or the US. As Barn notes:

> The issue of identity for children from a minority ethnic background living in a county such as Britain is particularly poignant. The negotiation and assertion of a black identity becomes a daily struggle in a country which is largely incongruous with one's self-image. Britain's credentials as a predominantly white, Christian country with a history of slavery and colonialism, and continuing racial disadvantage and discrimination play a significant role.

(Barn, 2001: 60)

Hence, their presence in Britain has been viewed as 'problematic, temporary and conditional' (Alibhai-Brown, 1999: 3), and damaging to ideas of Britishness, which themselves are often built on racist constructions.

Because ideas about nationhood are by their very nature 'defined in an exclusive relationship of difference' (Weedon, 2004: 20), a key marker of a difference used is that of race and colour. So identifying oneself as *Black* in such an environment may be seen as an important way of fighting racism, as was seen with the US Black Power Movement in the 1960s (Alibhai-Brown, 2001: 98). However, it is important to note that within this space there are political struggles, which transform the social meanings of race (Omi and Winant, 1986: 68). For example, consider the transition from the American usage of the terms 'Negro', 'coloured', 'Black', 'African-American', and 'people of colour', and in particular note their shift from being used as allocated terms of abuse to self-adopted terms of empowerment. Also note the wider context of their 'different imaginings and different group boundaries' (Pilkington, 2003: 20).

Children of mixed (interracial) parentage

'The controversial new 'mixed' category in the 2001 census attracted 400,000 ticks. One in ten ethnic minority Britons is the product of 'mixed' parents . . . Britain has one of the highest rates of interracial relationships in the Western world. Whether you view this as a positive sign of a new multi-ethnic melting pot, or a negative watering down of the UK's minorities, it is a fact' (*Observer*, 25 November 2001, in Spencer, 2006: 222). According to the 2001 Census, it has been estimated that mixed-race children make up approximately 1.2 per cent of the total population in the UK,[1] which is 14.6 per cent of the UK minority ethnic population (Office for National Statistics, 2001). In the US, their size has been given at 2.4 per cent of the population, which represents over 6.8 million people (Census Scope, 2000).

Diversity and difference

Without doubt, as a racialised group, their numbers are increasing and their make-up containing the most diversity. For example, consider the case of US professional golfer Tiger Woods, who once used the self-defined acronym of 'Cabalinasian' to reflect that he is 'one-fourth Black, one-eighth American Indian, one-fourth Thai, and one-fourth Chinese' (Schaeffer, 2006: 26).

In the light of this diversity, it is argued that mixed-race individuals should be recognised as a racialised group in their own right, neither black nor white, but as a varied group whose identities are taken from both heritages. However, this is not so. As Alibhai-Brown notes, many mixed-raced individuals feel that 'one of the most pernicious effects of living in a racially divided and unequal society is that all sides conspire to rob you of your own individuality' (Alibhai-Brown, 2001: 118). Thus, children of mixed-race largely continue to be viewed as being black. For example, as Small argued: 'in this society, any child who has the slightest taint of black is seen by the majority as black . . . for those children there are no 'in-betweens' (Small, 1986: 91). Indeed, many use such essentialist ideas to insist that

---

[1] See Tizard and Phoenix (2002) for a factual and thought provoking in-depth discussion of the history and presence of children of mixed parentage.

children of mixed-race should be viewed as black, and only when they themselves adhere to this can they develop a healthy sense of self. It is of little surprise then that interest in mixed-race individuals has centred on their social experiences and their racial identity, as discussed in Chapter 1.

Many of these studies have claimed that mixed-race people experience difficulties due to racism and their sense of living between two binary opposites, that of the black world and the white world; for example, consider the ideas of Stonequist (1942), and more recently the arguments forwarded by Small (1986). Other studies, however, have highlighted the uniqueness that their position brings, for example, as noted in the early work of Park (1928), and how the expected problems of self-identification and low self-esteem have not actually materialised (Bagley and Young 1979; Wilson, 1987). As such, it is argued that the imposing of the black label is problematic (Alibhai-Brown, 2001; Owusu-Bempah and Howitt, 2000). This view has especially been borne out of 'insider research', which are 'studies that focus on insider accounts . . . publications by people who are themselves 'insiders' to mixed parentage' (Tizard and Phoenix, 2002: 50).

Child and family placement services
Within child and family placement services, mixed-race people pose a 'placement dilemma' (Barn, 2001: 23). Who should they be placed with, especially if they have been cared for by their white mother prior to entering the care system? Is both an ethnic and racial match possible? What about those mixed-race children who are not as visibly of mixed-race parentage? (Barn, 2001: 23). Commentators such as Small (1986) and Barn (1993) have argued that these children should be treated as black.

It has been widely recognised that there is a disproportionate number of mixed-race children entering the public care system (Barn, 1993; Tizard and Phoenix, 1994). Often, they come from a single parent, white, female-headed family, where the black African Caribbean father is absent, and little or no contact has been made with their black relatives or members of the black community (Barn, 2001; Tizard and Phoenix, 1994). In addition, they enter the system at a much younger age, compared with white children, and once in the system, end up spending more time there (Barn, 1999: 269). This particular mixed-race group (white mother and black African Caribbean father) is highly represented in the general population in comparison to other mixed counterparts. According to the 2001 Census 237,000 mixed-race individuals ticked the white and black Caribbean box and another 79,000 selected the white and black African box (ONS, 2001). Nevertheless, their highly disproportionate representation in the public care system has been questioned.

As is the case with transracial adoptees, the black-white continuum can also be used to understand the racial identity development of mixed-race people. This is supported by Tizard and Phoenix, who from their own findings, noted: 'it should by now be clear that the racial identities of our sample of mixed parentage young people differed widely, and that the main influences on them that we were able to show were social class, type of school, gender and the degree of politicisation of the young people' (Tizard and Phoenix, 1994: 21). Those of mixed-race heritage utilise the same variables in very much the same ways as transracial adoptees, in order to embark on a similar identity development process, where racialised labels are presented, negotiated and re-defined to ones that the individual feels more comfortable with and is a more accurate reflection of how they view themselves. Settling on a particular mixed-race identity can also be positive. For example, as Tizard and Phoenix note: 'young people with a 'mixed' identity were just as likely as those with a black identity to feel positive about their colour and proud of their inheritance' (Tizard and Phoenix, 1994: 21).

These racialised identities are not fixed, but flexible, fluid and in a constant state of change. They are open to modification and are re-negotiated according to the racialised meanings of the particular space, time and context that the mixed-race individual may find themselves in. Harris and Sim, who examined the 'magnitude and fluidity of racial identity' (Harris and Sim, 2000: 13), and the ways in which the members of the mixed-race population define themselves, especially when in different racialised contexts, such as the home and the school, also found that race assigning depends on several factors, some of which were very similar to those outlined above, that is, the individual's ancestry and the context in which they find themselves, for example, the other's race, ideology, familiarity with the individual, racial composition of the context, and their own personal history (Harris and Sim, 2000: 4–5).

Of significance is the view that there is no one mixed-race category, as there is no one black category. Indeed, as Root (1996, in Tizard and Phoenix, 2002: 50) argues, there is enough commonality of experience by mixed-race people for what she calls, 'multiraciality' to be considered as a racial identity category. However, Root also adds that this should not be taken as another singular racialised category (Root, 1996, in Tizard and Phoenix, 2002: 50). Thus, there is a vast range of hybrid forms of mixed-race identity, which not only varies according to context, but also depends upon the particular 'racial mix' of the birth parents. Tizard and Phoenix (2002) agree when they say:

> . . . it is difficult to generalise about the mixed parentage young people in our study . . . their mixed origins carried a wide range of meanings . . . we have shown that the different meanings of their mixed parentage for the young people were related to a wide range of factors. Their gender, social class, the type of school they attended, the extent to which their views on race were politicised, and the amount of family communication about race, were all significantly related to their identities and experiences.
>
> (Tizard and Phoenix, 2002: 232–3)

This is also supported by Harris and Sim who found that the processes involved in the racial identification of different racially-mixed groups vary. This suggests that there is no one universal mixed-race identity. Instead 'there are overlapping mixed-race populations whose membership depends on what identity is measured – expressed or external – and the social context in which identity is assessed' (Harris and Sim, 2000: 28).

Children of settled immigrant families

In talking about the growing trend of young British Asian couples to request money at weddings from guests as opposed to presents, Rahman notes:

> Young British Asians don't wish to live the rootless, in-between lives of their elders. By requesting cash instead of gifts, the new generation is showing that it intends to stamp its personality on to its homes, invest its identity in every stylised detail, and lay down roots to foster memories and belonging. British Asians see themselves as being here to stay, and what better way of emphasising this than exercising control over every aspect of their symbols of permanent residence: their homes.

> (Rahman, in *New Statesman*, 25 April 2005: 28)

In this excerpt Rahman is using requesting money as wedding gifts as an indication that many of today's settled immigrant children, especially in this case, those from a South Asian background, have developed themselves racial, cultural and ethnic identities that incorporate a fairly strong sense of being British, here demonstrated by their feelings of right to permanent residency in the country. As Anwar notes: 'They are British and can no longer be considered as 'immigrants', 'foreigners', or 'outsiders'. They are an integral part of Britain' (Anwar, 1998: 182).

The next generation

The term 'settled immigrant children' is used here to refer to individuals who have been born and raised in Britain, but whose parents or grandparents came from other countries, the vast majority of these being countries in the African and Asian subcontinents. Figures on their numbers in Britain are difficult to obtain. For example, according to the 2001 Census it has been estimated that 7.9 per cent of the population, which translates into 4.6 million people, are from ethnic minority groups (ONS, 2001). Although the Census does not provide any further indication as to how many of these are settled immigrant children, another national statistical source, the *British Labour Force Survey*, indicates that 2.8 per cent of the black minority ethnic population in Britain are the direct descendants of ethnic minority immigrants, such as those from the African and Asian subcontinents (British Labour Force Survey, 2001, in Dustmann and Theodoropoulos, 2006: 2).

It should be recognised that while the presence of such minority ethnic groups (i.e. Africans, West Indians, Pakistanis, Indians, Chinese and Irish), appears to have taken place due to the forms of increased visible migration, or what is often referred to as *mass migration*, since the mid-1940s, their actual presence in Britain is long established. For example, Fryer (1984) and Visram (2002) have been able to document in some detail the presence of these groups in Britain since the 17th century. The contribution of this 'immigrant community' to the British labour market and business economy, as well as their everyday cultural input, has been invaluable (Visram, 2002).

In terms of examining the mixed racialised identities of these settled immigrant children this discussion takes the period of increased visible migration (1945 onwards) as a key point of reference. This is because the group which is being examined here often use this as a key point of reference in terms of their own historical roots in Britain. Racism and hostility towards black minority ethnic people in Britain has always existed. Immediately after World War II though, there was some acceptance of black minority ethnic people coming into Britain. Indeed, to some degree they were 'welcomed by the British people as allies who had defended their national survival' (Cabinet Papers, 1950, in Anwar, 1998: 2), not only during the war but immediately afterwards, when they were used to fill gaps in the British labour market. They were therefore seen as of key importance to the survival of the British nation and its economy. However, this relative acceptance soon turned to hostility. In particular, concern was raised about the *large numbers* of 'coloured' immigrants, who were bringing with them a supposed inferior, problematic and alien culture that would infect British life.[2] This was most clearly illustrated by the 'rivers of blood' speech given by Enoch Powell in April 1968.

It was clear at this time that this immigrant community, and indeed their children and grandchildren, and now a new generation of their great-grandchildren, would always be viewed as immigrants and outsiders. This is despite the fact that their offspring were born and raised in Britain, contributed to the running of the country and in many ways often considered themselves to be part of British society. This led to a feeling that although all generations face 'the same type of prejudice and discrimination', the second and third generations, 'unlike their parents . . . are not prepared to accept hostility and discrimination as an inevitable part of living in Britain' (Anwar, 1998: 148).

Old and new forms of racism

In terms of racialised identity studies have analysed the type of discrimination experienced by these settled immigrant children. They have also tried to understand the difficulties that immigrants faced as a result of living between two cultures and the mechanisms they have utilised for overcoming them (Anwar, 1998; Dudrah, 2002; Hall, 2002; Modood, 1994; Phillips, 2007). These writers highlight the role that negotiation and social construction plays in the formulation of identity, especially ethnic and racialised identity. In many ways, then, development of their identities can be likened to that of transracial adoptees and mixed-race individuals. In doing so, it also demonstrates how essentialist notions of a unified singular black racial identity, even as a political reference point, are no longer valid. For example, as

---

[2]It was initially thought that these immigrants would assimilate themselves into British society, a key part of which was that they would in effect shake-off and forego everything about their own ethnic culture.

Alibhai-Brown notes: 'The Muslim and Hindu women were no longer happy with the term 'Asian' and black women said they were not interested in the 'culture wars' of the Asians' (Alibhai-Brown, in *New Statesman*, 4 April 2005: 12). Modood also highlighted this when he noted the danger of the 'assumed homogeneity' that the blackness concept actually imposes on British Asians (Modood, 1994: 859).

Essentialist thinking views such a diversity of experience and interests as a problem, misinterpreting it as a rejection of blackness and thus as an attempt to become more white and hence more acceptable. For example, in talking about his televised documentary broadcasted in August 2004, Darcus Howe commented:

> *I remember that during the age of black militancy all the old immigrant groups were comfortable with the definition 'black'. But our friends from the Indian subcontinent came to prefer 'brown' and 'Asian', which put them nearer to whites in the colour coding. Now, young Pakistani men have gone further and demand that they be referred to as Pakistanis, which by inference includes Islam, and implies a lighter shade of brown. This hierarchy of skin colour presumes that all Caribbeans are darkies, which places us at the bottom of the pile.*

(Howe, in New Statesman, 16 August 2004: 10)

The implications of Howe's attack on Asians, in particular young Pakistani men, is based on his essentialising of identity as well as pushing for a unified black singular racial identity. His lack of appreciation for the diversity of identities, and the need for groups to control the naming of racialised selves is of concern. So too is his lack of attention to the desire to negotiate more an identity that takes into account religion and ethnicity, as well as notions of race or colour.

Despite the diversity of experiences and hence the choice to re-define labels, even if those labels take into account self-assigned feelings of Britishness, the offspring of immigrants still find themselves experiencing racial discrimination and disadvantage. For example, as Alibhai-Brown noted: 'There is mounting evidence of overt racism in institutions and generally towards immigrants. Settled people as well as newcomers are feeling increasingly threatened by both obvious and subtle manifestations of xenophobia' (Alibhai-Brown, in *New Statesman*, 4 April 2005: 12). These settled immigrant children and the multi-cultural British society which their presence has helped to create, continue to be viewed as problematic in that they are considered to be unwelcome aliens in British society. In addition, their presence has been viewed as a threat to the well-being of the British nation. This has been a popular view in response to uprisings in Northern England in 2001 and the recent focus on 'Islamic terror threats' and 'home grown terrorists' following the London bombings in 2005.

Re-negotiating belonging
Many of the studies on the racialised identity development of settled immigrant children highlight the negotiation processes embarked on and the ways in which these groups are

able to negotiate the different cultures in order to emerge with an identity that they feel comfortable with and which best reflects who they are and how they view themselves. Often, this is an identity that considers both the immigration heritage, such as the heritage of their parents or grandparents' country of origin, as well as the settlement heritage, that is the heritage of the country in which they themselves have been raised. Indeed, public figures illustrate ways in which these identities are presented to us. For example, consider boxer Amir Khan's choice of national symbolism on his uniform in his fight for the Commonwealth lightweight title in July 2007. Here, Khan, who was born and raised in the North-East region of England, and whose parents came from Pakistan, proudly fought, and won, whilst wearing black shorts bearing both the British flag and the Pakistani flag. His surname, Khan, a popular Pakistani Muslim name, spelt out across his waistband in the design of the Union Jack represented the significance and unification of both his immigrant and settlement heritages.

Hall argues that such individuals are able to do this via embarking on negotiations, or as Hall calls it, participating in the 'symbolic play' of 'cultural identities and images' according to given 'cultural fields', these being 'socially inhabited spaces' such as the school, familial home, places of worship and entertainment venues (Hall, 2002: 170). Consequently, she noted, with reference to the British-Sikhs in her own study, individuals 'become more or less English, more or less Indian or more or less 'black' by situationally performing identities and creating lifestyles that differentially articulate race, class, gender, and cultural markers' (Hall, 2002: 190). In doing so, they settled on an identity that best suited who they were in that given context at that particular point in time:

> . . . they move through their lives understanding that, as one young woman phrased it, there is 'a time to act English and a time to act Indian'. In their everyday lives, second generation Sikhs participate in a number of cultural fields in which they 'act Indian' or 'act English' or, more accurately, within the limits of normative constitutive constraints, perform identities that produce something in between.
>
> (Hall, 2002: 171)

As Anwar states, it is 'a new culture which is a synthesis of the "old" and the "new"' (Anwar, 1998: 192). In this way, the settled immigrant children can be likened to transracial adoptees and mixed-race individuals. The black-white continuum can therefore also be used to show how a variety of key factors are influential in developing a racialised identity and the ways in which such racialised identities are presented and re-defined. The flexible nature of these identities means that there can be no one fixed or singular identity, as space, time and context are constantly shifting the boundaries within which racialised meanings are given. This includes the significance that the individual gives to their cultural, ethnic and racial heritage. These all combine to play a role in how they choose to define their very selves, as does the degree to which they feel a sense of connection with the birth country of their parents or grandparents. For example, many of these children make regular visits to the country from which their parents came and often keep in regular contact with the family that they still have in these countries. They talk of being 'born and bred' in Britain, and yet still are aware of where their family came from and the physical, cultural and political route they took after arriving in Britain. Indeed, Ghuman and Kamath (1993) recognise this negotiation process in their observation that black minority ethnic people are beginning to develop their own adapted and culturally diverse identities, in comparison to their parents. However, they still nevertheless experience racial abuse and discrimination and 'mixed feelings about belonging in Britain' (Ghuman and Kamath, 1993: 7). It is therefore commonplace for hyphenated labels to be used, such as Asian-British, Black-British, Black-African, Caribbean-British, or even self made acronyms, such as Tiger Woods' 'Cabalinasian' (Schaeffer, 2006: 26), to indicate the development of identities that take into account both the immigrant and settlement heritages. The hyphenated use of labels has also been formally recognised if one considers the categories used in the 2001 UK Census. However, self-defined acronyms, and the right to develop them, is yet to be widely accepted, for example, Tiger Woods is still often referred to as being an 'African American' (Schaeffer, 2006: 25).

It is also important to note that different groups, who can be classed as settled immigrant children, also have within them a multiplicity of identification layers and ways of being. These differences are tied up with their own cultural, historical and political issues. Similarly, it is not correct to assume that, for example, the grandchildren of immigrants who came from India in the 1960s would actually identify themselves in the same ways as their parents. Neither is it correct to assume that two siblings whose grandparents came from India in the late 1960s would identify themselves in similar ways. This is because there are different meanings attached to a different set of personal, social and cultural experiences. This illustrates the complex and fluid nature of racialised identity development.

Ownership of multi-racial identities

The cases of transracial adoptees, children of mixed (interracial) parentage, and the settled immigrant children all share in a common theme, namely that they are bogged down by a restrictive essentialised view of racial identity. In particular, it is a view that their very being and development of multi-racial identities, as opposed to an adherence to a singular Black racial identity, is problematic. It is argued that because they have been brought up by white parents or parents who have moved away from politicised notions of Blackness, this is a problem because the child will suffer from a lack of skills to protect themselves from racism, suffer from identity confusion and so fail to develop a healthy black identity (Katz, 1996: 198–9).

This is a seriously outdated position, because the development of multi-racial identities that are neither black nor white, but instead contain elements of both, are not acknowledged.

Indeed, the processes that occur in the development of such flexible identities, many of which are actually positive and healthy, are not being granted rights of ownership and recognition. As Katz notes:

> All this points to a simple view of black identity which is possessed by all black children, no matter what their background, which needs to be nurtured by an identity worker. Any definitions by the children of themselves which contradict the identity worker's view are seen as a result either of identity confusion or of immaturity
>
> (Katz, 1996: 194)

The existence of such a mixed identity, or what Katz calls a 'brown identity' (Katz, 1996: 193) over a singular essentialised Black identity is important, as is the fact that such multi-racial identities bring with them a different set of flexible and diverse meanings for the owner.

New racialised spaces

Diverse identities, or what can be called *hybrid identities*, are 'positioned as an antidote to essentialism' and for this reason have some importance: 'Hybridity is a further acknowledgement of the complex multi-faceted nature of human identity, and particularly of the fact that different identities are uniquely melded together within individual biographies' (Downing and Husband, 2005: 18). The creation of such multi-layered, flexible, dynamic and diverse identities can be viewed as complex ways of being, as well as taking into account the equally complex routes of construction borne out of racialising processes.

The existence of healthy hybrid identities is a matter of fact, and a fact that should be catered for. That is not to say, however, that the course of its development and its projection in some contexts is problem free. It brings its own set of dilemmas and struggles. As Anwar says ' . . . young Asians are part of both worlds, which sometimes leads to tensions and conflict within Asian families' (Anwar, 1998: 148).

However, the historical development of the term *hybrid* and the negative connotations in which it is bound, is here viewed as problematic: 'In colonial discourse, hybridity is a term of abuse for those who are products of miscegenation, mixed-breeds. It is imbued in nineteenth-century eugenicist and scientific-racist thought' (Young 1995, in Meredith, 1998: 1). Thus, although *hybridity* can be viewed as an advance on essentialist racialising of identity, the problem which this itself creates should be addressed. It is suggested, therefore, that usage of hybrid identity theorisation should go beyond its traditional scientifically racist and problematising thinking. This is because such a traditional view of a hybrid racial identity may bring with it recognition of a new racial identity that is neither wholly black nor white. However, there is also the danger of still being tied to notions of an essentialised racial space located between black and white – it therefore creates a new essentialised racial category; *in between space*, where some of the conflicting parts of two polarised opposites attempt to join together. For example, often in this place, hyphenated labels, such as *Black-British* are used. In doing so, the complex biography behind that multi-racial identity is still being hidden. Indeed, as Bolatagici (2004) rightly notes, the hyphen 'simplifies and reduces the individual to the sum of their parts and the hyphen stands to represent a juncture; a chasm that cannot be united' (Bolatagici, 2004: 75).

Rather, this updated theorisation of hybrid identities and their existence in what Bhabha called a 'third space' (2004) to which transracial adoptees, children of mixed (interracial) parentage and the settled immigrant children belong to, should be seen as valid spaces in which particular types of non-essentialised multi-racial identities exist. Such 'third spaces' act as 'a site of translation and negotiation' (Bolatagici, 2004: 78). In doing so, it 'eludes the politics of polarity' (Bhabha, 1991, in Bolatagici, 2004: 75), and then brings with it the ability to move away from a restrictive understanding and defining of multi-racial identities as something that is 'not as half of two things, but a whole 'new' entity that is not reducible to its components' (Bolatagici, 2004: 78).

The wider black minority ethnic and mixed-race populations

Adopting this view of racial identity is also of significance for what is seen as the wider black minority ethnic and mixed-race community. This is especially so for those residing in racially diverse, yet discriminatory societies such as the UK. By viewing racial identity as something that is actively socially constructed and negotiated on an ongoing basis, depending on symbols, meanings and language, not only offers a more accurate reflection of reality, but also lays the first important foundations for empowerment, that of existence recognition. This is the right to name oneself, and to have this selection recognised as valid.

It is important to note that this would not necessarily act as a hindrance to the overall struggle of the black minority ethnic community as a whole with respect to anti-oppressive practices. This is because access to a unified black label, which in its politicised sense provides one way of fighting racism, and which as highlighted in other chapters is still valid and important, remains available if and when one chooses. Indeed, following the point being made here, it is one of a variety of available racialised identities that can be utilised and mobilised.

In offering a fairer representation of the diversity of the black minority ethnic and mixed-race community, the politics of skin shade is also important. As highlighted in other chapters, this also plays a key role in the ways in which individuals are not only identified, but also the ways in which as a racialised sub-group they experience privilege or disadvantage. Calling attention to the ways in which these politics are actually created, or socially constructed, allows their discriminatory nature to be questioned, challenged, resisted and re-negotiated on a more level playing field. It also allows whiteness, and those akin to whiteness, to be dislodged from its position of desire, power and authority.

This also brings with it the ability for challenging racialised ideas about whiteness as the norm and its centrality as a position of power, in that it represents humanity and civilisation, as well as being a barometer against which everything else, such as other racialised groups, are measured, but can never quite match. An intentional by-product of this would be a questioning of the racialisation of national identity, this being the idea that to be truly British one must be white. This would bring a greater level of access to British identity by those who, in many ways, consider themselves to be British, but have largely been denied full access.

Utilising this view of racial identity would also mean that a more accurate body of child, family and community support services can be delivered to members of the black minority ethnic community, who, as highlighted in other chapters, too often experience discrimination and marginalisation as service users. This is because a service package can be constructed on a more informed basis. It would be tailored to the specific requirements of the service user and thus remove racially inaccurate, offensive and stereotypical ideas. Instead, it would be better informed by a consideration of all the user's needs, including those of welfare, financial and health, as well as being able to facilitate their rights to the development of a healthy and positive racial identity. On a wider scale, if the development of such services was made more publicly accountable, it could highlight more clearly when cases of racial discrimination do occur.

Allowing a consideration of ethnicity

Consideration of these arguments about the social construction of racial identity and the development of multi-racial identities also brings with it the benefit of allowing a progressive and meaningful discussion of ethnicity to enter the debate. A basic analytical distinction between *race* and *ethnicity* is offered by Van den Berghe (1978, in Song, 2003: 10), who notes that 'race is socially defined but on the basis of physical criteria' and in comparison, ethnicity is 'socially defined on the basis of cultural criteria'.

As briefly noted in the introduction, the focus of this book remained on how markers drawn on the basis of race, as in 'physical markers such as skin pigmentation, hair texture, facial features' (Pilkington, 2003: 11), informed identity development. Although ethnic indicators, such as 'language, religion and shared customs' (Pilkington, 2003: 11), were also seen as important to how one constructed a sense of self, notions of race, because of their obvious and often ever-present visible presence for the groups discussed, were considered as the overriding factors. This has been noted by Song (2003: 6) who, in providing a clear illustration of this, stated:

> Racial categorizations of people can sometimes, though not always, 'trump' or override ethnic designations. That is, people's ethnic identities may be subsumed within broader racial identities which are imposed by others. For instance, West Indian immigrants in the USA may find themselves labeled Black, first and foremost because the White majority may not recognise their ethnic identities as Jamaicans or Trinidadians, but rather see them in racial terms, as Black people. While many Black Jamaicans,

Trinidadians, and Haitians think of themselves in these specific ethno-national terms, they can also be highly aware of being seen as Black in many social contexts in the USA.

Because lay society as a whole, and many support services, still largely refer to matters in terms of race, as opposed to ethnicity, it was necessary in this book to update and clarify the race and racial identity debate before a valid discussion of ethnicity could be generated. This indicates how race could be viewed as one element in how ethnicity is defined. It also highlights how the two terms are not mutually exclusive. This is because their very flexibility means that their boundaries overlap and blur. Indeed, policy research indicates this in reference to minority ethnic groups being 'differentiated based on a combination of categories including 'race', skin colour, national and regional origins, and language' (Office for National Statistics, 2003).

This incorporation of race has also been hinted at by Bulmer who describes it as:

. . . a collectivity within society having real or putative common ancestry, memories of a shared past, and a cultural focus on one or more symbolic elements which define the group's identity, such as kinship, religion, language, shared territory, nationality or physical appearance. Members of an ethnic group are conscious of belonging to that group.

(Bulmer, 1996: 54)

Paying particular attention to the shared belief element of this understanding helps to avoid biological determinism found in references to a racial identity. In addition, Cohen (1978, in Bolaffi et al., 2003: 95) argues that belonging to an ethnic group is no longer defined solely in religious and cultural terms, but is now also structured around political and economic factors. This means that ethnicity is ever more flexible, situational and in a constant state of negotiation. For example, Wallman evidenced this flexibility when he looked at the way that ethnic boundaries in London are drawn differently depending on their given contexts:

. . . two sets of people with common cultural origins placed in similar minority positions [will not] necessarily use the same elements of their traditional culture to mark themselves off from non-member 'others'. What they do use will depend on the resources they have, on what they hope to achieve (whether consciously or not) and on the range of options available to them at the time.

(Wallman, 1979: 5–6, in Mason, 2000: 94)

Within a sociological and even lay consideration of identity, this updated understanding of race and its relationship with ethnicity, rooted in an acknowledgement of both their largely socially constructed nature,[3] brings with it an opportunity for members of the wider black

---

[3]See Song (2003) for an insightful examination into how individuals are able to exercise ethnic options and socially construct for themselves ethnic identities, albeit within a framework of choices and constraints.

minority ethnic and mixed-race population to further identity themselves more accurately. However, in order for this to be truly progressive, the term *ethnicity* needs to incorporate a serious consideration of race, and move away from the tendency for it to be used as a replacement term or as a euphemism for race, especially by those who seek to distance themselves from any allegations of crude racism when making points that are hostile to minority groups (Mason, 2000).

Conclusion

This book has shown the ways in which consideration of matters relating to child, family and community support need to be revisited as a matter of urgency. In focusing on child and family placement services, with particular reference to the case of the transracial adoption of black minority ethnic and mixed-race children, it is argued that this needs to be done using an updated sociological analysis of the racial identity development process. This is based on using a social constructionist perspective over an essentialist one. The argument presented here is that this would assist a better and more accurately informed thinking of how racial identity is flexible, diverse and possesses a multiple status. To add weight to the validity of this claim, the cases of children of mixed (interracial) parentage and settled immigrant children have also been considered. It has been argued that approaching the issue in this way would progressively lead to an improvement in the child, family and community support services which seek to assist some of the most vulnerable and marginalised members of society, namely black minority ethnic and mixed-race children. Additionally, it would also allow the space for them to develop healthy, positive racially diverse identities.

Facilitating identity rights

Child, family and community support services, particularly in the area of race and adoption, have been dominated by those whose arguments are based on politicised ideas of an essential black identity. The problem with this approach is that the complexity of racialised identities, in terms of their flexible and diverse nature are not being sufficiently taken into account. This means that there is a lack of serious consideration of the reality of how and why black minority ethnic and mixed-race children within the public care system actually:

* Have a diverse background, in terms of race, ethnicity, religion and culture.
* Need space to identify themselves in their own ways and on their own terms.

The type of children discussed here are able to work within a framework of choices and constraints, and embark on a series of negotiation processes to develop, sooner or later, a racial identity that reflects their experiences and is illustrative of how they most comfortably identify themselves. In this sense they follow a self-acceptance process as outlined by Kich (1992, in Okitikpi, 2005: 73). This states that such individuals work through three key stages, after which they emerge with complete self-acceptance:

1. Initial awareness of being different. Also awareness of dissonance between self-perceptions and other people's perceptions.

2. The individual's wish to be accepted by others.
3. Gradual self-acceptance as a multi-racial person.

This acceptance process certainly fits in with the negotiation processes outlined in the black/white continuum presented in this book.

Utilising symbolic interactionism to understand racial identity development

In response to the lack of consideration given to the socially constructed nature of racial identity this book has provided an indication of the developmental stages of a fixed racial identity. It has done so by examining the ways in which a group of adults who had been transracially adopted as children, had negotiated a racial identity for themselves with which they felt comfortable and understood as most accurately representing who they were. Unlike existing studies, there has not been an assumption that a Black racial identity is the natural one, to be obtained at any cost. Hence, the study on which this book is based did not attempt to measure the supposed successful ownership of this Black identity. Rather, this book has examined the flexible status of racial identity development and in doing so it has looked at how the interviewed adoptees constructed for themselves a multi-racial identity, and one that was neither wholly white nor wholly black. To do this, the social constructionist perspective has been used, which involved a theorisation of racial identity based on the works of Symbolic Interactionist theorists Mead (1995) Blumer (1969) and Goffman (1982). This views race labels, such as black and white, as bringing with them a series of meanings and expectations, which are socially constructed in a process involving ongoing interaction between:

- The individual.
- The individual's social contact with other individuals.
- How the individual thinks others perceive them.
- The individual's social environment.

In deconstructing, evaluating and updating existing ideas about racial identity and, in particular, the notion of an essential black identity, and re-considering the debate in this way, a significant claim has been made. This relates to how some individuals move beyond definitions of appearance and colour, to identify themselves in flexible, diverse and mixed ways. In doing so, they are able to comfortably develop and positively settle on a racialised identity and culture of their own that they feel is a more accurate representation of who they are.

This was certainly illustrated by the racial biographies and narratives of the adoptees in this book. Here, it was argued that all the adoptees had a different set of experiences, not only of their transracial adoption experience but also due to:

- Variances in their *racial* biographies, for example, whether they were of mixed-race, or the offspring of immigrants.

- Variances in their *adoptive* biographies, for example, experiences in the adoptive home, contact with the birth family, experience of the birth heritage.
- Variances in their *social* biographies, for example, gender, class, age, religion, geographical location, and so on.

Therefore, each had a varied racial identity. However, all of them had gone through a similar process of having to negotiate racialised similarities and differences in order to settle on a racial identity that they felt comfortable with and which best represented how they saw themselves. The racial identity that emerged was one that was based on a multi-layered *hybrid* identity, created in a 'third space' away from racial polarity (Bhabha, 1991, in Bolatagici, 2004: 75). This constituted a new racial category, that of the multi-racial identity.

The possession of what is here categorised as a multi-racial identity, is significant. The sample of adoptees clearly felt that their own adoption circumstances and life experiences were deemed to be *transracial*. This was so because arguments about a polarised racially divided society were commonly thrown at the adoptee. In this sense, although the adoptees saw their own experiences as *transracial* they were uneasy with the term. This was because the term brings with it the suggestion of a permanent movement from one race to another. It was felt that the term was therefore not only inaccurate, but also often applied in a negative and offensive context. It was also restrictive in the degree to which each transracial adoptee is able to project their own multi-racial identity. Rather, the adoptees had emphasised their preference for a term that more accurately described the flexible, complex, diverse, and multi-layered nature of their racial identity.

Re-visiting terms of reference
In terms of race and family placement, this book questions the continuing use of the term *transracial* to describe the racial identity of individuals involved in these types of adoptions. Instead, a call is made for an alternative term. This new term would have to recognise the multiplicity of racial heritages, and their role in creating a multi-racial identity. It is also important that the term identifies the reality of the growing presence of the people to whom it refers, and the acceptance of them as a distinct racial group in their own right. From a sociological and social work perspective, the replacement term should be one that does not further marginalise this population. It also should be a term that is accurate, and yet readily useable by professionals and the wider society.

In seeking a replacement term, the best source to consult is the current population of transracial adoptees. As such, the adoptees, whose narratives form the basis of this book, suggested that the replacement term should incorporate the words '*mixed*' or '*multiple*', as to accurately describe the diverse and numerous stages of their racial identity development process. They also demonstrated their agreement with the decision to use the term *heritage* throughout the study to describe the adoptees' family, culture and racial group. Taking this into account, the suggested and preferable alternative term presented here, which better describes the adoptees, their racial identity development and the nature of their adoption, is that of 'mixed heritage'.

This replacement term emphasises the move away from restrictive essentialist ideas about race and blackness. It also moves beyond the problem of developing a 'tripartite system' within a black/white paradigm, that the term 'mixed-race' may produce (Ifekwunigwe, 2000: 180). There are also several other distinct advantages in utilising the term, not only with respect to child and family placement services, but also more generally for community work and effective service delivery, i.e. youth justice, welfare, housing, education and employment. Firstly, use of the replacement term mixed heritage would allow for the recognition of the complexity of the race and identity issue. Secondly, it would mean an accurate description of the experiences for a labelled group of people, who do not identify themselves in singular racial ways. Thirdly, the replacement term would enable policy makers and practitioners to make more accurately informed decisions in their service delivery. In the case of transracial adoption this would mean black minority ethnic and mixed-race children could be placed in a social context where there is more of a representative familial and social match, which would then offer the space, in terms of information, experience and support, for a more accurately fitting mixed racial identity to be developed. However, this is not without its limitations, in that these identities would still have to be constructed in what is, in the main, a racially discriminatory society. Rather, it offers a step forward for accurate matching in child and family placements, as well as facilitating identity rights.

Questioning essentialised notions of a Black racial identity

As mentioned in Chapter 5, the existing body of literature on race, identity and the family is dominated by essentialist ideas. This is the view that for those who are of black minority ethnic or mixed-race origin, there is a set of distinct universal 'black characteristics', unique to all black people and which do not alter across time. The argument is that these characteristics must be satisfied via membership and active participation if the individual is to develop a healthy racial identity (Ballis-Lal, 1999: 56).

The arguments presented in this book disagree with the essentialist theorisation of racial identity. That is not to say, however, that racism in contemporary society does not exist and that there is no benefit in being a member of a collective as a means of empowering oneself and being better placed to overcome racial discrimination. But the problem here is that the dominance of essentialist thinking about binary blackness and whiteness does not cater for:

- The presence of new racisms, which are not just based on crude notions of race or colour.
- The mixed population who do not see themselves as either black or white.

As a mixed population, whether it be by birth, such as being of mixed parentage, or through social circumstances, as in being adopted or the offspring of immigrants, they do not entirely support Cross's 'Nigrescence Model' (1971), nor Park (1928), nor Stonequists's (1937) ideas about the supposed identity problems faced by the 'Marginal Man' (Park, 1928). They would be condemned to living between 'two diverse cultural groups' and hence develop 'an unstable character' (Park, 1928: 881).

The case of adoption

The literature on race and adoption in particular is divided between two conflicting camps. Yet both camps focus on the attainment of a healthy black identity, as opposed to a healthy racial identity per se. This illustrates the dominance of essentialist thinking. On the one side there are those who support mixed heritage adoption, and maintain that white parents can teach black minority ethnic and mixed-race children about black issues and help them to develop a healthy black identity. In addition, they argue that because the most important thing is that children in care are provided with a secure and loving permanent home as soon as possible, mixed heritage adoption should not only be allowed, but actively pursued as opposed to them having to wait in care for long periods of time. They also argue that as well as meeting this need, racially sensitive white parents who have black friends or who live in a black or mixed neighbourhood, can also teach the black child about their birth heritage, provide them with experience of their black culture and help them to cope with racism (Bagley and Young, 1979; Bagley, 1993). For example, Simon and Alstein (2000), argued that mixed heritage adoptees have accurate racial self-definition and have no preference for white characteristics or any negative reactions to possessing a black identity.

This was the case for some of the adoptees in the study reported here. However, although some adoptees acknowledged their mixed-racial identity, others showed a preference for stereotypical white characteristics. Some adoptees even reported that at times they had felt negative towards the idea of a black identity, and even towards black people. Similarly, the adoptees highlighted how, although they were grateful to their adoptive parents for having raised and cared for them, they had nevertheless felt some degree of anger and loss at having missed out on what they saw as their black minority ethnic birth culture. This was largely due to the lack of information and experience of their birth heritage given to them by their adoptive parents whilst growing up.

On the other side of the race and adoption debate, there are those who argue that mixed heritage adoption of this type only occurs due to the decrease in available white babies for those white couples who are seeking to adopt (Gill and Jackson, 1983: 2), and it therefore puts the needs and wants of the adopters before the needs of the child. It is also seen as another form of slavery, in that the black community are still seen as serving the white community (Abdullah, 1996: 259). Critics of transracial adoption go on to argue that this is also a problem because the needs of the black child to know about, and experience their black birth heritage, is being denied, and which has serious consequences for their identity development in terms of self-awareness and self-esteem. In this sense, it is argued by critics that only black parents can teach black children about issues related to the development of a healthy and positive black identity.

In these debates, critics make no distinction between those adoptees born to two black parents from those born to one black parent and one white parent. Rather, these mixed-race children are referred to and treated as if they were born to two black parents. This is because critics of mixed heritage adoption argue that mixed-race people are treated as black by the white majority and will therefore face the same discrimination. Therefore, these mixed-race adoptees will suffer from misidentification and serious identity difficulties if they do not wholly identify with the black part of their birth heritage (Small, 1986).

The same arguments are also used in cases where mixed heritage adoption is also intercountry. Indeed, the consequences are deemed to be even worse, because the intercountry adoptee not only has to adjust to a new culture, but in addition they are more likely to face discrimination, marginalisation and identity conflict as a result of having to adjust to life in a new country (Bagley, Young and Scully, 1992).

A sociological consideration

In the case of mixed heritage adoption, the essentialist based arguments that have dominated adoption practice have been challenged. In its place, a sociological analysis in the form of a social constructionist perspective, which involved the use of the Symbolic Interactionist theorisation of identity development, has been developed. This argues that the construction, meanings and usage of race concepts such as black and white, have been based on ideas that have been developed and maintained in social human interaction through dialectical and behavioural processes. Here, black and white are held as distinct polar opposites, where the individual either belongs to one category or the other. Other individuals who actively choose to move away from such essentialist notions, such as mixed heritage adoptees, mixed-race children or the offspring of immigrants, are mislabelled, marginalised and assumed to have racial identity problems. This book contests the idea that race is a fixed and essential category, and therefore questions many of the arguments and assumptions used by those who base their arguments on outdated, politicised and essentialist based notions of identity formation.

Those opposing mixed heritage adoption have tended to rely heavily on the idea of a fixed and essential black identity that must be lived in order to develop a healthy identity, that is having good levels of self-awareness and self-esteem. These individuals have also highlighted the importance of a lived black experience in order to feel a sense of belonging with the black community, and thereby survive living in a racist society (Maximé, 1986; Small, 1991). This assumption of a total adherence to a black identity is also seen to be relevant to those who are of mixed-race (Small, 1986).

However, the adoptees in the study discussed here, who were mixed-race by birth, did not see themselves as just black in the sense that critics argue. Rather they saw themselves as being of mixed biological origin, and mixed in terms of their socially constructed racial identity, which although at times was black, and at other times was white, they largely tended to situate themselves somewhere in between. Such a mixed racial identity was viewed as positive. The same was also felt by the adoptees born to two black minority ethnic parents, who indicated that in terms of their socially constructed racial identity, they had felt both black and white. This was not only because of the mixed heritage aspects of their adoption, but also because of the influence of other variables, such as physical features, birth heritage, experiences of different forms of racism, religion and other cultural factors.

This challenges the idea that such individuals need to develop a full black identity in order to have a positive and healthy sense of self. It also disputes the idea of a fixed and essential black identity. This is because the adoptees' negotiation of a racial identity highlights that identities are open to interpretation and modification. However, in saying this, the adoptees did report a constant feeling of difference and isolation due to their experience of the adoption process. This sometimes led to them feeling as if they did not wholly belong with the black people of their birth community, with whom they shared some physical similarities, but not social and cultural experiences, or with the white people of their adoptive community, with whom they shared social and cultural experiences, but not physical similarities. The adoptees' felt that despite their adoptive parents' efforts, overall the strategies for reducing negative perceptions of difference was inadequate. However, it should be noted that not all perceptions of difference were negative. This is because, at times, it made adoptees the focus of special attention, which brought its own set of benefits. Neither did the perceived differences seriously damage the adoptees' sense of belonging. This is because, like the flexible nature of their racial identity, the adoptees felt that they were able to make active choices when settling on their sense of place, which they were able to change, modify and renegotiate as and when they desired.

Critics also argue that black minority ethnic and mixed-race children who are adopted by white families suffer from low self-esteem and poor identity development. Indeed, some of the adoptees in this study reported having experienced some self-esteem difficulties, which were tied to them having felt different to others in their immediate white social world, being misidentified, or to them having to constantly answer the racialised questions or correct the racialised stereotypes of others. However, most of the adoptees reported good self-esteem levels. Similarly, although some of the adoptees searched for their birth heritage in order to develop their sense of identity and deal with their negative perceptions about the adoption and the racialised differences between them and their adoptive parents, they did not view themselves as having suffered from poor identity development. Rather, the adoptees reported having a positive sense of self and in particular a sound multi-racial identity due to their achievements and their ability to assert their own sense of pride as a mixed heritage adoptee.

The study findings reported here indicate that although some black minority ethnic or mixed-race adoptees experienced difficulties as a result of the racialised differences due to the mixed heritage aspects of their adoption, and although they had a different racial identity development, they were able to emerge with positive self-perceptions and a racial identity that they felt comfortable with.

Accurate service delivery

Within social welfare and support services, there has been an overwhelming and unhealthy tendency to view social order, relationships and self-concept in rather narrow terms. This has had a particularly negative impact on those sections of society that already experience exclusion and marginalisation, such as members of the black minority ethnic communities. For them, services are based on crude essentialised and discriminatory ideas about perceptions of self, despite sound evidence and valid arguments being presented about the development of healthy, positive and accurately representative racial identities. The context in which these multi-racial identities are created is also ignored, along with the calls made for access to space and recognition rights.

Child and family placement services

In matters relating to race and adoption, consideration needs to take account of the racially mixed aspects of a child's biological, social and cultural background. The closer the match the better, but meeting the child's welfare needs sooner rather than later is also important. In essence, an exact racial match is not vital, but it should be as close as possible and be able to seriously cater for the child's mixed racial biography. The match should also seek to cater for other considerations, such as the special needs of the child, or whether they have come from an abusive home.

The findings of this study support this view. In talking about experiences in the adoptive home, the adoptees' narratives revealed that they were grateful to their adoptive parents for having provided them with a secure and loving home sooner rather than later in their lives, or perhaps even not at all. To different degrees, however, they also felt that there would have been particular benefits if they had been raised by an adoptive family where there was a closer racial match. Such benefits were thought to include a greater understanding of the racism experienced by them, knowledge, contact and experience of their birth heritage at a much earlier age, and the comfort of a greater sense of sameness by being around people who looked like them. In this vein, some adoptees had sought to explore their birth heritage, largely as an attempt to feel more complete with their racial identity and sense of self.

However, an important theme that emerged from this study was that although adoptees had experienced some difficulties as a result of the mixed heritage aspects of the adoption, most of them had not begrudged being adopted in the way that they were, nor considered it to have seriously damaged their racial identity development. The overriding message that emerged from the narratives was that the adoptees had wanted to be recognised and accepted in their own right as mixed heritage adoptees. They did not have a singular essential black or white identity, but a multi-racial identity which incorporated both their birth and adoptive heritages. This, they insisted was *their* biography.

In the light of the arguments presented in this book, the following recommendations offer realistic and readily useable policies for the development of best practice in adoption. They are applicable at both central and regional levels, and with some appropriate modifications certainly have international relevance. They are underpinned by a desire to see an updated re-think of the racial identity development process to enter the arena of debate, namely the social construction of a multi-racial identity that is flexible, diverse and in a constant state of negotiation. Debates therefore need to include references to its existence, as opposed to prioritising decisions based on a belief that conformity to a singular essentialised black racial identity must be satisfied. It is recognised that some of these recommendations are in the current context difficult to consider, let alone implement. However, highlighting and calling for them to be considered is one small, yet significant step towards:

- Providing those involved in mixed heritage adoption, with the appropriate support in order to limit the difficulties they face.
- Encouraging a more sophisticated level of thinking about racial identity development.
- Helping to empower a growing section of the population by providing a means through which they can name their multi-racial identity.

The recommendations for policy changes are as follows:

Adoption legislation

Current legislation on child placement has two key positive points. First is the way in which it calls for 'due consideration' to be given to 'the child's religious persuasion, racial origin and cultural and linguistic background' (*Children Act 1989*, section 22). Second is the recognition for welfare needs to be catered for (DoH, 1998, sections 12–14). These two points together can help the development of a healthy sense of self. This is because on one level a safe space is being provided where the child's welfare needs can be met, whilst on another level, information and experience of some sort is being provided for the adoptee on an important part of their pre-adoptive heritage. However, the current legislation needs to be updated to make one significant change. The 'fresh start' view of adoption, as introduced by the *Adoption of Children Act 1950* and actively supported by the Acts which later followed, should be modified or removed altogether. Doing so would allow adoptees to feel more comfortable in being able to draw upon their pre-adoptive heritage and to use their biographical roots for development of self, in an open and transparent way that is not compounded by incomplete information.

National guidelines

Although national guidelines on adoption offer some useful suggestions and direction, there should be a closer connectivity between central policy recommendations and regional practice. On the part of central office, recommendations need to sufficiently take into account the local conditions such as geography, population and politics, within which the regional agencies work. One way of doing this would be to ensure that the guidelines offered at national level are firm enough to put in place a universal and workable set of priorities, yet be flexible enough to provide room at a regional level for any necessary local variances and conditions to be catered for.

Balancing needs

The significance of race and the discriminatory boundaries it creates in contemporary society is something that is still prevalent today. It is therefore an important factor to consider. However, placement needs to move beyond a crude colour decision that is based on outdated essentialised ideas about the polarised colouring of society. Instead, it should acknowledge that although a close match is preferred, meeting the child's welfare needs as soon as possible is also important. What should be pursued then is a placement that is able to seriously cater for the child's mixed racial biography, as well being able to serve the child's welfare needs, whether these are special needs, mental health issues or having come from an abusive home.

Matching regulations

There should be a consistent clarification of matching regulations, in particular the need to agree on an interpretation and the application of guidelines and any situations which may be the exception (Parker, 1999: 115). Agreement should be reached on what constitutes multi-racial matching, including social and cultural factors such as religious and ethnic background. One suggestion could be the formulation of a priority list or 'close matching' itinerary (Parker, 1999: 115), which would consider both racial biography and welfare needs.

Recruitment campaigns

Further recruitment campaigns should be set up in order to provide a pool of readily available adopters from a variety of multi-racial backgrounds. Such campaigns should be undertaken with a long-term view and a commitment to their implementation and maintenance (Prevatt Goldstein and Spencer, 2000). Resources and financial support needs to be provided by central government to initiate these campaigns, both on a national and regional level. Consideration should also be given to the informal child care methods found within other communities which have proven to be a success, as in the informal fostering systems found amongst African communities.

Support system

A specifically tailored system of support should be established which offers both mixed heritage adopters and adoptees help and advice in dealing with the types of difficulties experienced by the adoptees in this study. One way of doing this would be through the establishment of a *buddy system* for both adopters and adoptees in similar situations, and who could act as a regular point of contact and be supportive of one another. In addition, their adoption history 'needs to be kept in trust for them' (Parker, 1999: 108), and so a more organised system of data holding and post-adoption support should also be provided for those adoptees who may later decide to search for information about their birth heritage. The use of the adopted child's life-story work and information or contact through letters are ways of pursuing this policy.

Roots and routes

It should be acknowledged that the birth heritage and the adopted heritage should not be seen as two distinct and separate parts of the adoptee. Neither should adoption be seen as *a new start* per se. Placement should be considered as a continuation of the child's biography. It is important to acknowledge that although every child has the right to the knowledge and experience of their birth heritage, they also, however, have the right to the knowledge and experience of the heritage in which they are raised, and further, to have access to a space in which they can comfortably negotiate themselves a racial identity that they are comfortable with. This basic identity right, that of access to both roots and routes should be accepted, respected and supported.

A broader application for child, family and community support services

These recommendations also have relevance for child, family and community support services whose remit goes beyond adoption. Here, services in health, welfare, housing, education, employment and justice would benefit from this updated re-conceptualisation of the racial identity development process and acknowledgement of multi-racial identities over singular essentialised ones. This is particularly true of the recommendation calling for a more informed balancing of needs. In addition to recognising this multi-racial status, support services should also have a genuine desire for progressive change in order to better the lives of the individuals which it serves. This is vital for the empowerment and successful transition of those who are marginalised and excluded from the mainstream of society.

Admittedly, to some degree, this is a fairly romantic idea. And, if one stops to critically reflect upon its existence and achievement, it is possible to legitimately question whether such a state can ever be fully achieved. However, it is argued in this book that it *is* a realistic goal that must be actively pursued if there is to be any meaningful change for a growing section of the population. In this sense, its pursuit would benefit from the incorporation of the formulation and delivery of service packages that are tailored for specific personal and social needs. These should consider individual emotional, psychological and welfare requirements, as well as regional variances. It should carefully consider the role played, at different times in different ways and to different degrees, by variables such as physical features, gender, age, immediate family, friends, social networks, religion, history and geographical location, in the construction of racial identity. Doing so would allow the social constructionist consideration around race and identity to move beyond academia, and to be able to enter the social work arena, both on policy and practice level.

On a cautionary note, though, it is important to highlight the way in which support for consideration of multi-racial identities and the questioning of essentialised racial categories are no longer misused by those who see it as a way of being able to mask the failure of a welfare system to respond to the discrimination and marginalisation of the black minority ethnic population. In this sense, the conclusions reached in this book recognise the value of black minority ethnic communities as an important resource of social capital for black minority ethnic people (Mirza and Reay, 2000; Wright et al., 2005). Episodes of my own personal biography are a testimony to this. The book also recognises the hard work of some black minority ethnic social workers who have themselves endured much discrimination and struggled to gain access to positions of power and influence, where they are able to correct discriminatory practices. Support is therefore given to the continued need to 'recruit welfare workers in a proportion that reflects the ethnic make-up of the location in which they work' (Frost and Stein, 1989: 137). Rather, the book has argued that in order to move forward, an updated consideration of the racial identity process and the existence of a diverse multi-racial category should now be acknowledged and catered for.

Appendix 1: Data collection

A truly representative sample is very difficult to produce because of the diversity of the backgrounds, experiences and views of the researched population. Although the adoptees' experiences would in many ways be comparable to the research reported here, it could not produce a comparative study because it did not focus on comparing the lives, experiences and identities of a sample of identical transracial adoptees. This has already been well covered in the literature (Bagley, 1993; Bagley and Young, 1979; McRoy and Zurcher, 1983; Johnson, Shireman and Watson, 1983). Rather, this study wanted to take a randomly selected small sample of individuals who had been transracially adopted, and then seek to understand how their social experiences had informed their racial identity development. Therefore, in the process of selecting a sample, the first question asked was: *Were you transracially adopted?* as opposed to: *Were you transracially adopted, and if so, have your experiences been negative or positive?*

An acknowledgment was made of the importance and value of interviewing children and in doing so there was support for the work of those who have provided a strong and convincing case for the necessity of involving children in research that affects them. The work of Thomas, Beckford, Lowe and Murch (1999), and Christensen and James (2000), provides guidelines on how to best do this. However, Roberts (2000), who also recognises the importance of researching children and child participation in research, highlights the ethical issues of doing so. Roberts argues that some 'young children (and indeed many adults) may not always have the judgement to know what the consequences will be of exposing their feelings ... children participating in research ... may (therefore) well suffer distress' (Roberts, 2000: 228). Taking into consideration these arguments and the nature of the research reported here, that is, to gain a deeper insight of the adoptees' whole life, a decision was made not to interview children. This is because it was felt that the topic was highly emotional and likely to have a strong impact on children, many of whom who would have already faced disruption and troubled backgrounds.

It was also recognised that it might be difficult to gain access to a sample of transracially adopted adults who would be willing to talk about their experiences at some length and in some depth. Apart from the usual word of mouth approach, other attempts at meeting adoptees included making contact with organisations with interests in this area and placing advertisements in various journals and magazines. A combination of these approaches provided the subjects of this study. A total of about 40 hours, representing over 600 pages of transcript, of in-depth information covering the lives of six transracial adoptees was recorded.

The research study sought to understand a variety of transracial adoption experiences, and to use these experiences to critically assess existing literature and policy. This meant that the sample was not representative in that adoptees were not selected on the basis of whether their experiences had been positive or negative. The adoptees were all transracially adopted. In particular they were of black minority ethnic or mixed-race background by birth and were adopted by white families, and this represents the vast majority of transracial adoptions.

Appendix 2: The sample profile

The following six adoptees made up the final sample. Pseudonyms have been used to protect their identities.

Alison Ridley, at the time of interviewing, was a 40-year-old female living in Worcester, England. She had been born to a white European mother from Ireland and a black African Caribbean father, who was living in London. Having received no support from her parents and the baby's birth father after Alison's birth, her birth mother reluctantly abandoned her on a train, a decision she immediately regretted. However, Alison's birth mother was unable to get her daughter back because the abandonment had meant that she had committed a criminal offence. Alison then went into foster care and spent nine months with a family. A month later the foster mother fell pregnant so Alison went back into foster care. It was then, at the age of 16 months, that her adoptive parents fostered her. At 18 months, Alison was adopted by her foster parents. In Alison's adoptive family, there were already three boys, who were all older than Alison and the biological children of her adoptive parents. The adoptive family were all white European and lived in a white, middle-class village in England. Whilst growing up, Alison received no cultural input of her birth heritage. Alison contacted members of her birth family when she was in her mid-twenties. Overall, Alison's experiences in her adoptive family were positive.

Katherine Hee Yun Muller was female, 26 years old and living in Sheffield, England. She preferred to be called Hee Yun (part of her birth name which was incorporated into her adoptive name by her adoptive parents). Hee Yun was born to a Korean mother. The racial background of her birth father was unknown, although Hee Yun strongly suspected that he was also Korean. Hee Yun was placed in an orphanage soon after her birth, and then put up for an intercountry adoption, where, at the age of three, she was adopted by a German family. The adoptive family were white European and lived in a predominantly white area of Germany. Although there were some Turkish families living in the area, there were no other Koreans. Hee Yun's adoptive family already had a biological son who was older than her. Hee Yun wanted to search for her birth mother in her youth, but had been seriously restricted by both the poor record-keeping of the orphanage and Korea's history regarding the stigmatisation of single mothers. Hee Yun received no cultural input of her birth heritage whilst growing up in her adoptive family. Hee Yun's experiences in her adoptive family was largely positive, although she suffered some serious problems during her teenage years, which was related to her having been an intercountry adoptee and having no access to information about her birth family.

Barbara Julie Shepherd, who preferred to be called by her middle name (part of her birth name), was female, 43 years old and living in Bristol, England. Julie had been born to a black African Caribbean mother, who may herself have been mixed-race, and a white European father. Her birth mother was unable to care for her and privately placed her for temporary foster care with a white European couple when Julie was about two years old. This later changed to a full adoption. Julie had been an only child in her adoptive family, and grew up in a predominantly white village in England. Julie had no interest in her birth family and received no cultural input of her birth heritage whist growing up. Overall, Julie had felt that she had a positive experience in her adoptive family.

Natasha Sue Agatha Dionne Baldwin (Agatha Dionne being two parts of her birth name) was female, 22 years old and living in Sheffield, England. She had been born to a black Caribbean mother living in the Seychelles. The racial background of her birth father had been unknown, although Natasha was sure that he was not black Caribbean, but possibly white. Natasha was adopted by a British family when she was about six months old. Although the adoptive parents spent a lot of time travelling around the world with their work, when in England they lived in a predominantly white area. Natasha's adoptive parents were white and already had five biological children, who were all older than Natasha. This family was also a step-family. Three of the biological children had been from the adoptive mother's previous marriage. These children were also mixed-race, because their birth father was black African Caribbean. The other two of the biological children were white European, and from the adoptive father's previous marriage. Natasha received no cultural input of her birth heritage as a youngster growing up in her adoptive family. She was curious about her birth family and the circumstances surrounding her birth, but failed to actively seek information because she feared upsetting her adoptive parents. Overall, Natasha had felt that she had a positive experience growing up in her adoptive family.

Robert Danjuma (Danjuma being his birth father's name) was male, 41 years old and living in Nottingham, England. His birth mother was a white European woman from Ireland, and his birth father a black African man from Nigeria. The mother had entered a Catholic mother and baby home for the birth, and at six weeks old, Robert was fostered. He was then fostered another two times, until he was adopted, at the age of two, by an Anglo-Irish Catholic family who were living in a predominantly white working-class area of London. The adoptive family already had five biological children, who were all older than Robert. Despite there having been no cultural input of his birth heritage, Robert recalled having a positive childhood in his adoptive family, where he felt as if he was treated as a biological child. Robert decided to search for his birth family in his twenties, in an attempt to develop his black racial identity.

Will Harris was male, 21 years old and living in Wolverhampton, England. He was born in the West Midlands region to parents who were both black African Caribbean. Will was abandoned in a hospital soon after his birth by his mother. He was then adopted by his white European adoptive parents, who separated soon after the adoption was made, meaning that Will was also raised in a female headed single-parent family. Will had two older siblings in his adoptive family, who were both the biological children of the adoptive parents. The area in which Will had grown up had been predominantly white. He received no cultural input of his birth heritage as a youngster. Will contacted his birth family, who were still living in the region, when he was 20 years old and largely had negative experiences with them. Will found growing up in his adoptive family difficult, although he recalled some positive experiences.

Appendix 3: Useful contacts

Below are the details of some organisations based in the UK who offer expert support, advice and guidance on some of the issues covered:

Adoption Information Line 204 Stockport Road, Altrincham, WA15 7UA Phone: 0800 783 4086 www.adoption.org.uk

Adoption Net East Point, Cardinal Square, 10 Nottingham Road, Derby, DE1 3QT www.adoption-net.co.uk

British Agencies for Adoption and Fostering Saffron House, 6–10 Kirby Street, London, EC1N 8TS Phone: 020 7421 2600 Fax: 020 7421 2601 Email: mail@baaf.org.uk www.baaf.org.uk

Association of Transracially Adopted and Fostered People Unit 35, King's Exchange, Tileyard Road, London, N7 9AH Phone: 020 7619 6220 www.atrap.org.uk

Black and in Care 300 Moss Lane East, Moss Side, Manchester, M14 4LZ Phone: 0161 226 9122

Post Adoption Centre 5 Torriano Mews, Torriano Avenue, London, NW5 2RZ Phone: 020 7284 0555 E-mail: advice@postadoptioncentre.org.uk www.postadoptioncentre.org.uk

National Organisation for the Counselling of Adoptees and their Families 112 Church Road, Wheatly, Oxfordshire, OX33 1LU Phone: 01865 875000.

Adoption UK 46 The Green, South Bar Street. Banbury, OX16 9AB Phone: 01295 752240 Fax: 01295 752241 www.adoptionuk.org.uk

After Adoption Canterbury House, 12–14 Chapel Street, Manchester, M3 7NH Phone: 0161 839 4932 Fax: 0161 832 2242 Email: information@afteradoption.org.uk www.afteradoption.org.uk

NORCAP (Adults Affected by Adoption) 112 Church Road, Wheatley, Oxfordshire, OX33 1LU Phone: 01865 875000 Email: enquiries@norcap.org www.norcap.org.uk

Intercountry Adoption Centre 64–66 High Street, Barnet, Hertfordshire, EN5 5SJ Phone: 020 8449 2562 Fax: 020 8440 5675 Email: info@icacentre.org.uk www.icacentre.org.uk

Transnational and Transracial Adoption Group Email: enquiries@ttag.org.uk www.ttag.org.uk

References

Abdullah, S.B. (1996) Transracial Adoption is Not the Solution to America's Problems of Child Welfare. *Journal of Black Psychology*. 22: 2, 254–61.

Abortion Act 1967

Adoption (Intercountry Aspects) Act 1999

Adoption Advocates International (2007) *Adoption Advocates International* – Washington, United States. (http://www.adoptionadvocates.org). 2 August 2007

Adoption and Children Act 2002

Adoption of Children Act 1926

Adoption of Children Act 1950

Adoption of Children Act 1958

Adoption of Children Act 1976

After Adoption (2007) *After Adoption: Reaching More People*. Manchester. After Adoption Online (www.afteradoption.org.uk). 3 August 2007

Ahmad, B. (1989) Child Care and Ethnic Minorities. In Katan, B. (Ed.) *Child Care Research, Policy and Practice*. London: Open University Press.

Ahmad, B. (1990) *Black Perspectives in Social Work*. Birmingham: Venture Press.

Albers, L. (1997) Health of Children Adopted from Former Soviet Union and Eastern Europe. *Journal of American Medical Association*. 278: 11, 922.

Ali, S. (2005) Uses of the Exotic: Body, Narrative, Mixedness. In Alexander, C. and Knowles, C. (Eds.) *Making Race Matter: Bodies, Space and Identity*. London: Open University Press.

Alibhai-Brown, Y. (1999) *True Colours: Public Attitude to Multiculturalism and the Role of the Government*. London: IPPR.

Alibhai-Brown, Y. (2001) *Mixed Feelings: The Complex Lives of Mixed-Race Britons*. London: The Women's Press.

Alibhai-Brown, Y. (2005) The Most Important Election Ever. *New Stateswoman*. Special Edition of New Statesman. 4 April 2005, 12.

Almas, T. (1992) After Recruitment: Putting the Preparation and Training of Asian Carers on the Agenda. *Adoption and Fostering*. 16, 25–9.

Anthias, F. and Yuval-Davies, N. (1992) *Racialized Boundaries: Race, Nation, Gender, Colour and Class in the Anti-Racist Struggle*. London: Routledge.

Anwar, M. (1998) *Between Cultures: Continuity and Change in the Lives of Young Asians*. London: Routledge.

Association of Black Social Workers and Allied Professionals (2007) *The Association of Black*

Social Workers and Allied Professionals. London: ABSWAP Online (http://www.abswap.org/). 10 October.

Bagley, C., Young, L. and Scully, A. (1992) *International and Transracial Adoptions: A Mental Health Perspective.* Aldershot: Avebury.

Bagley, C. (1993) Transracial Adoption in Britain: A Follow Up Study with Policy Considerations. *Child Welfare.* 72: 3, 285–99.

Bagley, C. and Young, L. (1979) The Identity Adjustment and Achievement of Transracially Adopted Children: A Review and Empirical Report. In Verma, G.K. and Bagley, C. (Eds.) *Race, Education and Identity.* London: MacMillan.

Baker, M. (1997) South Korea Struggles to Free Itself from Adoption Stigma. *Christian Science Monitor.* 89, 246.

Baldwin, J.D. (1986) *George Herbert Mead: A Unifying Theory for Sociology.* London: Sage.

Ball, C. (1998) Adoption: A Service for Children? In Hill, M. and Shaw, M. (Eds.) *Signposts in Adoption: Policy, Practice and Research Issues.* London: BAAF.

Ballis-Lal, B. (1999) Why the Fuss? The Real and the Symbolic Significance of Transracial and Intercountry Adoptions. In Morgan, P. (Ed.) *Adoption: The Continuing Debate.* London: Civitas – Institute for the Study of Civil Society.

Banton, M. (1997) *Ethnic and Racial Consciousness.* London: Longman.

Barn, R. (1993) *Black Children in the Public Care System.* London: Batsford BAAF.

Barn, R. (1999) White Mothers, Mixed-Parentage Children and Child Welfare. *British Journal of Social Work.* 29, 269–84.

Barn, R. (2001) *Black Youth on the Margins: A Research Review.* York: Joseph Rowntree Foundation.

Barn, R. (2006) *Improving Services to Meet the Needs of Minority Ethnic Children and Families.* Quality Protects Research Briefing Number 13. London: DFES/Research in Practice.

Barn, R., Sinclair, R. and Ferdinand, D. (1997) *Acting on Principle: An Examination of Race and Ethnicity in Social Services Provision for Children and Families.* London: BAAF.

Barton, C. and Douglas, G. (1995) *Law and Parenthood.* London: Butterworths.

BBC News (1998) *Adoption Rules to End Misguided Practices.* BBC Online (http://news.bbc.co.uk/hi/english/uk/newsid_160000/160106.stm). 18 November.

Bebbington, A. and Miles, J. (1989) The Background of Children who Enter Care. *British Journal of Social Work.* 19, 349–68.

Benyon, J. and Solomos, J. (Eds.) (1987) *The Roots of Urban Unrest.* Oxford: Pergamon Press.

Besag, V.E. (1989) *Bullies and Victims in Schools.* Milton Keynes: Open University Press.

Best, S. (2005) *Understanding Social Divisions.* London: Sage.

Bhabha, H.K. (2004) *The Location of Culture.* London: Routledge.

Black and in Care (1984) *Black and in Care.* Conference Report. London: Blackrose Press.

Blumer, H. (1969) *Symbolic Interactionism: Perspective and Method.* New Jersey: Prentice Hall.

Bolaffi, G. et al. (Eds.) (2003) *Dictionary of Race, Ethnicity and Culture.* London: Sage.

Bolatagici, T. (2004) Claiming the (N)either/(N)or of 'Third Space': (Re)presenting Hybrid Identity and the Embodiment of Mixed Race. *Journal of Intercultural Studies.* 25: 1, 75–85.

Bourdieu, P. (1986) The Forms of Capital. In Richardson, J.G. (Ed.) *Handbook of Theory and Research for the Sociology of Education.* New York: Greenwood Press.

British Agencies for Adoption and Fostering (1987) *The Placement Needs of Black Children.* Practice Note 13. London: BAAF.

British Sociological Association. (2007) *Equality and Diversity: Language and the BSA.* BSA Online (http://www.britsoc.co.uk/equality/intro.htm). 30 July.

Britton, N.J. (1999) Racialised Identity and the Term Black. In Roseniel, S. and Seymour, J. (Eds.) *Practising Identities: Power and Resistance.* London: MacMillan.

Brooks, M.S.W. and Barth, R.P. (1999) Adult Transracial and Inracial Adoptees: Effects of Race, Gender, Adoptive Family Structure, and Placement History on Adjustment Outcomes. *American Journal of Orthopsychiatry.* 69: 1, 87–99.

Bulmer, M. (1996) The Ethnic Group Question in the 1991 Census of Population. In Coleman, D. and Salt, J. (Eds.) *Ethnicity in the 1991 Census of Population.* London: HMSO.

Butt, J. and Mirza, K. (1997) *Social Care and Black Communities.* London: HMSO.

Campbell, L.H., Silverman, P.R. and Patti, P.B. (1991) Reunions Between Adoptees and Birth Parents: The Adoptees' Experience. *Social Work.* 36: 4, 329–35.

Census Scope (2000) *United States Multiracial Profile.* MC: University of Michigan, Social Science Data Analysis Network. Census Scope Online (http://www. http://www.census-scope.org). 1 August.

Chahal, K. (2004) *Experiencing Ethnicity: Discrimination and Service Provision.* York: Joseph Rowntree Foundation.

Chand, A. (2000) The Over-Representation of Black Children in the Care Protection System: Possible Causes, Consequences and Solutions. *Child and Family Social Work.* 5: 1, 67–77.

Channel 4 History (2007) *Untold Black History Season: Riots.* Channel 4 Television Online: (http://www.channel4.com/history/microsites/U/untold/programs/riot/timeline.html). 21 January.

Cheetham, J. (1986) Introduction. In Ahmed, S., Cheetham J. and, Small, J. (Eds.) *Social Work with Black Children and their Families.* London: Batsford/BAAF.

Children Act 1975

Children Act 1989

Children First in Adoption and Fostering. (1990) *Transracial Adoption: The Issues.* London: Children First in Adoption and Fostering.

Chimezie, A. (1975) Transracial Adoption of Black Children. *Social Work.* 20: 4, 296–301.

Christensen, P. and James, A. (Eds.) (2000) *Research with Children: Perspectives and Practices.* London: Routledge.

Clark, K.B. and Clark, M.P. (1939) The Development of the Consciousness of Self and the Emergence of Racial Identity in Negro Preschool Children. *Journal of Social Psychology.* 10, 591–9.

Clark, K.B. and Clark, M.P. (1940) Skin Colour as a Factor in Racial Identification in Negro Preschool Children. *Journal of Social Psychology.* 11, 159–69.

Clark, K.B. and Clark, M.P. (1947) Racial Identification and Preference in Negro Children. In Newcomb, T.M. and Hartley, E.L. (Eds.) *Readings in Social Psychology.* NY: Holt, Rinehart and Winston.

Clark, K.B. and Clark, M.P. (1950) Emotional Factors in Racial Identification and Preference in Negro Children. *Journal of Negro Education.* 19, 506–13.

Cohen, P. (1994) Yesterday's Words, Tomorrow's World: From the Racialisation of Adoption to the Politics of Difference. In Gaber, I. and Alridge, J. (Eds.) *In the Best Interests of the Child: Culture, Identity and Transracial Adoption.* London: Free Association Books.

Cohen, S. (1972) *Folk Devils and Moral Panics.* London: MacGibbon and Kee.

Commission for Racial Equality (2002) *The Voice of Britain.* London: CRE/MORI.

Courtney, M.E. (1997) The Politics and Realities of Transracial Adoption. *Child Welfare.* 76: 6, 749–79.

Cross, W.E. Jr. (1971) The Negro-to-Black Conversion Experience: Toward a Psychology of Black Liberation. *Black World.* 20: 9, 13–27.

Dagoo, R. et al. (1993) *Thoughts on Adoption by Black Adults Adopted as Children by White Parents.* London: Post Adoption Centre.

Darwin, C. (1872) *Origin of Species.* Reprinted in 1996. Oxford: Oxford University Press.

Department for Education and Skills (2006a) *Care Matters: Transforming the Lives of Children and Young People in Care.* London: TSO.

Department for Education and Skills (2006b) *Promoting Good Campus Relations: Working With Staff and Students to Build Community Cohesion and Tackle Violent Extremism in the Name of Islam at Universities and Colleges.* London: TSO.

Department of Health (1990) *Interdepartmental Review of Adoption Law: The Nature and Effect of Adoption.* London: DoH.

Department of Health (1998) *Adoption: Achieving the Right Balance.* London: DoH.

Department of Health (1999) *Explanatory Notes for the Adoption (Intercountry Aspects) Act 1999.* DoH Online (http://www.legislation.hmso.gov.uk/acts/en/1999en18.html) 5 May.

Department of Health (2000a) *Prime Minister's Review of Adoption – A Report from the PIU.* LAC(2000)16. DoH Online (http://www.cabinetoffice.gov.uk/innovation/2000/adoption/html) 10 June.

Department of Health (2000b) *Adoption: A New Approach.* (A White Paper). London: DoH.

Department of Health (2000c) *The Children Act Report.* London: DoH.

Donald, J. and Rattansi, A. (1992) *Race, Culture and Difference.* London: Sage.

Downing, J. and Husband, C. (2005) *Representing 'Race': Racisms, Ethnicities and Media.* London: Sage.

Dudrah, R. (2002) Drum 'n' Dhol: British Bhangra Music and Diasporic South Asian Identity Formation. *European Journal of Cultural Studies.* 5: 3, 21.

Dustmann, C. and Theodoropoulos, N. (2006) *Ethnic Minority Immigrants and their Children in Britain.* London: Centre for Research and Analysis of Migration.

Dutt, R. and Sanyal, A. (1991) Openness in Adoption or Open Adoption – A Black Perspective. *Adoption and Fostering.* 15: 4, 111–15.

Dyer, R. (1997) *White.* London: Routledge.

Ely, P. and Denney, D. (1987) *Social Work in a Multi Racial Society.* Aldershot: Gower.

Engel, M., Phillips, N.K. and Dellacava, F.A. (2007) International Adoption: A Sociological Account of the US Experience. *International Journal of Sociology and Social Policy.* 27: 5/6, 257–70.

Feast, J. and Howe, D. (1997) Adopted Adults who Search for Background Information and Contact with Birth Relatives. *Adoption and Fostering.* 21: 2, 8–15.

Feigelman, W. and Silverman, A.R. (1984) The Long-Term Effects of Transracial Adoption. *Social Service Review.* 58: 4, 588–602.

Fisher, M., Marsh, P. and Phillips, D. (1986) *In and Out of Care: The Experiences of Children, Parents and Social Workers.* London: Batsford/BAAF.

Forced Marriage (Civil Partnership) Act 2007

Frost, N. and Stein, M. (1989) *The Politics of Child Welfare: Inequality, Power and Change.* London: Harvester Wheatsheaf.

Fryer, P. (1984) *Staying Power: The History of Black People in Britain.* London: Pluto Press.

Galton, F. (1869) *Hereditary Genius: An Inquiry into its Laws and Consequences.* Reprinted 1962. London: Fontana.

Genero, N.P. (1998) Culture, Resiliency and Mutual Psychological Development. In McCubbin, H.I. et al. (Eds.) *Resiliency in African-American Families.* London: Sage.

Ghuman, P.A.S. and Kamath, A. (1993) Bicultural Identities: Study of Asian Adolescents. *Bilingual Family Newsletter.* 10: 1, 3–7.

Gill, O. and Jackson, B. (1983) *Adoption and Race: Black, Asian and Mixed-Race Children in White Families.* London: Batsford.

Gilroy, P. (1992) The End of Anti-Racism. In Rattansi, A. and Donald, J. (Eds.) *'Race', Culture and Difference.* London: Sage/Open University.

Gilroy, P. (1995) Roots and Routes: Black Identity as an Outernational Project. In Harris, H.W., Blue, H.C. and Griffith, E.E.H. (Eds.) *Racial and Ethnic Identity: Psychological Development and Creative Expression.* NY: Routledge.

Goffman, E. (1963) *Stigma: Notes on the Management of a Spoiled Identity.* London: Penguin.

Goffman, E. (1982) The Interaction Order. *American Sociological Review.* 48, 1–17.

Goodyer, A. (2005) Direct Work with Children of Mixed Parentage. In Okitipki, T. (Ed.) *Working with Children of Mixed Parentage.* Lyme Regis: Russell House Publishing.

Guillaumin, C. (1999) The Changing Face of Race. In Bulmer, M. and Solomos, J. (Eds.) *Racism.* Oxford: Oxford University Press.

Gupta, A. (2003) Adoption, Race and Identity. In Douglas, A. and Philpot, T. (Eds.) *Adoption: Changing Families, Changing Times.* London: Routledge.

Hall, K. (1995) There's a Time to Act English and a Time to Act Indian: The Politics of Identity Among British Sikh Teenagers. In Stephens, S. (Ed.) *Children and The Politics of Culture.* Chichester: Princeton University.

Hall, K. (2002) *Lives in Translation: Sikh Youth as British Citizens.* Philadelphia: Penn.

Hamwi, M. (2006) Sending Babies Abroad. *Newsweek.* 148: 20, 17.

Harris, D.R. and Sim, J.J. (2000) An Empirical Look at the Social Construction of Race: The Case of Mixed-Race Adults. *American Sociological Conference.* University of Michigan, MC, USA.

Harris, H.W. (1995) A Conceptual Overview of Race, Ethnicity and Identity. In Harris, H.W., Blue, H.C. and Griffith, E.E.C. (Eds.) *Racial and Ethnic Identity.* London: Routledge.

Hayes, M.V. (1988) How to Tell Your Children That They Are Black. *Foster Care.* December 1988, 14–15.

Hayes, M.V. (1998) Placing Black Children. In Hill, M. and Shaw, M. (Eds.) *Signposts in Adoption: Policy, Practice and Research Issues.* London: BAAF.

Helms, J.E. (Ed.) (1990) *Black and White Racial Identity.* London: Greenwood Press.

Hill, R. (1971) *The Strength of Black Families.* New York: Emerson-Hall.

Hill, R. (1977) *Informal Adoptions Among Black Families.* Washington DC: National Urban League.

Hollinger, J.H. (2004) Intercountry Adoption: Forecasts and Forebodings. *Adoption Quarterly.* 8: 1, 41–60.

Hollingsworth, L. (1998) Adoptee Dissimilarity from the Adoptive Family: Clinical Practice and Research Implications. *Child and Adolescent Social Work Journal.* 15: 4, 303–19.

Holman, R. (1975) The Place of Fostering in Social Work. *British Journal of Social Work.* 9: 1, 3–29.

Hong, S. (1999) Subsidy for Families Adopting Disabled Orphans to Double. *The Korean Times.* Korea, 12–13. 17 January.

Howard, A., Royse, D.D. and Skerl, J.A. (1977) Transracial Adoption: The Black Community Perspective. *Social Work.* May, 184–9.

Howe, D. (2004) The Hierarchy of Skin Colour Presumes that Caribbean Folk are at the Bottom of the Pile. *New Statesman.* 16 August.

Howe, D. and Feast, J. (2000) *Adoption, Search and Reunion: The Long Term Experience of Adopted Adults.* London: The Children's Society.

Howell, S. (2006) *The Kinning of Foreigners: Transnational Adoption in a Global Perspective.* Oxford: Berghahn Books.

Humphreys, C., Atkart, S. and Baidwin, N. (1999) Discrimination in Child Protection Work: Recurring Themes in Work with Asian Families. *Child and Family Social Work.* 4: 4, 283–91.

Hunter, M.L. (2005*) Race, Gender and the Politics of Skin Tone.* NY: Routledge.

Hussain Sumpton, A. (1999) Communicating with and Assessing Black Children. In Barn, R. (Ed.) *Working with Black Children and Adolescents in Need.* London: BAAF.

Hylton, C. (1997) *Family Survival Strategies: Ways of Coping in UK Society.* London: Exploring Parenthood.

Ifekwunigwe, J. (2000) *Scattered Belongings: Cultural Paradoxes of 'Race', Nation and Gender.* London: Routledge.

Ignatiev, N. (1995) *How the Irish Became White.* London: Routledge.

Islamic Fostering Service (2004) *Islamic Fostering Service Launch.* London: Foster Care Link.

Jacobs, B. (1986) *Black Politics and Urban Crisis.* Cambridge: Cambridge University Press.

James, S.M. (1993) Mothering: A Possible Black Feminist Link to Social Transformations? In James, S. and Busia, A. (Eds.) *Theorizing Black Feminisms: The Visionary Pragmatisms of Black Women.* London: Routledge.

Jardine, S. (2000) In Whose Interests? Reflections on Openness, Cultural Roots and Loss. In Selman, P. (Ed.) *Intercountry Adoption: Developments, Trends and Perspectives.* London: BAAF.

Jenkins, R. (1996) *Social Identity.* London: Routledge.

Johnson, L.B. (1997) Three Decades of Black Family Empirical Research: Challenges for the 21 Century. In McAdoo, H.P. (Ed.) *Black Families.* London: Sage.

Johnson, P.R., Shireman, J.F. and Watson, K.W. (1987) Transracial Adoption and the Development of Black Identity at Age Eight. *Child Welfare.* 66, 44–55.

Jones, A., Jeyasingham, D. and Rajasooriya, S. (2002) *Invisible Families: The Strengths and Needs of Black Families in which Young People Have Caring Responsibilities.* York: Joseph Rowntree Foundation.

Katz, I. (1996) *The Construction of Racial Identity in Children of Mixed Parentage: Mixed Metaphors.* London: Jessica Kingsley.

Keating, J. (2001) Struggle for Identity: Issues Underlying the Enactment of the 1926 Adoption of Children Act. *Journal of Contemporary History.* 3, 1–9.

Kirton, D. (1999) Perspectives on 'Race' and Adoption: The Views of Student Social Workers. *British Journal of Social Work.* 29: 5, 779–96.

Kirton, D. (2000) *Race, Ethnicity and Adoption.* Buckingham: Open University Press.

Kirton, D., Feast, J. and Howe, D. (2000) Searching, Reunion and Transracial Adoption. *Adoption and Fostering.* 24: 3, 6–18.

Knowles, C. (2003) *Race and Social Analysis.* London: Sage.

Kowal, K.A. and Schilling, K.M. (1985) Adoption Through the Eyes of Adult Adoptees. *American Journal of Orthopsychiatry.* 55, 354–62.

Lambert, L. and Streather, J. (1980) *Children in Changing Families: A Study of Adoption and Illegitimacy.* London: Macmillan.

Lewis, G. (1996) Black Women's Experiences and Social Work. *Feminist Review.* 53, 24–56.

Lifton, B.J. (1988) *Lost and Found: The Adoption Experience.* New York: Harper and Row.

Linnaeus, C. (1735) *General System of Nature.* Reprinted 2002. Maryland: University Press of America.

Logan, S.L. (1996) Strengthening Family Ties: Working with Black Female Single-Parent Families. In Logan, S.L. (Ed.) *The Black Family: Strengths, Self-help and Positive Change.* Kansas: Westview Press.

MacAnghaill, M. (1999) *Contemporary Racisms and Ethnicities: Social and Cultural Transformations.* Buckingham: Open University Press.

Macionis, J.J. and Plummer, K. (2002) *Sociology: A Global Introduction.* London: Prentice Hall.

MacPherson, W. Sir (1999) *The Stephen Lawrence Inquiry.* London: HMSO.

Malik, K. (2001) *The Changing Meaning of Race.* Keenan Malik Online Papers (http://www.kenanmalik.com/lectures/race_oxford1.html). 23 September.

Marsh, P. (1999) Leaving Care and Extended Families. *Adoption and Fostering.* 22: 4, 6–14.

Mason, D. (2000) *Race and Ethnicity in Modern Britain.* Oxford: Oxford University Press.

Maximé, J.E. (1986) Some Psychological Models of Black Self-Concept. In Ahmed, S., Cheetham, J. and Small, J. (Eds.) *Social Work with Black Children and their Families.* London: B.T. Batsford.

Maximé, J.E. (1994) Teach Your Children. *Community Care.* 21 April 1994, 22–3.

Maza, P. (1983) Characteristics of Children in Foster Care. *Child Welfare.* December 1983.

McAdoo, H.P. (1998) African-American Families: Strengths and Realities. In McCubbin, H.I. et al. (Eds.) *Resiliency in African-American Families.* London: Sage.

McAdoo, H.P. (Ed.) (1997) *Black Families.* London: Sage.

McGhee, D. (2005) *Intolerant Britain: Hate, Citizenship and Difference.* Berkshire: Open University Press.

McRoy, R.G. and Zurcher, L.A. (1983) *Transracial and Inracial Adoptees: The Adolescent Years.* IL: Charles C. Thomas.

Mead, G.H. (1995) Self. In Anthias, F. and Kelly, M.P. (Eds.) *Sociological Debates: Thinking About the Social.* Kent: Greenwich University Press.

Mech, E.V. (1983) Out-of-Home Placement Rates. *Social Services Review.* 57, 659–67.

Meredith, P. (1998) Hybridity in the Third Space: Rethinking Bi-cultural Politics in Aotearoa/New Zealand. Paper Presented to: Te Oru Rangahau Maori Research and Development Conference, 7–9 July 1998. Massey University Online. (http://lianz.waikato.ac.nz/PAPERS/paul/hybridity.pdf). 12 September.

Miles, R. (1990) Racism, Ideology and Disadvantage. *Social Studies Review.* 5: 4.

Mirza, H.S. and Reay, D. (2000) Spaces and Places of Black Educational Desire. *Sociology.* 34: 3, 521–43.

Modood, T. (1994) Political Blackness and British Asians. *Sociology*. 28: 4, 859–76.

Modood, T., Beishon, S. and Virdee, S. (1994) *Changing Ethnic Identities*. London: Policy Studies Institute.

Modood, T. et al. (1997) *Ethnic Minorities in Britain Diversity and Disadvantage*. London: Policy Studies Institute.

Morrison, A. (2004) Transracial Adoption: Pros and Cons – The Parents' Perspective. *Harvard Black Letter Law Journal*. 20, 163–202.

National Association of Black Social Workers (1972) *Our Stand*. Detroit, MI: NABSW.

National Association of Black Social Workers (1994) *Position Statement: Preserving African American Families*. Detroit, MI: NABSW.

Neal, L. (2003) *The Case Against Transracial Adoption*. New York: NABSW.

O'Neal, V. (2000) *Excellence Not Excuses: Inspection of Services for Ethnic Minority Children and Families*. London: Social Services Inspectorate.

Office for National Statistics (2001) *Census 2001*. London: HMSO.

Office for National Statistics (2003) *Ethnic Group Statistics: A Guide for the Collection and Classification of Ethnicity Data*. London: HMSO.

Okitikpi, T. (2005) Identity and Identification: How Mixed Parentage Children Adapt to a Binary World. In Okitipki, T. (Ed.) *Working with Children of Mixed Parentage*. Lyme Regis: Russell House Publishing.

Okitikpi, T. (2005) Working with Children of Mixed Parentage. In Okitipki, T. (Ed.) *Working with Children of Mixed Parentage*. Lyme Regis: Russell House Publishing.

Omi, M. and Winant, H. (1986) *Racial Formation in the United States*. London: Routledge.

Owusu-Bempah, K. (2005) Mulatto, Marginal Man, Half-Caste, Mixed Race: The One-Drop Rule in Professional Practice. In Okitipki, T. (Ed.) *Working with Children of Mixed Parentage*. Lyme Regis: Russell House Publishing.

Owusu-Bempah, K. and Howitt, D. (2000) *Psychology Beyond Western Perspectives*. Oxford: Blackwell/The British Psychological Society.

Park, R.E. (1928) Human Migration and the Marginal Man. *The American Journal of Sociology*. 33: 6, 881–93.

Park, S.M. and Green, C.E. (2000) Is Transracial Adoption in the Best Interests of Ethnic Minority Children? Questions Concerning Legal and Scientific Interpretations of a Child's Best Interests. *Adoption Quarterly*. 3: 4, 5–34.

Parker, P. (1999) *Adoption Now: Messages from Research*. London: DoH.

Phillips, D. (2007) British Asian Narratives of Urban Space. *Transactions of the Institute of British Geographers*. 32: 2, 217–34.

Pilkington, A. (2003) *Racial Disadvantage and Ethnic Diversity in Britain*. Hampshire: Palgrave MacMillan.

Prevatt Goldstein, B. (1999) Black, with a White Parent, a Positive and Achievable Identity. *British Journal of Social Work*. 29, 285–301.

Prevatt Goldstein, B. (2000) Ethnicity and Placement: Beginning the Debate. *Adoption and Fostering*. 24: 1, 9–14.

Prevatt Goldstein, B. and Spencer, M. (2000) *Race and Ethnicity: A Consideration of Issues for Black, Minority Ethnic and White Children in Family Placement*. London: BAAF.

Putnam, R.D. (2000) *Bowling Alone*. NY: Simon and Schuster.

Putnam, R.D. (1995) Bowling Alone: America's Declining Social Capital. *Journal of Democracy*. 6: 1, 65–78.

Rahman, S. (2005) Please, No More Flock Wallpaper. *New Statesman*. 25 April, 28.

Rashid, S.P. (2000) The Strengths of Black Families: Appropriate Placements for All. *Adoption and Fostering*. 24: 1, 15–21.

Ratcliffe, P (2004) *'Race', Ethnicity and Difference*. Open University Press.

Raynar, L. (1970) *Adoption of Non-White Children: The Experience of a British Adoption Project*. London: George Allen and Unwin.

Reynolds, T. (2001) Black Mothering, Paid Work and Identity. *Ethnic and Racial Studies*. 24: 6, 1046–64.

Roberts, H. (2000) Listening to Children and Hearing Them. In: Christensen, P. and James, A. (Eds.) *Research with Children: Perspectives and Practices*. London: Routledge.

Rothschild, M. (1988) Babies for Sale: South Koreans Make Them, Americans Buy Them. *The Progressive*. 16th August.

Runnymede Trust. (2000) *Commission on the Future of Multi Ethnic Britain*. Runnymede Trust Online (http://www.runnymedetrust.org/meb/thereport.html). 11 October.

Ryan, S.D. (2004) Romanian Adoptees: A Cross-National Perspective. *International Social Work*. 47:1, 53–79.

Schaeffer, R.T. (2006) *Racial and Ethnic Groups*. 10 edn. NJ: Pearson/Prentice Hall.

Schechter, M.D. and Bertocci, D. (1990) The Meaning of the Search. In Brodzinsky, D.M. and Schechter, M.D. (Eds.) *The Psychology of Adoption*. New York: Open University Press, 62–90.

Schor, E.L. (1982) The Foster Care System and Health Status of Foster Children. *Pediatrics*. 69, 521–8.

Selman, P. (2000) The Demographic History of Intercountry Adoption. In Selman, P. (Ed.) *Intercountry Adoption: Developments, Trends and Perspectives*. London: BAAF.

Selman, P. (2001) The Movement of Children for Intercountry Adoption: A Demographic Perspective. Poster Presentation. *XXIVth IUSSP General Population Conference*, Salvador, Brazil, 18–24 August.

Selman, P. (2004) Intercountry Adoption in the New Millennium: The Quiet Migration Revisited. *Population Research and Policy Review*. 22: 3, 205–25.

Selman, P. and White, J. (1998) Mediation and the Role of 'Accredited Bodies'. In Hill, M. and Shaw, M. (Eds.) *Signposts in Adoption: Policy, Practice and Research Issues*. London: BAAF.

Shekleton, J. (1990) *A Glimpse Through the Looking Glass*. London: PAC.

Shyne, A.W. and Schroeder, A.G. (1978) *National Study of Social Services to Children and their Families.* Washington, DC: Department of Health, Education and Welfare.

Silverman, P.R., Campbell, L.H. and Patti, P.B. (1994) Reunions Between Adoptees and Birth Parents: The Adoptive Parents' View. *Social Work.* 39:5, 542–9.

Simon, R. and Alstein, H. (1991) Intercountry Adoptions: Experiences of Families in the United States. In Simon, R. and Alstein, H. (Eds.) *Intercountry Adoption: A Multi-National Perspective.* NY: Praeger.

Simon, R. and Alstein, H. (1996) The Case for Transracial Adoption. *Children and Youth Services Review.* 18: 1/2, 5–12.

Simon, R. and Alstein, H. (2000) *Adoption Across Borders: Serving the Children in Transracial and Intercountry Adoptions.* London: Rowman and Littlefield Publishers.

Simonton, A. (2000) *Issues on Interracial Adoption.* University of Maine Online (http://www.umm.maine.edu/BEX/Lehman/HomePage.Stuff/text/beh450/An_/asessay.html) 10 August.

Small, J. (1982) New Black Families. *Adoption and Fostering.* 6:3, 35–9.

Small, J. (1986) Transracial Placements: Conflicts and Contradictions. In Ahmed, S., Cheetham, J. and Small, J. (Eds.) *Social Work with Black Children and their Families.* London: Batsford.

Small, J. (1991) Ethnic and Racial Identity in Adoption Within the United Kingdom. *Adoption and Fostering.* 15:4, 61–9.

Small, J. (1998) Ethnic and Racial Identity in Adoption within the UK. In Hill, M. and Shaw, M. (Eds.) *Signposts in Adoption: Policy, Practice and Research Issues.* London: BAAF.

Smith, H.Y. (1996) Building on the Strengths of Black Families: Self-Help and Empowerment. In Logan, S.L. (Ed.) *The Black Family: Strengths, Self-Help and Positive Change.* Kansas: Westview Press.

Social Services Inspectorate (1997) *For Children's Sake, Part 2: An Inspection of Local Authority Post-placement and Post-adoption Services.* London: DoH.

Song, M. (2003) *Choosing Ethnic Identity.* Cambridge: Polity Press.

Song, M. and Edwards, R. (1997) Raising Questions About Perspectives on Black Lone Motherhood. *Journal of Social Policy.* 26: 2, 233–44.

Soul Kids (1977) *Report on the Steering Group of the Soul Kids Campaign, London, 1975–1967.* London: Waterloo Press.

Spencer, S. (2006) *Race and Ethnicity: Culture, Identity and Representation.* London: Routledge.

Stonequist, E.V. (1937) *The Marginal Man: A Study of Personality and Culture Conflict.* New York: Russell.

Stonequist, E.V. (1942) The Marginal Character of the Jews. In Graeber, I. and Britt, S.H. (Eds.) *Jews in a Gentile World.* New York: MacMillan.

Sudarkasa, N. (1997) African American Families and Family Values. In McAdoo, H.P. (Ed.) *Black Families.* London: Sage.

Sunmonu, Y. (2000) Why Black Carers are Deterred from Adoption. *Adoption and Fostering*. 24: 1, 59–60.

The Independent Newspaper (2008) Girl Who Fled Arranged Marriage 'Was Smothered or Strangled' by Mark Hughes. *The Independent Newspaper*. 9 January.

Thoburn, J., Norford, L. and Rashid, S.P. (2000) *Permanent Family Placement for Children of Minority Ethnic Origin*. London: Jessica Kingsley.

Thomas, C. et al. (1999) *Adopted Children Speaking*. London: BAAF

Thompson, A. (2000) Going Back to Their Roots. *Community Care*. 17 May 2000, 23–9.

Tizard, B. (1977) *Adoption: A Second Chance*. London: Open Books.

Tizard, B. (1991) Intercountry Adoption: A Review of the Evidence. *Journal of Child Psychology and Psychiatry*. 32: 5, 743–56.

Tizard, B. and Phoenix, A. (1989) Black Identity and Transracial Adoption. *New Community*. 15: 3, 427–37.

Tizard, B. and Phoenix, A. (1994) Not Such Mixed Up Kids. *Adoption and Fostering*. 18: 1, 17–22.

Tizard, B. and Phoenix, A. (2002) *Black, White or Mixed-Race? Race and Racism in the Lives of Young People of Mixed Parentage*. London: Routledge.

Triseliotis, J. (1993) Intercountry Adoption: In Whose Best Interest? In Humphrey, M. and Humphrey, H. (Eds.) *Intercountry Adoption: Practical Experiences*. London: Routledge.

Triseliotis, J. (1998) Adoption: Evolution or Revolution? In Hill, M. and Shaw, M. (Eds.) *Signposts in Adoption: Policy, Practice and Research Issues*. London: BAAF.

Triseliotis, J. (2000) Intercountry Adoption: Global Trade or Global Gift? *Adoption and Fostering*. 24: 2, 45–54.

Triseliotis, J., Shireman, J. and Hundleby, M. (1997) *Adoption, Theory, Policy and Practice*. London: Cassell.

Turner, S. and Taylor, J. (1996) Under-Explored Issues in Transracial Adoption. *Journal of Black Psychology*. 22: 2, 262–5.

United Nations (1960) *Leysin Report*. European Seminar on Inter-Country Adoption, Leysin, Switzerland. (May 23–31). NY: United Nations Technical Assistance Office.

United Nations (1989) *United Nations Convention on the Rights of the Child*. NY: United Nations Technical Assistance Office.

Vincent, J.A. (2000) Age and Old-Age. In Payne, G. (Ed.) *Social Divisions*. Basingstoke: Palgrave.

Visram, R. (2002) *Asians in Britain: 400 Years of History*. London: Pluto Press.

Weedon, C. (2004) *Identity and Culture: Narratives of Difference and Belonging*. Berkshire: Open University Press.

Weeks, J. (1993) *Sexuality*. London: Routledge.

Whitfield, R. (1999) Secure Tender Loving Care as Soon as Possible, Please. In Morgan, P. (Ed.) *Adoption: The Continuing Debate*. London: IEA Health and Welfare Unit.

Wilson, A. (1987) *Mixed Race Children: A Study of Identity*. London: Allen and Unwin.

Worotynee, Z.S. (2006) *Child Interrupted: International Adoption in the Context of Canadian Policy on Immigration, Multiculturalism, Citizenship and Child Rights*. Centre of Excellence for Research on Immigration and Settlement. Toronto: CERIS

Wright, C. et al. (2005) *Overcoming School Exclusion and Achieving Successful Youth Transitions within African Caribbean Communities*. York: Joseph Rowntree Foundation.

Zastrow, C.H. (1977) *Outcome of Black Children – White Parents Transracial Adoptions*. San Francisco, CA: Reed and Eterovich.

Index